4   **Twilight of Princes**

1601   **1609**   **1620**

Newsweek New York N.Y.

Editor   Christopher Hibbert

1631   1649   1661

4 Twilight of Princes

1666   1683   1698   1713

1720

1751

1755

1770   1776   1789

Contents

Introduction

Before the French Revolution every major European state except Venice was a monarchy, and every monarch except the King of Poland succeeded to his throne by right of birth. It was the Age of Absolutism; it was an age in which a monarch could claim—as Louis XIV is alleged to have done—"*L'état c'est moi*"—"I am the state;" it was an age in which an autocrat might, in his will, bequeath his country to his sons as though it were his own personal property. It was, moreover, an age in which a monarch might bestow vast estates and innumerable peasant-slaves upon his favorites—as Catherine the Great did when she retired her violent lover, Count Grigori Orlov, with a fortune of 17 million rubles, a marble palace and estates staffed by 45,000 serfs.

Yet by the beginning of the eighteenth century there were indications in Europe and throughout the civilized world that the long era of the hereditary despot—even of the enlightened despot who considered himself, in the words of Frederick the Great, "the first servant of the state"—was drawing to a close. No future Emperor of China was to govern with such serene confidence as Ch'ien-lung, Son of Heaven; no future King of France was to shine as brightly as the Sun King; and no future King of Sweden was to lead victorious armies through the plains of Germany as did Gustavus Adolphus.

In the two centuries covered in this volume, the slow process of transforming the fractured territories of medieval Europe into a relatively small number of powerful, centrally governed states was finally completed, and Europe's dominant position in the world—foreshadowed by the skills and daring of the early navigators—was firmly established. During those centuries of gradual consolidation, the map of the world was transfigured: some states grew, others shrank, and a few were altogether effaced. In the Levant the ancient Ottoman Empire began to crumble; in India and North America the French and British fought to control and expand new colonies; in the South Pacific a whole new world was discovered; and in China a foreign dynasty vastly extended the frontiers of the empire by driving the Gurkhas from Tibet, conquering Turkistan and reducing the Burmese to suzerainty.

When thirty years of religious wars were ended by the Treaty of Westphalia in 1648, Europe's public law seemed settled and its national frontiers seemed securely fixed. Yet by the close of the following century—an era that Goethe considered the dawn of a new age in the history of the world—the well-trained armies of the old order had been turned aside by the massed forces of revolution, public law had been flouted time and again, and almost every frontier had been obliterated and redrawn by Europe's ruling dynasties as they pursued their conflicting ambitions.

The Turks, thrown back from Vienna in 1683, lost Hungary to Austria and the Crimea to Russia, and ceased to be a threat to the Christian world; Spain's European empire disintegrated as Sardinia fell to the House of Savoy, Franche-Comté to France, and the Netherlands to the growing power of Austria. Sweden's power had been eclipsed; Poland, soon to be entirely dismembered, was already being cut up by her neighbors; and two new powers—which later became the most powerful in all Europe—had emerged with ruthless force. Those two were Russia, which had pushed southward to the Black Sea and westward to the Baltic, and Prussia, which had been created by the vigor of the House of Hohenzollern. Of the great maritime powers of Western Europe, France had not yet recovered the glory that the later years of Louis XIV had so sadly tarnished; Holland's power was in decline through competition with larger states; and England—now known as Great Britain—was creating the strong outlines of an overseas empire that was to decide the fate of North America and Australia and to

Introduction

leave its indelible mark on the subcontinent of India.

The drive and forcefulness of the despot were decisive in transforming those frontiers and effecting those transfers of power in Europe. "Kings are absolute lords and have full authority over all people," wrote Louis XIV, whose practical example deeply influenced the rulers of eighteenth-century Europe. His opinion was shared by Peter the Great and Frederick the Great, different though their concepts of autocracy were. It was Frederick the Great's belief that "a well-conducted Government must have a system as coherent as a system of philosophy, so that finance, police and the army are coordinated to the same end, namely the consolidation of the state and the increase of its power. Such a system can only emanate from a single brain, that of the sovereign." Catherine the Great, who continued Peter's work in modernizing and westernizing Russia, insisted in her *Instructions to the Commissioners for Composing a New Code of Laws* that while all men were equal before the law, the sovereign was absolute: "The extent of the empire necessitates absolute power in the ruler. Any other form of government would bring it down in ruins."

The effective exercise of absolute power required immense resources of energy and application. Catherine the Great, though she delighted in good food, good conversation and good lovers, would often work for fifteen hours a day, beginning at five o'clock in the morning. Frederick the Great also got up at five, and allowed himself no more than two hours a day for relaxation. "I rise at five in the morning," said Charles III of the Two Sicilies, who "thought himself the most absolute monarch in Europe" according to the British ambassador. Following the death of Maria Theresa of Austria, her son, Joseph II, threw himself into his work with such astonishing avidity that he was able to issue more than six thousand long decrees on all manner of subjects in the ten years before his own death. Louis XIV, whose life appeared to revolve around the choreographic ceremonial of an enervating court, had a real talent and taste for administration: his ministers were forbidden to seal anything without his order or to sign anything without his consent. His successor, Philip, Duke of Orleans, who ruled as regent for eight years after Louis' death, worked all day and—in the opinion of more than one observer—simply wore himself out.

But although they stride across the years with such vitality, setting their mark for good and ill upon the history of their times, those absolute monarchs provide but one fitting title for their era—*Twilight of Princes*. For the Age of Absolutism was also the Age of Reason, the Age of Enlightenment and the Age of Scientific Revolution—an age in which Newton's discoveries were more important than the conquests of Frederick the Great, and Diderot's *Encyclopédie* was more influential than the triumphs of Louis XIV. It was the age of French *philosophes* as well as French despots; an age in which the new scepticism was disseminated and the secularization of society and thought were all but completed; an age in which thoughts of international revolution were already in the air, and in which the princes, moving slowly into the twilight, were ultimately brought to their end.

CHRISTOPHER HIBBERT

The tragic legend of Denmark's Prince Amleth had fired the imaginations of European storytellers long before England's famous playwright, William Shakespeare, began work on his Revenge of Hamlett Prince of Denmark *in 1600 or 1601. In fact, the tale of Hamlet's bloody demise was already a familiar folk legend when Saxo Grammaticus, a Danish scholar, first committed it to paper in 1186, and its popularity had not diminished four centuries later when Thomas Kyd produced his melodrama based on the tale. Drawing heavily upon Kyd's action-filled but otherwise inconsequential drama, Shakespeare created what is certainly his most famous tragedy and quite possibly the most famous play in world literature. In the centuries since* Hamlet *was first performed, its title role has been coveted—and attempted—by nearly all leading actors.*

No play has had a more enduring impact on the world than Shakespeare's *Hamlet*. It has been acted in every country where there is a serious interest in the theater, and leading actors the world over have been eager to play the part of the melancholy Prince. In the chronicles of writing and performance for the stage, *Hamlet* has become a part of world history.

The saga of the Danish Prince Amleth was first recorded in the twelfth century by the Danish scholar Saxo Grammaticus, but it has its origins in Scandinavian legend. In Saxo's story the murder of Amleth's father by his uncle is common knowledge. Amleth pretends to be insane to save his own life until he can avenge the murder. Revenge, when it comes, is bloody and violent: while the members of the court are celebrating a false report of Amleth's death, Amleth tricks them into drunkenness, sets fire to the hall, kills his uncle and proclaims himself king.

In the late sixteenth century an English play about Hamlet appeared in London. That play, which was probably written by Thomas Kyd, was a bloody, old-fashioned melodrama, complete with a ghost that went about wailing "Hamlet, revenge." The play was in the repertory of the Chamberlain's Men—one of London's two leading acting companies—for some time. In fact the type of melodrama it represented was spoofed in another play produced by the same company:

> A filthy whining ghost
> Lapt in some foul sheet, or a leather pilch,
> Comes screaming in like a pig half sticked
> And cries, *Vindicta*–Revenge, Revenge!

This English *Hamlet* was the play that Shakespeare rewrote in creating his own play.

Documented records of Shakespeare's tragedy begin in 1602, although the exact date of its composition is unknown. The date 1601 is usually given, but the author may have begun work on the play in 1600. In July, 1602, "a booke called the Revenge of Hamlett Prince Denmarke, as it was latelie Acted by the Lord Chamberlayne his servantes" was "entered" at Stationers' Hall in London. The practice at the time was for new books, including the texts of plays, to be sent to the headquarters of the Stationers' Company, whose members—all the booksellers and most of the printers in London—had the sole right of publication.

The application for the right to print *Hamlet* did not give the author's name. It did, however, clearly indicate that the play was already popular, and it identified the company of actors performing the play as the Chamberlain's Men. Of this troupe or "fellowship" Shakespeare had been a leading member and a shareholder for eight years. Shakespeare's writing skill—more of an asset than his acting—and the great ability of Richard Burbage, the troupe's leading player, had won renown and prosperity for the Chamberlain's Men. They were favored by Queen Elizabeth and had the acclaim of the general public. A rhymed epitaph that appeared after Burbage's death in 1618 named "young Hamlet" as one of his principal roles.

Thus we know that the most famous of Shakespeare's tragedies started with every advantage. Its author had been well established by his histories and comedies, and by the tragedy *Romeo and Juliet*. Further, the play was performed by a renowned company headed by Burbage.

It became immediately apparent that *Hamlet* was one of those rare works of art with nearly universal appeal. The play was great melodrama, with blood and violence and pageantry. But it was much more, for Shakespeare had taken an old, familiar plot and had shifted the emphasis from external events to Hamlet's character. And the man he revealed— paralyzed by gloom and indecision, torn between the flesh and the spirit, with shifting moods, uncontrolled passions, sharp insights and haunting fears—proved frighteningly real not just to seventeenth-century audiences but to every later generation.

Yet, while *Hamlet* has impressed and gripped audiences down the centuries, it is nonetheless a play of its own period. It is the first of the four great

The Globe Theater in London: for many years the home of the Chamberlain's Company, of which Shakespeare was a leading member.

Opposite The print of Shakespeare used as the frontispiece to the First Folio edition of his plays, published in 1623.

Elizabeth I at Blackfriars, surrounded by her guard of honor.

The Earl of Essex, one-time favorite of Elizabeth I.

Shakespearean tragedies that reveal an increasingly dark and pessimistic view of human nature. Shakespeare was to write light romantic pieces after that phase, but he never returned to the old gaiety of his "high fantastical" comedies, which had their happiest, finest—and final—hour in *Twelfth Night*, which was almost certainly produced in 1601.

The first years of the seventeenth century in England were dominated by the twilight of the reign of the great Queen Elizabeth. The glory of Gloriana was being dimmed by her years, and her heart had been bruised, if not broken, by a shattering event. In February, 1601, her former favorite the Earl of Essex had led a foolhardy rebellion. With him was a clique of malcontents, including Shakespeare's early patron, the Earl of Southampton.

The challenge to the Queen's sovereignty found little public support and failed miserably. Essex was convicted of treason and beheaded; Southampton, lucky to escape with his life, was imprisoned in the Tower of London. Some of the insurgents had paid Shakespeare's company a special fee to revive *Richard II* at the Globe Theater, and even—as the Queen later alleged—to play it in the streets. Their purpose was to show that the deposition of a monarch could be successful—and it was absurdly stupid of the players to accept their bribe. There was an official inquiry into the company's conduct, but they were not penalized and they were quickly returned to royal favor. A subsequent remark of the Queen's —"Know ye not that I am Richard the Second?"— indicated that the wound had been deep.

Elizabeth's death came in March, 1603. The nation mourned and wondered. The Protestant succession was assured—there would not be a revival of civil and religious war to ravage public life with blood and hatred. But none could be sure how King James VI of Scotland would behave when he became also King James I of England. Doubts and fears gathered, and thus *Hamlet* was born in stormy weather, in a country under a cloud.

Even amid the eager, ardent and creative energy of the Elizabethan Age there had been a cult of melancholy. It had been more of a fashionable pose than a considered philosophy, but during the reign of the new king there was a growing wave of bleak pessimism. In his *History of the World* Sir Walter Raleigh noted that "the long day of mankind draweth fast towards an evening and the world's tragedy and time are near at an end." Raleigh was a prisoner—and probably knew that he was doomed —when he wrote his *History*, but bishops and clerics who were not in danger also preached decay and disaster. In one of his sermons, John Donne, dean of St. Paul's, told his listeners that the sun was "fainter and languishing, men less in stature and shorter lived. No addition, but only every year new sorts of worms and flies and sicknesses which argue more and more putrefaction." Other divines urged the saving of souls before the darkness thickened.

Those dismal forebodings came after *Hamlet* was written. By then Shakespeare had entered a period in which his despair about human character and

The smell of corruption in the English air

destiny was far more prominent than his faith in charity and the saving power of mercy. That view is found in his last plays. If something was rotten in the state of Denmark, there was also a smell of corruption in the English air—and Hamlet's bitter commentary on life anticipate a generally felt insecurity.

The settled philosophy and faith of the Middle Ages had cracked. To question authority in Church and State once had been strange and sinful; it was now familiar and fashionable. The stage of national life had become full of questioning Hamlets.

Had *Hamlet* been no more than a projection of sad scepticism, it could never have pleased as it did. It has lived by the dramatic values of its fast-moving story and still more by the character of the Prince, so quicksilver in his moods, so sharp of wit, so profound in reflection, and, above all, so ready with the perfect phrase and the perfectly chosen word. Whatever were the failings of the new reign and the degradation of court life, the English language reached its summit of power and richness in the Authorized Version of the Bible, which was suggested by and dedicated to King James. The old Anglo-Saxon or Anglo-Norman English had a special strength, and the classical culture of the Renaissance brought new

Above left James I: he took the Chamberlain's Company under his patronage and plays were often performed at court.

Above right The Third Earl of Southampton, an early patron of Shakespeare.

Pirated versions of "Hamlet"

The title page of the Second Quarto of *Hamlet*.

Far right William Kemp, a famous Shakespearian comedian, from a woodcut of 1600.

Richard Burbage, the leading player of the Chamberlain's Company. He was the first actor to play the role of "Hamlet."

THE
Tragicall Historie of
HAMLET,
Prince of Denmarke.

By William Shakespeare.

Newly imprinted and enlarged to almost as much againe as it was, according to the true and perfect Coppie.

AT LONDON,
Printed by I. R. for N. L. and are to be sold at his shoppe vnder Saint Dunstons Church in Fleetstreet. 1604.

decoration to its sinewy frame. Hamlet is a university student with a gift of golden words. He commands a thundering eloquence in his parley with the ghost. He can be as brief as poignant: "The Rest is silence." And he dies with a sigh, not a swan song. His part was written in the dusk of Elizabethan glory, and in the high noon of the English language.

There is no question that the play pleased its audiences. In fact, *Hamlet*'s reception was so gratifying that a "pirated" version was thought to be worth printing in 1603. There was then no copyright of plays, and the manuscripts were keenly guarded by the companies for which they were written in order to prevent performance by rivals. If a piece were popular, a bogus text could usually be dishonestly obtained by bribing one of the minor players. Such players were known as "hired men" to distinguish them from "sharers," who took the chief roles. The hired men's wages were very low, and they could be bribed to provide rough scripts based on memories of parts taken by themselves or others. There were also shorthand writers who took surreptitious notes at performances in order to get out a text.

The pirated version of *Hamlet*, a truncated travesty of the play, was known as the First Quarto. The Quarto named Shakespeare as the dramatist, and therefore either he or his company decided to print the full and genuine text. Doing so involved the risk of its being used by other teams of players, but since the play had been published with a text grotesquely unfair to the author, it was decided to issue a correct version. In 1604, therefore, the Second Quarto— which described the play as "Newly imprinted and enlarged to almost as much againe according to the true and perfect Coppie"—was issued. There were two reprintings in 1611.

In 1623 John Heminges and Henry Condell, Shakespeare's fellow sharers in the Chamberlain's Men, printed a slightly abbreviated form of the Second Quarto, omitting four hundred lines out of four thousand. They were probably using a play-house text in which some cuts had been marked, for the complete version occupies the stage for nearly four hours—or nearly double "the two hours' traffic of our stage" mentioned by Shakespeare in his prologue to *Romeo and Juliet*. Uncut, *Hamlet* is the longest of Shakespeare's plays.

The unauthorized first edition of the text stated that the play had already been performed both in and out of London, and it is certainly true that *Hamlet* appealed not just to the regular playgoers or to the students at Oxford and Cambridge. In 1607, when Captain Keeling of the East India Company's ship *Dragon* was sailing east with two other vessels, *Hector* and *Content*, they were becalmed off Sierra Leone. There Keeling recorded in his diary that he entertained Captain Hawkins of *Content*. There was a fish dinner and then he had "Hamlet acted abord me: which I permitt to keepe my people from idlnes and unlawful games, or sleepe." That they managed to improvise a stage on the tiny ships of the period is remarkable. So is the fact that the Captain had taken a copy of *Hamlet* with him. The performance by the crew, organized for the sake of discipline rather than in devotion to drama, must have been extremely crude. The impact of *Hamlet* had indeed been wide.

There is no record of command performances of *Hamlet* at court, even though King James constantly made requests to see other plays. If *Hamlet* was never in demand at court, that is understandable. James had married a Danish wife, and neither the story of the murder and revenge nor the remarks about the drinking habits of the Danes were complimentary to the Queen's nation. But the play remained in the repertory of the King's Men (the name the Chamberlain's Men had taken upon the accession of James I).

English actors frequently toured in Europe, where

they had a high reputation. As early as 1586, the Earl of Leicester had taken players with him when he was with an army in Holland, and the Shakespearean clown William Kempe was among them. Fynes Moryson (1566-1630), a Cambridge scholar and traveler, met English actors at Frankfurt. "The Germans," he wrote, "not understanding a word they said, flocked wonderfully to see their gesture and action." The English standard of performance was thought exemplary. In 1626 an English company led by John Green played *Hamlet* in Dresden. They used a shortened version: *Der Bestrafte Brüdermord, Prinz Hamlet ans Dannemark.*

English theaters, closed by the Puritans for nearly twenty years during the civil war and the Commonwealth, were reopened after the restoration of the monarchy in 1660. *Hamlet* was one of the first plays to be revived. The diarist Pepys noted that Thomas Betterton played the Prince "beyond imagination" in "the best part I believe that man ever acted."

In recent years classics have been subjected to the whims of directors who want to prove their ability by giving old plays a new look. *Hamlet* has been dressed in the costumes of many periods, including our own. It has received new interpretations and been staged according to strange theories. Through all that, it has held its position at the summit of English drama, continually examined by scholars while continually fascinating the general public. More than any of Shakespeare's plays, it has justified Ben Jonson's promise of the author's survival, "not for an age but for all time."

IVOR BROWN

Thomas Betterton, a well-known actor after the Restoration of 1660. *Hamlet* was one of his favorite roles.

Left The title page of John Donne's *Sermons*, published in 1640.

John Donne, poet and divine.

4/17

While *Hamlet* was being performed for the first time in London, an impoverished fifty-six-year-old Spaniard who had once been a soldier and had lately been in prison was writing "just such a book as might be begotten in a jail." The Spaniard's name was Miguel de Cervantes Saavedra and the book was *Don Quixote*, the first modern novel. Cervantes' work was in the tradition of the picaresque romances that had been popular in Spain since the middle of the sixteenth century, when the anonymous *La Vida de Lazarillo de Tormes y de sus fortunas y adversidades* was published. *La Vida* had been followed by the equally popular works of Mateo Alemán, Agustin de Rojas, and Francisco López de Úbeda, whose *La Pícara Justina* appeared in 1605. Indeed, the Spaniards have been credited with inventing the picaresque novel —a genre that takes its name from the Spanish word for rogue, *picaro*.

Don Quixote was much more than a picaresque novel, however: Cervantes' work was soon recognized as the greatest social romance of the early seventeenth century. The Spaniard's highly moralistic masterpiece succeeded not only in ridiculing the picaresque novel and its chivalric sentiments, but also in demonstrating the follies of prejudice and the real dangers behind an exaggerated contemporary regard for pure blood and nobility of birth—a regard that was coupled with widespread disdain for work.

Cervantes himself led a hard and vigorous life. He joined the army in 1568 and served in Italy, where he was badly wounded at the Battle of Lepanto in October, 1571. On his return to Spain he was captured by Barbary corsairs and taken to Algiers, where he was sold as a slave to a Greek renegade. Ransomed after five years, Cervantes returned to his homeland in 1576. He tried and failed to make a living as a playwright and eventually found employment as a collector of provisions and stores for the Spanish Armada of 1588. After the fleet's defeat, he was retained as an ill-paid and overworked commissary to the galleys—but his unbusinesslike methods soon led to his imprisonment. Out of that experience grew Cervantes' great literary panorama of Spanish society, *Don Quixote*, which was published in 1605. In 1614 a spurious sequel to *Don Quixote* appeared, and a year later Cervantes himself published an authentic second installment.

On April 23, 1616, Cervantes died in Madrid; on that same day Shakespeare died in Stratford, England. Like his contemporary, Shakespeare may also have been a soldier—and may even have fought against Cervantes' countrymen in the Netherlands. Indeed, Spain and England were at war for most of the two authors' lives, and the rivalry between the two countries was not over at the time of their deaths.

Cervantes: soldier, slave and author.

Spain under Philip II

Although the Spanish Empire was far less extensive than it had been in the splendid days of Charles V (1500-58), it was still the largest and most widespread empire on earth. Apart from her rich possessions in Italy and Sardinia, Spain still retained several key European possessions — including Franche-Comté and the Netherlands — whose feudal estates had come into Spanish hands through purchase, marriage, treachery and violence at the beginning of the fifteenth century. Spain still held her rich empire across the Atlantic, and she had extended her dominions in Western Europe and America.

In 1581, Philip II, son of Emperor Charles V, forcibly annexed Portugal after declaring himself heir to the decrepit and scarcely sane Henry II, who had died leaving no direct heirs. There were four other claimants to the Portuguese throne, all of whom were grandchildren or great-grandchildren of King Emanuel I. The strongest claim was that of the Duchess of Braganza, whose father was one of Emanuel's younger sons. All the other contenders—with the exception of Don Antonio, Prior of Crato, who was illegitimate —were descended through the female line. The Church favored

union with Spain, as did several prominent members of the Cortes, or parliament — and when the Duchess of Braganza was won over to their side by large grants of land and by the promise that her husband would be made King of Brazil when Philip II became King of Portugal, the success of the Spanish party seemed assured. In order to forestall the Spanish, Don Antonio proclaimed himself King and occupied Lisbon. But a Spanish army commanded by the great Duke of Alva invaded Portugal and soon overwhelmed Don Antonio's forces at Alcantara.

Sixty years of captivity

After his coronation as King of Portugal, Philip promised to recognize the constitutional rights of the Portuguese people, particularly those of the influential *hidalgos*. He agreed to summon the Cortes regularly and to create a Portuguese privy council with responsibility for Portuguese affairs. The country's possessions in Brazil, Africa and Asia were to be held by Portugal, which was to be considered not as a conquered province but as a separate kingdom, joined with Spain in a mutually profitable political union.

Few of Philip's promises were observed: the Cortes was summoned only once; the government of the country was left to the grasping favorites of the Spanish court; and the union with Spain—known in Portugal as the "Sixty Years of Captivity"—led to incessant involvement in wars with Spain's maritime enemies. There were two serious insurrections in the 1630s, and in 1640 the lazy Duke of Braganza, grandson of the Duchess whose claims had been bought out by Philip II, rode a wave of national discontent to the throne. As King John IV, he expelled the Spanish garrisons from his country.

The empire crumbles

Despite the size of her empire, Spain's power at the beginning of the seventeenth century was already in decline. The defeat of the Armada in 1588 had exposed the incompetence of the Spanish navy and had given Spanish self-esteem a severe shock. Since that time it had become increasingly clear that Spain no longer had the strength to maintain the position she had presumed to occupy in the world. The con-

THE
HISTORY
OF THE
VALOROUS and WITTY
Knight-Errant,
DON QUIXOTE
Of the MANCHA,

Written in *Spanish*
By MICHAEL CERVANTES.

Translated into *English*
By THOMAS SHELTON.
And now printed *Verbatim* from the Quarto Edition
of 1620.

With a curious SET of CUTS from the French
of COYPEL.

VOL. II.

LONDON:

Printed for D. MIDWINTER, W. INNYS, R. ROBINSON, A. WARD, J. and P. KNAPTON, S. BIRT, T. LONGMAN, T. WOTTON, C. HITCH T. OSBORNE, H. LINTOT, J. DAVIDSON, C. BATHURST, H. KNAPLOCK, and A. CONYERS. M.DCC.XL.

Don Quixote : more than a picaresque romance.

The Delightful
HISTORY
Of the moſt Witty KNIGHT
Don QUIXOTE
Of the MANCHA.

BOOK IV.

CHAP. I

Wherein is diſcourſed the new and pleaſant Adventure, that happened to the Curato *and* Barber *in* Sierra Morena.

MOST happy and fortunate were thoſe Times, wherein the thrice audacious and bold Knight Don *Quixote* of the *Mancha* was beſtowed on the World; by whoſe moſt honourable Reſolution, to renew and revive in it the already worn-out, and well night deceaſed Exerciſe of Arms, we joy in this our ſo niggard and ſcant an Age of all Paſtimes, not only the Sweetneſs of his true Hiſtory, but alſo of the other Tales and Digreſſions contained therein,

Vol II.   B   in,

American empire

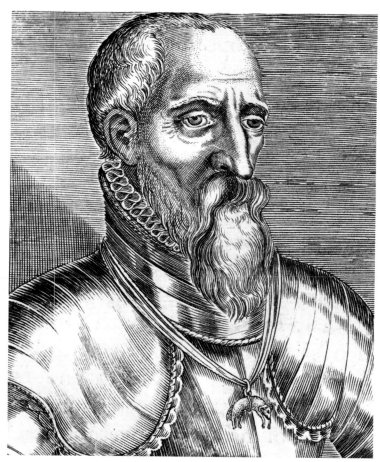

The Duke of Alva, who almost destroyed the Dutch revolt.

Philip III

Philip II died at the Escorial a few months after the Treaty of Vervins was signed and he was succeeded by his son Philip III, a pious, extravagant, incapable monarch who was content to leave the government in the hands of the worthless Duke of Lerma. The unscrupulous Duke encouraged the King's extravagances while acquiring a vast personal fortune and involving his impoverished country in disastrous foreign entanglements. Fearing that they might support a Mohammedan invasion of Spain, Lerma expelled the Moriscos, or Spanish Moors, from the country. His move was almost as damaging to Spain as Louis XIV's expulsion of the Huguenots would later be to France; for the half-million Moriscos whom Lerma forced into exile were among the most skilled members of the community.

Hoping to strike a blow against England in 1602, Spain landed an army in Ireland to bolster the cause of the Earl of Tyrone. The intervention was wholly unsuccessful, and by the time Don Juan del Aguila, the Spanish general, had evacuated Kinsale, Spain's finances were all but exhausted.

The accession to the English throne of James I, who "naturally loved not the sight of a soldier nor any violent man," saved Spain from further expensive involvement with England; for Elizabeth's successor achieved a peace settlement between the two countries in 1604. Thereafter, despite the strength of anti-Spanish feeling in England, relations between Madrid and London became more friendly. Philip's skillful diplomat, the Count of Gondomar—whose task was to keep James from aiding the Protestant states in their quarrels with Spain and to prevent English attacks on Spanish possessions in America—helped maintain this amicable relationship. Negotiations were eventually entered into for a marriage between James I's son Charles and the Infanta Donna Maria, sister of the Spanish King.

Spain had been saved by the pacific policies of James I and the skills of Count Gondomar—but nothing could save her from the loss of her possessions in the Netherlands, where Dutch rebels, supported by England and subsidized by France, had been resisting all attempts to crush them for over thirty years. On April 9, 1609, a treaty was signed that recognized the Dutch Republic as an independent state.

tinuing war with England was but one of the constant strains on her resources.

Toward the end of his reign, Philip II added to his country's fiscal burden by intervening in France in support of the Catholic League, a group that sought to unseat Henry of Navarre. The Duke of Parma was ordered to march across France to help raise the siege of Paris, and Don Juan del Aguila was directed to land in Brittany at the head of two thousand men. The siege of Paris was successfully raised, as was the siege of Rouen; but Parma, Philip's most valued servant, was wounded during an attack on Caudebec and died on December 2, 1592. Subsequent Spanish victories—the capture of Doullens and Cambrai by the Count of Fuentes, Parma's successor, and the reduction of Calais and Amiens—counted for little when weighed against Henry of Navarre's superior diplomatic skill. And by the Treaty of Vervins, signed in May of 1598, Philip was obliged to recognize the failure of his schemes in France and to return all his conquests except Cambrai.

The Escorial, capital of a world empire.

HAERLEM.

Revolt of the Netherlands 1609

The revolt that erupted in the Spanish Netherlands in 1568 pitted a small band of vastly out-numbered, militantly Protestant Dutch nobles against the armies of Spain's Catholic King, Europe's mightiest monarch, Philip II. The contest was a lopsided one, and Philip's victory over the Dutch troops led by William of Orange should have been a swift one. Instead, the fighting dragged on for forty years before a temporary truce was agreed upon in 1609. William of Orange had been assassinated in 1584 and Philip died in 1598—but the dream of an independent Dutch state lived on. Sporadic fighting continued for forty years after the truce, however. Not until 1648, by the terms of the Treaty of Munster, was the former Spanish possession divided into the independent Dutch Republic in the north and the "obedient" southern provinces (later known as Belgium).

The Dutch nation achieved its independence through a war that lasted for eighty years—from 1568 to 1648. If a single day can claim to be the turning point in that long struggle, it is probably April 9, 1609, the day when Spain was compelled to sign a twelve-year truce with the Dutch rebels and thereby recognize that the war had reached a state of complete deadlock. The truce acknowledged, *de facto*, what forty years later was to be recognized *de jure*: that the Dutch Republic was an independent state. Before the final Treaty of Münster was signed in 1648, there were to be military threats to that independence from Spain and more serious threats from France. Frontiers were to be adjusted by military action but subject only to these relatively minor changes in territory and law, 1609 marked the emergence—through political revolt and armed conflict—of a new state in Europe, unique in its constitution, its social structure and its economy.

In its earliest phase, the resistance to Philip II of Spain, who had succeeded his father Charles V as sovereign of the Burgundian Netherlands in 1555, came from the great aristocrats. Charles had scarcely abdicated when the trouble began. The high Netherlands nobility resented Philip's assumption that he "ruled" their territories and could treat them as he liked. They protested against the presence of Spanish troops on Dutch soil, the enforcement of the Inquisition by persecuting Edicts, the rationalization of the Netherlands bishoprics and the general disregard of their traditional feudal rights and privileges. Of the three leaders, Egmont, Hoorn and William, Prince of Orange, it was the latter who rapidly developed the habit of command and the exercise of authority. Yet even Orange, desperately trying to maintain reasonable relations with Philip and also—after the King's departure for Spain in 1559—with his regents and deputies, could not prevent the spread of more violent protest. Some five hundred lesser nobles banded together in a league that was by no means inclined to moderation. Neither

were the fanatical Protestants who went on a wild spree of iconoclasm in the churches of Antwerp and other cities in 1566.

Philip's answer was to send the Duke of Alva to suppress the revolt in 1567. Orange fled, Egmont and Hoorn were executed, and thousands were burned or killed. Alba subsequently proposed a turnover tax, known as the "Tenth Penny," that turned the powerful merchant class in cities like Antwerp, Ghent and Bruges against Spain. Nevertheless, Alba's brutal measures seemed to be working when, in 1572, a band of Dutch rebels—ordered out of Dover harbor by Queen Elizabeth I—fell upon the Dutch port of Brill and succeeded in capturing it. These "Sea Beggars" then went on to take the nearby communities of Flushing, Middelburg and Zierikzee. They swiftly established control over the entire Scheldt estuary and the approaches to Antwerp. That region was not only the center of Spanish government in the Netherlands but also the largest commercial entrepôt in the world. And although Alba successfully laid siege to Haarlem, the dogged resistance of Leyden and Alkmaar led to the liberation of most of Holland and Zeeland.

In 1573 Alba retired to make way for two successors, Luis de Requesens and Don Juan of Austria. Neither succeeded in quelling resistance nor in stemming the growing mutinies among the 60,000 unpaid Spanish troops stationed in the Netherlands. Between 1578 and 1579—amid growing Spanish confusion—Orange consolidated the rebel forces and strengthened their grip on the northwestern Netherlands. Unfortunately for him, religious quarrels between Dutch Catholics, moderate Erasmians and extreme Protestant groups like the fanatical Calvinists of Ghent made national unity impossible; the Prince's opportunity for an early victory was lost amid factional squabbling.

In 1577 Philip sent Alexander Farnese, later Prince of Parma, to join Don Juan. Farnese was not only one of the greatest military commanders of the

Alexander Farnese, Prince of Parma and Governor of the Netherlands; he was one of the military geniuses of his age, but was unable to hold Spain's northern possessions together.

Opposite Spanish soldiers executing Dutch rebels in Haarlem, from *de Leone Belgica* by Francis Hogenberg 1585.

century, he was also an adroit diplomat. By military genius and skillful bribery, Farnese reunited a large part of the south and east for Spain, and in 1579 he signed the Treaty of Arras with the leaders of the southern provinces. That treaty was, in effect, an answer to the Union of Utrecht—an accord signed by most of the northern and some of the southern provinces and towns that is regarded as the foundation charter of the Dutch Republic.

From 1578 to 1589 Farnese pushed north, recapturing most of present-day Belgium—including the great cities of Ghent, Bruges and Antwerp—for Spain. He reached the region where the Rhine, Maas and Lek rivers cross the Low Countries from east to west before his progress was checked by Philip's orders to divert troops to the 1588 invasion of England. Just before Antwerp fell, the rebels' great leader, Orange, was struck down by an assassin. Orange was succeeded by his son Maurice, who proved to be an even greater military commander. With the political help of another republican leader, Jan van Olden Barneveldt, Maurice regained much of the territory to the south and east that Farnese had captured, but he could not break the siege of Ostend. Its surrender to Spinola, another brilliant Italian commander in the pay of Philip II, ended the first half of the war and made the truce of 1609 inevitable.

Little of real consequence happened after hostilities were resumed in 1621. In a protracted and dreary struggle, the Dutch, under Maurice's successor, Frederick Henry, managed to capture 's Hertogenbosch, Maastricht and the surrounding country. Neither a French alliance nor the marriage of Frederick's daughter Mary to James, Duke of York, enabled them to do more. The 1648 Treaty of Münster irrevocably divided the Netherlands into the obedient Provinces of the South, which remained loyal to Spain, and the Dutch Republic, which became a monarchy in 1813.

Nineteenth-century historians assumed that the rebellion was Protestant and liberal, and that there was something about the ethos of the "Teutonic" north that predestined it to lead the Netherlands out of the decadent, Catholic, persecuting Spanish Empire. The explanation is obviously defective. In the early stages—and indeed as late as 1578—the revolt drew much of its strength from the south: the southern city of Ghent was, from the beginning, a violent, unrepentant center of Calvinism—and Calvinism itself entered the Netherlands from the south (from France, via the Walloon provinces). The original center of Orange's resistance movement was in

4/22

A difference of social structure

Brabant, or Brussels, a city that lay far south of Holland and Zeeland. The Sea Beggars drew much of their strength from Flanders, Brabant and Wallonia, and many southern Catholic nobles were as strong in defense of their privileges as their poorer northern neighbors—until they were bribed back into loyalty by Farnese.

Such obstinate facts caused the most famous twentieth-century historian of the revolt, Peter Geyl, to reject the religious or "racial" explanation of the rising in favor of a quite different one. The Netherlands, he argued, had already formed a natural cultural unity before the revolt; the country was on its way to becoming a political unit before the fighting began. Thus the revolt began as a medieval, feudal, noble protest and ended as a conquest of the north by Protestant forces working through the Sea Beggars. The north was able to fight off Spanish attempts at reconquest because it was protected by a defense line of great rivers that even Farnese failed to breach.

Geyl's interpretation has become virtual orthodoxy, although after forty-odd years it seems oversimplified. Unquestionably the rebels were helped by geography. Yet other factors must be taken into account. For one, the era was one of siege warfare, not mobile warfare. Southern cities like Ghent, Bruges and Antwerp were well fortified and capable of self-defense. For another, the pattern—even in the north—was inconsistent: the northern city of Haarlem fell, but Amsterdam remained pro-Spanish and Catholic until 1578, when it fell to the rebels by an internal coup d'état. The truth is that Antwerp and the other southern cities succumbed through muddle, bribery and loss of morale—rather than through absolute indefensibility.

Nor should one ignore another important feature of the revolt that does not fit Geyl's theory of a united Netherlands disrupted solely by Spanish military force. The fact is that even before Philip's accession there were marked differences of social structure between south and north. The south was more prosperous, more commercial, more industrial—and yet more subject to feudal, aristocratic influence—than the north, which was a poorer society, dependent upon shipping and fishing. From the beginning of the revolt in 1567, merchants, manufacturers and workers began to move north, sensing that the north was likely to be safer and less exposed to the risk of princely or aristocratic looting than the south was. Perhaps ten per cent of the southern population— and a far higher percentage of its most dynamic members—emigrated during this period, and by the 1590s they were prominent among the professors, printers, artists, bankers, clothiers, silk spinners, shipbuilders and overseas traders in Amsterdam, Haarlem, Leyden, Middelburg and many other ports and cities of the north.

The southern aristocracy, immobilized by their investments in land and property, could contribute little to the revolt. Shamefaced, they stayed put and allowed themselves to be bribed into renewing their loyal pledges to Spain. On the other hand, there can be no doubt about the fanatical sincerity of the

Frederick Henry, Prince of Orange; it was ironic that Holland's struggle for liberty should be led by German nobles such as the princes of Orange.

southern Calvinists, most of whom came from the lower or middle classes.

There was little homogeneity among the classes that supported the revolt, and it is difficult to determine the motives that drove them on. Simple hatred of Spanish occupation and Inquisitional persecution was widespread among the middle and upper classes. (Among other things, persecution, war, dynasticism and all the costs that accompanied them were bad for business—and Dutch society was already a business society.) At the other end of the scale, frustration and mistrust were increased by a new phenomenon of the age: unprecedented inflation, which afflicted aristocracy and working men alike. Nobles living on incomes derived from more or less fixed rents found themselves caught between rising costs and falling receipts at a time when court jobs and army appointments were going to Spaniards. And as industry deserted the old guild-dominated towns for the Flanders countryside, a growing force of workers found itself turned adrift, workless and starving. As a result, the extremes of Dutch society were united in their discontent and unanimous in their support of both political and religious dissent. They were soon joined by the potentially less vulnerable and certainly more circumspect middle class, whose members were disturbed by the prospect of damaging and unlimited Spanish taxation. This class took control of the new Republic.

It is that combination of social classes and political motives which distinguishes the revolt of the Netherlands from the feudal protests, Protestant rebellions and peasant uprisings that occurred in France, England, Germany, Italy, Spain and Scandinavia in the late sixteenth and early seventeenth centuries. The Dutch revolt represents the one successful rising of a mercantile republic against the centralized,

Francis Gomarus: leader of the Calvinist extremists.

Mercantilism succeeds against monarchical absolutism

A Dutch merchant with his wife in Java. The Dutch colonial empire, like that of England, grew during the seventeenth and eighteenth centuries, while those of Spain and Portugal stagnated.

Right The Mayor of Delft. Dutch domestic life, after independence was officially acknowledged by Spain, became far more prosperous than it had previously been.

The Rise of the Dutch Republic to 1648

- ○ Holy Roman Empire
- ● United Provinces
- ○ Remained Spanish Netherlands

Dutch open dykes 1573
Alkmaar
Amsterdam
Haarlem
Besieged by Alba 1572-73
The Hague
Assassination of William the Silent 1584
Rotterdam
Brill
Leyden
Utrecht
Delft
Zutphen
Defeat of Sir Philip Sidney 1586
Breda
Bruges
Ghent
Nieuwport
Antwerp Sacked 1576
Maastricht
Brussels
Louvain
Liége
Mons
Cateau-Cambrésis
River Rhine

FRANCE

monarchical absolutism typified by the states of early modern Europe—Spain, France, England and Prussia. Curiously, the Dutch example did not spread. (John Adams, scraping the bottom of the barrel for money to finance the American Revolution, appealed to the spirit of comradeship between the American "federation" and its Dutch "originals" —and got nowhere.)

The chronicle of the Republic's economic and cultural history is an altogether different story. Before the 1590s the northern provinces were poorer than their southern neighbors, but after 1590 they rapidly overtook them. Amsterdam soon replaced Antwerp as the world's foremost entrepôt, and the Dutch *fluit*—an unarmed, cheap, sea-going barge— introduced a technological revolution in shipbuilding. The Dutch *fluit* fleet soon established a virtual monopoly on the trade in grain, timber and naval stores from the Baltic to Europe.

In the early seventeenth century Dutch merchants opened new markets in Russia, Greenland, Newfoundland, India, Java, Sumatra and Australasia. At New Amsterdam (renamed New York after its capture by the English) and at the Cape of Good Hope, the Dutch left colonies that helped to shape the character of future settlements. In India, Ceylon and the East they founded a great trading company, the East India Company. And in North and South America and the West Indies the Dutch West India Company flourished for a time.

Dutch colonial history has been emphasized in Western history books, yet statistically it was never as important as Dutch trade within Europe. The

"new drapery"—carried by Belgian emigrants from Ypres to Leyden, and then to Norwich and Colchester—revolutionized Europe's textile trade, replacing old, heavy, expensive cloths with bright, light, cheaper textiles. Antwerp silk weavers and linen bleachers carried their skills to Amsterdam and Haarlem, and cohorts of merchants and bankers followed King William and Queen Mary to England. In ensuing decades, Dutch bankers helped to shape the structure and finance of the Bank of England, and the loans by which England financed her wars— including the American Revolution—were underwritten by men named Vanneck, Van Notten, and Capadose.

Almost every country in Europe profited from Dutch immigration. From London to Rome and Danzig to Warsaw, Dutch settlers used their engineering skills to clear swamps and marshes and to build dams, locks and canals, water works and pumping systems. Colbert employed Dutchmen in Bordeaux to reclaim land and build textile factories, and in Sweden Dutch immigrants negotiated contracts with the Crown that gave them a virtual monopoly of iron and copper mining, the manufacture of munitions, the cutting of timber and the export of tar, hemp and rope. Export of Dutch capital and skill to less-developed economies is a recurrent feature of economic life in the seventeenth century.

Along with the economic tide went ideas, philosophy and works of art. Grotius was the spokesman, advocate and historian of the patrician governing class, but his principles—among them *mare liberum*, or freedom of the seas—were adopted by England

and later by the entire civilized world. (Indeed Grotius' claim to the title Father of Modern International Law has never been challenged.) Philosophers like Descartes, Spinoza and Locke took refuge in the relatively tolerant climate of Holland.

Rembrandt, the greatest of the hundreds of Netherlands artists whose works have become part of Europe's cultural heritage, lived not far from Spinoza in Amsterdam's Jewish quarter. Dutch art, like many Dutch innovations, grew up under strong Italian influence, yet it developed its own unique and unmistakable style. Seascapes, domestic interiors, flower paintings, portraits, landscapes—all demonstrate a miraculous absorption of detail into broad and satisfying patterns that has rarely been equaled before or since.

The capacity for combining detailed observation with significant generalization links seventeenth-century Dutch artists with their scientific contemporaries—men like Leeuwenhoek, Boerhaave, Huyghens and Stevin—who brought scientific methods to microscopy, biology, zoology, medicine, astronomy, architecture, ballistics and navigation.

Economic decline set in with the eighteenth century, as competition from larger states, high defense costs and heavy taxation combined to check Dutch prosperity and diminish Dutch power. But in their heyday, Dutch capital, Dutch enterprise and Dutch technology—all by-products of the Dutch revolt— served as a powerful driving force, propelling a predominantly agrarian, semifeudal Europe toward industrial revolution and socio-economic modernity.

CHARLES WILSON

The ratification of the treaty of Münster, 1648, which finally gave Holland independence from Spain.

The perverse fragmentation of

While Spain was signing a truce with the Dutch rebels in 1609, King James of England was entertaining vague but grandiose notions of peacefully uniting the whole of Europe and establishing himself and the Pope as joint presidents of a great council of the Church. James' ambitious design far exceeded his rather limited talents and powers, however, and seventeenth-century Europe remained as perversely fragmented as it had been at any time in its history.

In the south, the unwieldy Ottoman Empire, slowly recovering from the shattering defeat of its navy at Lepanto, sprawled across the southern shore of the Mediterranean from Algiers to Egypt and Syria, and stretched northward across Anatolia and the Bosphorus—through Greece, Bulgaria and Hungary—to the Black Sea and the Crimea. This vast empire was ruled by Sultan Ahmed I, a sickly king who was to die before he was

James I welcomes his son Charles home after his visit to Spain.

thirty. Ahmed's decadent and corrupt Empire had long since lost the vitality that had made it the terror of Christendom in the days of Suleiman the Magnificent. Nonetheless, its confidently predicted

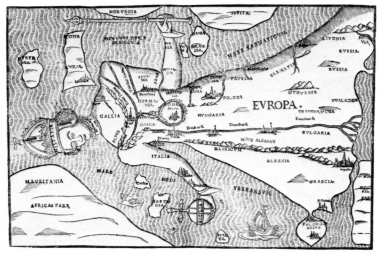
Europe and Asia through the eyes of the early-seventeenth century.

demise was to be postponed for more than three centuries.

Beyond the Empire's northern boundaries were the three largest states in Europe—Poland, Russia and Sweden. Of these, Sweden—under the stern military rule of the aggressive Charles IX—was by far the most powerful. By 1609 she had seized Estonia, and with the conquest of Livonia and Ingria she pushed Poland out of the eastern Baltic.

Barbarous Russia

Russia, shut out of the Baltic by Sweden, cut off from the Black Sea by the Turks and engaged in interminable disputes with Poland, was reckoned of small importance in European affairs. "If a man consider the natures and manner of life of the Muscovites, he will be forced to allow that there cannot be anything more barbarous than that people," a German visitor decided. "They never learn any art or science or apply themselves to any kind of study; on the contrary they are so ignorant as to think that a man cannot make an almanack unless he be a sorcerer, nor foretell the revolution of the moon and the eclipses unless he have some communication with devils."

The few schools that existed in the primitive, thinly populated country were in the hands of superstitious and narrow-minded monks; there was no parliament; there was no justice worthy of the name; there was no freedom of thought, no intellectual life, no economic development. Instead there was sloth and prejudice, corruption, violence and wholesale drunkenness. Ivan the Terrible—the Grand Duke of

Muscovy who had bestowed the title of Tsar upon himself and who had ruthlessly imposed an autocratic government of the most oppressively despotic kind upon the Russian people—had died in 1584, leaving a weak and pious heir who was content to place the administration of the country in the hands of his brother-in-law, Boris Godunov.

Godunov — who gained wide popularity among the landowning class by forbidding peasants to move from one estate to another, thus placing them at the mercy of their masters and accelerating their debasement into serfs—had himself chosen as his brother-in-law's successor. In 1598 he became Tsar of All the Russias. The accession of a

Ivan the Terrible: his death threw Russia into turmoil.

mere boyar aroused the anger and jealousy of the nobles, who conspired to overthrow Godunov. And thus, while the nobles plotted, while gangs of bandits terrorized the countryside, while hundreds of square miles were devastated by plague and famine, while an impostor who called himself Dimitri, the younger son of Ivan the Terrible, mustered an army in Poland —a disturbed Russia entered the seventeenth century.

To the west of Poland lay a conglomeration of over three hundred German states, all of them under the nominal protection of the ill and indolent Austrian Hapsburg Emperor, Matthias, who had succeeded his brother in 1602.

seventeenth-century Europe

Italy—a geographical expression

Like Germany, Italy was what Metternich would later call *"ein geographischer Begriff"* — "a mere geographical expression." In the northeast lay the Republic of Venice, whose lands stretched from Bergamo to Istria and down the eastern shores of the Adriatic. (Overseas they also included Crete, which was not to fall into the hands of the Turks until the end of the seventeenth century.) South of Venice were the Papal States, which cut Italy in half from Ancona to Rome and extended as far south as Terracina, sixty miles north of Naples. Naples itself was the capital of a kingdom that included Sicily and Sardinia and formed part of the vast possessions of the King of Spain.

The extensive Duchy of Milan was also part of the Spanish Empire. Milan's neighbors — aside from Venice to the east and Switzerland to the north—were the Duchy of Mantua, ruled by the Gonzaga family; the Duchy of Modena, governed by the House of Este; the Duchy of Parma, which was in the hands of the Farnese; the Republic of Genoa, to which Corsica belonged until it was sold to France in 1768; and the Piedmontese possessions of the House of Savoy. Victor Emmanuel III, a descendant of the King of Savoy, was to become the first king of a united Italy in 1861.

France's ascendancy

France, to whom the House of Savoy would one day lose both Savoy and Nice, was ruled by Henry IV, the most remarkable ruler of his time. The son of the

The execution of Henry IV's murderer Ravaillac.

Duke of Vendôme and Jeanne d'Albret, Queen of Navarre, he was educated as a Protestant and distinguished himself in the religious wars in France. On the death of his mother in 1572 he became King of Navarre, and following the assassination of Henry III in 1589 he became King of France.

Ten years of fighting intervened before Henry, who had become a Catholic convert, could claim his inheritance. From that time on, Henry, aided by his friend the Duke of Sully, concentrated his considerable talents upon restoring the fortunes of France. Riding over all opposition and ignoring all criticism, Henry drove through reforms of the administration, finances, industry and the army, and gave Paris new buildings of great beauty.

In his efforts to weaken the power of the Hapsburgs, the French King entered into a series of alliances with the Protestant princes of Germany, the King of Sweden, various Italian states, the Swiss cantons and the Duke of Lorraine. After the death of his first wife, Margaret of Valois, sister of Henry III of France, Henry married the formidable

Marie de' Medici, and thus gained the favor of her uncle, the Grand Duke of Tuscany. By the time of his assassination in May, 1610, Henry had prepared France for the fulfillment of her great destiny. Cardinal Richelieu, minister to Henry's son and heir Louis XIII, and Richelieu's successor, Cardinal Mazarin, were to achieve that destiny.

While France was rising to domination in Europe, Spain was becoming ever weaker. She was internally exhausted: her economy was unstable, her treasury was ruined, and the American gold that poured into her ports was grossly ill-distributed. In no country in Europe was there so marked a contrast between the magnificence of the rich and the abject poverty of the poor. The American colonies were also proving a liability to Spain.

England, for her part, had as yet made little attempt to colonize America. Her sixteenth-century voyagers had been more concerned with discovery, adventure and plunder. In 1583 Sir Humphry Gilbert had taken possession of Newfoundland in the name of Queen Elizabeth, and in 1584 a fleet sent out by Sir Walter Raleigh to explore the American seaboard north of Florida had occupied the district known as Virginia. But even such men as Richard Hakluyt, whose *Principal Navigations, Voyages and Discoveries of the English Nation* was published between 1598 and 1600, believed that a colony's main uses were as a promoter of trade or as a penal settlement. It was not until 1609, with the founding of Jamestown in Virginia, that the age of English colonization really began. Eleven years later, an even more significant landfall was made in New England.

Henry IV of Navarre and France: enemy of the Hapsburgs.

Marie de' Medici, widow of Henry IV, with her son Louis XIII.

The Pilgrims at Plymouth

Unlike their predecessors, who settled in Virginia at the end of the first decade of the seventeenth century, the religious dissidents who boarded the Mayflower *in September 1620 had no patron and no significant financial backing. Those expatriate Englishmen—most of whom had recently sought—and failed to find—ecclesiastical equanimity in Holland—sailed without a royal charter and without commercial backing. Their voyage was undertaken amid considerable uncertainty and at long odds—and when half the 102-man company died within six months of their arrival, Plymouth Colony appeared doomed. Indeed, the Colony never did prosper, and it was ultimately absorbed into the thriving Massachusetts Bay Colony—but not before America's most famous colonists had firmly established religious diversity and, to a degree, religious toleration as a fact of life in the New World.*

From September 6 to November 9, 1620, the merchant ship *Mayflower*, usually employed in the Anglo-French wine trade, sailed west across the Atlantic Ocean toward the coast of North America. On board were 102 men, women and children bound for a new life in a new world. (According to William Bradford, leader of the *Mayflower* company and first governor of Plymouth colony, the original passenger list totaled 102. Two children were born during the voyage.

The *Mayflower*'s passengers were predominantly poor men, drawn from the ranks of small craftsmen, artisans and petty tradesmen. Many of them came from Leyden, Holland, where they had made a meager living in and around the cloth industry. All were English—and although they were poor, their main reason for leaving Europe was not to improve their economic lot but to secure religious freedom. They had emigrated from England and settled in Holland to escape religious persecution, seeking and finding in Holland the right to organize their own church. But in Leyden other vexations had arisen: the immigrants feared that their children would quickly absorb Dutch ways, lose their attachment to the English community and abandon the "Pilgrim's" church.

The Pilgrims were a community centered upon a church. Like many other Englishmen of their time, they had grown discontented with the Church of England. The majority of its critics had remained within the Anglican Church, pressing for reforms; the Pilgrims were part of a small, weak minority which had decided that it could no longer profess allegiance to a corrupt Church. Following the lead of their ministers, a number of persons from Scrooby, in Nottinghamshire, had separated themselves from their parish churches and formed their own congregations. Their act was blatantly seditious—a challenge to Church and State alike—and rather than risk prosecution, the separatists had fled to Holland in 1607. Holland too had posed problems, and the

immigrants had therefore boarded the *Mayflower*, hoping that they would soon be beyond the reach of the English government—yet free to remain English in the New World.

In early November of 1620, the *Mayflower* reached Cape Cod. New England was not the Pilgrims' intended destination; their original plan had been to settle themselves in a remote and empty part of Virginia, which was already an English colony. The settlers attempted to sail free of the New England coast and proceed south, but the currents and winds hindered them and they returned to Cape Cod. On November 11, their ship lay safely at harbor. The Pilgrims had decided to settle in New England.

Winter was near, and the settlers were justifiably apprehensive about its coming and about the desolate look of the nearby coasts. William Bradford, their great leader and chronicler, noted in his journal the "violent and savage hue" of the "wilderness." Reconnoitering parties were put ashore to search for a suitable place to begin the long business of building a new settlement, but it was several weeks before such a place was found. The *Mayflower*, cruising down the inner coast of the Cape, reached a sheltered harbor. The inlet was safe for shipping, and its shores had "divers cornfields and little brooks"; all in all, "a place fit for situation." There the settlers would establish Plymouth Colony.

The long search for a suitable site for their future colony had been only one of the Pilgrims' troubles. Since they were outside the jurisdiction of Virginia, some of the passengers—those recruited in London, who were not members of the Leyden church—claimed that no government existed and that no one could exercise authority over them. Bradford and the other Pilgrim fathers resolved that dilemma by drafting the famous Mayflower Compact. In signing that document, the vast majority of the adult males on board the *Mayflower* pledged their obedience to an elected governor and to any laws on which they might agree. In effect, control was given to the

The seal of the Plymouth colony: it was used on official documents.

Opposite A reconstruction of the Plymouth Colony as it appeared in 1627.

The first Thanksgiving

Boston
Cambridge
Greenwich
Southampton
Plymouth
● Main emigrant areas
○ Secondary emigrant areas

William Laud, who became Archbishop of Canterbury in 1633. His rigid intolerance of Puritanism caused a wave of emigration to New England.

Below left The port of Southampton: one of several ports on the south and east coast of England from which emigrants set sail for America.

Below right The *Mayflower*, the ship in which the Pilgrim Fathers sailed to the New World.

Leyden group, the dissenting faction was suppressed, and the colony's chances of survival were enhanced.

Unity was necessary. The first years of the colony's existence were hard and cruel ones, as famine, disease and privation—all potential invitations to anarchy —overtook the little society. Half the *Mayflower*'s original passengers were dead by the spring of 1621, and the colony did not achieve even the most modest sort of security until two years later. Yet its internal life proceeded smoothly. The religious community of the Pilgrims acted as a stabilizing force, and so did their social homogeneity. After a few years the colony became a self-governing settlement—one in which there was a simple and unself-conscious legal and political equality.

During those first difficult years, the struggling colony received immeasurable assistance from several indigenous Indian tribes, notably the Wampanoag. Their chief, Massasoit, signed a mutual aid pact with the settlers in 1621. Legend credits Squanto, sole survivor of the Pawtuxet Indian nation, with teaching the colonists how to catch and dry herring, tap maple groves for their sugar, and plant the native corn—Indian style, four kernels to a mound. Squanto had been captured by an English slaver in 1614 and sold to a Spanish master, had escaped to England and, in 1618, had returned to his homeland—to find all the members of his tribe wiped out by a smallpox epidemic. Squanto's trans-oceanic travels had given him a knowledge of the English language and English customs that was to prove of inestimable value to Bradford and his company.

The Pilgrims, touched and astonished by the Indians' aid, reciprocated by inviting Squanto and ninety-odd members of Massasoit's tribe to the most famous alfresco buffet in American folklore—the first Thanksgiving dinner. That feast, held in mid-October of 1621 to celebrate the completion of the colony's first harvest, featured native turkey, duck, geese, deer, corn bread and wild berries. The Indians, obviously caught up in the spirit of the occasion, stayed for three days.

The Thanksgiving celebration was the lone bright spot in a year otherwise noted for famine, skirmishes with unfriendly Indians and uncontrolled epidemics —known collectively as the "General Sickness." The *Mayflower* passengers were not unique in their sufferings, however; Virginia's early settlers (1584 and 1607 at Jamestown) had had similar experiences. It was the radical nature of the Pilgrims' religious attitudes, their poverty and their lack of support from England that set them apart from other early American colonists. Virginia was the creation of English gentry and merchants, who financed voyages of colonization and supported New World colonies for commercial reasons. Massachusetts Bay, the third English colony in North America, had both a royal charter and financial backing from several quarters. Plymouth Colony, on the other hand, was the only North American settlement to be established with little aid from England and no influential friends.

Plymouth never became a particularly thriving colony. It remained a society of traders, small farmers and fishermen—poor and unpopulous. In 1630 the colonization of Massachusetts by the Puritans began in earnest, and that colony soon surpassed Plymouth in size and importance. In 1691 the Pilgrim colony was absorbed by its large and powerful neighbor (more or less willingly, since the two shared similar religious and political systems). The memory of Plymouth's founding remained a vivid one, however, and the story of those poor and humble settlers —who sailed three thousand miles across the storm-tossed Atlantic to find religious freedom and suffered in the wilderness to build their new homes—became a not unimportant part of American legend.

By the end of the seventeenth century, that legend had already become a politically useful tool in New England. The Pilgrims and the Puritans were frequently depicted as a poor, harassed minority that had fled the persecution of kings and bishops to secure freedom in the New World. There, at their own expense, they had built simple but godly societies that were antipathetic to monarchs—unless they were good Protestant ones who left them alone—and

to bishops, of any religion whatsoever. New England was naturally sympathetic to Cromwell, to the Parliamentary side in the English civil war and to the nonconformists exiled upon the return of the Stuarts. Their plight corresponded perfectly with the Anglo-American nonconformist tradition—a tradition that had its roots among the middle classes, was suspicious of ecclesiastical hierarchy, aristocracy and monarchy, and was devoted to representative assemblies that opposed any flavor of absolutism or princely power, whether exercised by kings or their ministers.

New England was only one region of America, and the Plymouth settlers were only part of a much larger migration of Englishmen to the New World—one that rapidly produced settlements along the entire Eastern seaboard. For the most part, those migrants were humble people: indentured servants, young men and women from the lower sections of

Colonists landing in Virginia: In 1607 the first permanent English colony in the New World was established at Jamestown in Virginia.

Left Indians celebrating a victory: in the early years, the Pilgrim Fathers received invaluable assistance from local Indian tribes.

4/31

Breaking down the concept of religious uniformity

Their rype corne

Their greene corne

Corne newly sprong.

Their sitting at meate.

the place of solemne prayer.

nese wherin the Tombe of their Herounds standeth.

SEGOTON.

A Ceremony in their prayers with strange iestures and songs dansing abowt posts carued on the topps lyke mens faces.

An Indian village, showing corn production: the Indians taught the colonists how to plant the native corn.

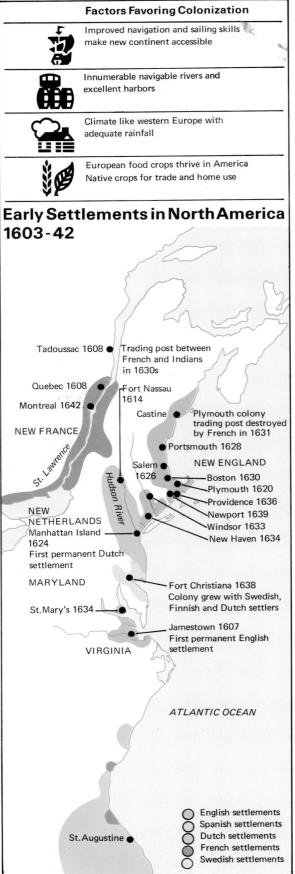

Factors Favoring Colonization

Improved navigation and sailing skills make new continent accessible

Innumerable navigable rivers and excellent harbors

Climate like western Europe with adequate rainfall

European food crops thrive in America Native crops for trade and home use

Early Settlements in North America 1603-42

Tadoussac 1608 — Trading post between French and Indians in 1630s

Quebec 1608 — Fort Nassau 1614

Montreal 1642

Castine — Plymouth colony trading post destroyed by French in 1631

NEW FRANCE

Portsmouth 1628

Salem 1626 — NEW ENGLAND

Boston 1630
Plymouth 1620
Providence 1636
Newport 1639
Windsor 1633
New Haven 1634

St. Lawrence

Hudson River

NEW NETHERLANDS
Manhattan Island 1624
First permanent Dutch settlement

MARYLAND

Fort Christiana 1638 Colony grew with Swedish, Finnish and Dutch settlers

St. Mary's 1634

Jamestown 1607 First permanent English settlement

VIRGINIA

ATLANTIC OCEAN

St. Augustine

○ English settlements
○ Spanish settlements
○ Dutch settlements
● French settlements
○ Swedish settlements

society, artisans and craftsmen. The hopelessly poor and degraded did not come. Nor—naturally enough —did the aristocracy, the gentry and the great merchants. A few men of property made the long voyage, but the colonial upper classes were largely recruited from within. In the process, many of the practices and institutions linked to the privileges of the European and English upper classes disappeared. Hereditary aristocracy was never introduced, nor was the concept of a professional army. Land tenure was simple in America, for the feudal complexity of European practices was rejected. Entailed estates were all but nonexistent, and attempts to introduce "quit rents" (rents paid in lieu of feudal services) and to link landownership to institutional privileges were unsuccessful.

The most remarkable alteration of all occurred in the area of religious toleration. During the first decades of the seventeenth century, the New World witnessed the breakdown of the concept of religious uniformity, a dream that was still cherished in most of the monarchies of Europe. European states had largely acted to choke off the proliferation of religious sects after the early years of the Reformation, but in the seventeenth and eighteenth centuries religious groups sought and found great opportunities in America. Maryland was settled by Catholics from

Protestant England; New England, of course, was colonized by Puritans and Separatists; Pennsylvania by Quakers fleeing Anglican repression; and Nova Scotia by Huguenots seeking security from French religious absolutism.

That massive migration was a remarkable phenomenon. By the end of the eighteenth century it had given America a reputation for profound and widespread religious tolerance. Such tolerance had not always been there—it was the growth of sects that forced its emergence. And grow they did—for once relieved of the weight of effective established churches, the original denominations rapidly splintered and multiplied. Old and New Light Congregationalists and Presbyterians, Baptists, Separate Baptists, Rogerenes, Methodists, Shakers and Quakers, Dunkers and Amish, Huguenots and Anglicans—all testified to the disintegration of European ideas of religious orthodoxy. The multiplication of sects evidenced the weakness of institutionalized religion and also lessened the formal influence of ministers and priests in government.

Diversity was also noticeable in the population of the New World. The French and the Spanish had their own national settlements—the former in Canada and the Ohio Valley, the latter in Florida and the Caribbean—but these were weak and fail-

An illustration from a discourse of 1636 outlining the heresies of two weavers.

Above left A seventeenth-century cartoon showing wrangling sects tossing a Bible in a blanket.

Below left The first church in Salem: Salem was founded in 1626 by discontented members of the Plymouth Colony.

Detail from a Puritan tombstone at Dorchester, Mass. The heavy symbolism of death reflects the tradition of Puritan religious severity.

Miles Standish, a leading
member of the Plymouth
Colony, although he was not a
Separatist but a member of the
Church of England.

Above right Signatures to the
Mayflower Compact which
served as the Pilgrim Fathers'
constitution in the New
World. It was signed on
November 21, 1620, before
the landing at Plymouth.

ing. After 1620, non-English settlers came to the
English colonies in increasing numbers. The Ulster
Scots—called Scotch Irish in America—and the
Germans—known as the Pennsylvania Dutch—were
the two largest groups; by 1790 they comprised
eighteen per cent of the colonial population. Catholic
Irish, French Huguenots, Swiss and Salzburger Protestants, Jews from Southern Europe, Lowland and
Highland Scots, and the remnants of early Dutch
and Scandinavian colonists made up another twelve
per cent. All these foreshadowed the variety of
national groups that flooded into nineteenth-century
America.

By the eighteenth century, colonial society was
moving in the direction of struggle and protest—
conditions that normally release social energies and,

for a time at least, increase political opportunities
for all classes. England had allowed her American
possessions large political freedoms while trying to
enforce a certain degree of economic control, and
that policy had produced strong local political institutions. Those institutions naturally opposed Britain's restrictions on colonial economic development, and for decades the royal governors of each
colony were forced to contend with strong and restive
representative assemblies.

The growth of the representative assembly was an
essential American development—one that could
trace its origins back to the Mayflower Compact.
Springing from privileges given to the early colonies
in their charters (which were intended to grant a
limited form of municipal self-government), the

John Winthrop.
He organized a Puritan
migration from England in
1630 to the Massachusetts
Bay area, finally settling
in Boston.

Right An early-seventeenth-
century map of America with
Indians decorating the border.

The South East Prospect of The City of Philadelphia By Peter Cooper Painter

assemblies had gradually arrogated parliamentary rights and immunities. Many of their members were fully conversant with the most extreme and advanced theories of eighteenth-century English politics and were as capable of using them as any English radical.

The final struggle came after 1763, when the British Crown, suddenly aware of the need for a revised colonial policy, decided to increase its regulation of American governments. The result was an intensification and universalization of the conflict between autocracy and personal liberty that had prompted the emigration of the Pilgrims more than a century earlier. Americans claimed to stand for the rights of man against the crimes of tyrants—for the people, and against their kings.

The largest non-English immigrant group shared none of the freedom or opportunity that the New World supposedly offered. That group consisted of more than half a million black slaves, nearly twenty per cent of the total population of North America in 1790. The economies of the southern colonies—and their profitable crops of tobacco, rice, indigo and cotton—were supported by the labor of men and women who were regarded as chattel and whose numbers were augmented each year by a thriving slave trade.

Henceforward the rhetoric of Americans would emphasize the differences between Europe and America. The Reverend Ezra Stiles proclaimed that Divine Providence "was making way for the planting and Erection in this land the best policied Empire that has yet appeared in the World. In which Liberty and Property will be secured." That empire, he asserted, would be renowned for "liberty civil and religious" and for "Science and Arts."

His opinion won widespread support among Europeans, for with the American Revolution, the New World had taken its place on the stage of history. Its institutions, and the prevailing opinions of its statesmen, placed it firmly in the "party of humanity"—the camp of the Enlightenment. Given time, the Old World might even catch up with the New.

OLIVER LEVY

Philadelphia. The territory of Pennsylvania was granted to William Penn in 1681, and Philadelphia rapidly grew to be the leading town and port.

Left The first Quaker temple in Philadelphia. Most of the early settlers in Pennsylvania were Quakers.

Quakers being tortured in London in 1656.

For several years after the sailing of the *Mayflower* in 1620, few Englishmen were adventurous enough to make the dangerous and fearfully uncomfortable Atlantic crossing. The prospects on arrival were bleak, and only those whose religious faith was certain, whose sense of adventure was acute, whose ambition was intense or whose debts were overwhelmingly pressing chose to hazard their future by making the long journey. As the colonies prospered, however, new companies were founded and new charters were granted. And as the determination of William Laud to impose uniformity upon the Church of England increased in intensity, the number of emigrants also increased. By the mid-1630s depopulation had become a serious social problem in several areas of England, and the government was obliged to issue proclamations against emigration. Those edicts notwithstanding, more than 60,000 people left England between 1630 and 1643, and a third of them settled in New England.

At first the English government and the Church were glad to see the Puritans leave the country, taking their heresies with them. America was thought of as a useful depository for tiresome, nonconforming Protestants who would otherwise stir up trouble at home. The American colonies, in the words of Peter Heylin, the Archbishop's influential High Church chaplain, were "like the spleen of the natural body, not unuseful and unserviceable to the general health by drawing to it so many sullen, sad and offensive humours."

Within twenty years of the *Mayflower*'s departure, that spleen had

Tradesmen were leaders of heretical protestant opinion in England.

become too full. There was a real fear in England that the offensive nature of the religion practiced in the American colonies—which had previously aroused little interest and had consequently gone unchecked—would spread to the home country. It was decided that an

Complaints against Puritan laws banning selling on Sundays.

Anglican bishop would have to be dispatched to New England and that troops would have to go with him to force the colonists to mend their ways and join the one true Church. The drastic proposal came to nothing, however, for there were troubles enough at home.

But even if a bishop had been dispatched, there can be no doubt that his mission would have met with small success, for Puritanism was by now an essential element in New England life, and New England was becoming increasingly independent of London. The New England Company, which had been organized in London in 1628 to provide a refuge for discontented Puritans as well as a profit for the shareholders, had been transformed into the Massachusetts Bay Company shortly thereafter. Within a matter of months the government of the extensive territories controlled by the Company was transferred from England to America, and it was soon established that no one could aspire to the privileges of a freeman unless he accepted the Puritan creed and conformed to Puritan morality. And since it was only freemen who could name "assistants"—the men who in turn named the governor — political power was lodged in Puritan hands from the beginning. It would have taken more than a lone Anglican bishop to wrest it from them.

Religious intolerance in America

Although the emigrants had gone to America to seek religious freedom, they had, upon arrival, been remarkably intolerant of those who

would not accept their own faith. Moreover, their elected leaders had been less than indulgent in their treatment of the sinners in their midst. Baptists were penalized, and in all of the New England colonies acts were passed to exclude or punish Quakers. The death penalty or various forms of mutilation were imposed for idolatry, blasphemy and adultery. A man who denied the existence of the Devil might have a hole bored in his tongue with a hot iron, and offenses as venial as smoking and wearing unseemly clothes were also considered crimes.

Yet cruel and absurd as their intolerance now seems to us, neither the Puritan colonists nor the zealots from whom they had fled were in conflict with the commonly held views of their time. Religious toleration was considered scarcely more acceptable in the first half of the seventeenth century than it had been in the days of Erasmus and Montaigne, for religion was not thought of as a private matter between God and a man's conscience, but was inextricably bound up with society and politics. It kept a king's subjects in obedience—and because it did so it became the direct concern of the State. (Such a view was not unique to England and the American colonies; it applied with even greater force on the Continent, where the fundamental issues had not yet been resolved.

The issue was not simply one of conflict between Roman Catholics and Protestants. On the Catholic side, for example, there were two rival defenders of the Church of Rome, two forces propagating the Counter-Reformation from different standpoints. There were the

A seventeenth-century contrast: the orthodox true minister (left), and the seducer and false prophet.

Europe and America

Townspeople fleeing to avoid the plague in 1530: England's troubles were exacerbated by this plague.

Capuchins, an order of friars who had broken away from the Franciscans and were particularly influential in France; and there were the Jesuits, members of the Society of Jesus founded by the Spaniard, Ignatius Loyola, in 1534. On the Protestant side there were also two movements, the Lutherans and the Calvinists. Those rival factions were as essentially different as the two men from whom they took their names—the earthy, ebullient, neurotically self-critical German monk and the austere, polite, reserved French scholar. John Calvin's teaching represented more than a new theology; indeed, what Calvin proffered was a new political theory. He envisaged a theocratic state in which the full privileges of the Church were reserved for those of proved godliness, a society in which pastors and laymen alike were subject to scrutiny and control by a council representative of the community and answerable to no one but God. It was a teaching that formed a direct challenge to monarchic government, one that allied itself entirely with the growing forces of Republicanism. Its followers were natural enemies of popery—and if there was one thing they detested as much as a papist it was a Lutheran. From the beginning of the seventeenth century the quarrel between Protestant and Catholic had been threatening to erupt into war, and when war did come at last, the reciprocated antipathy of the Calvinists and the Lutherans added to its protracted bitterness and tragedy.

Religious war in Europe

The inevitable battleground was Central Europe, where the Roman Catholic Hapsburg dynasty, still boasting—with good reason—that it was the greatest power in the world, maintained a weakening hold over a vast empire in which Protestants were growing in numbers, power and ambition. Several times in the early years of the century war seemed imminent. In 1608 there was an ominous riot in Donauwörth, a free city on the Danube northwest of Munich, and in its wake the *Reichshofrat*, a council of imperial advisers empowered to adjudicate in disputes within the vassal states, deprived Donauwörth of its rights and decreed that its church, which had been taken over by the Protestants, should be handed back to the Catholics.

War threatened again in 1610, when the death of the childless Duke of Cleves-Jülich left various provinces along the upper Rhine without a ruler. To prevent a clash between the two Protestant contenders for the dukedom, the Emperor sent in an occupying force—whereupon one of the contenders became a Catholic and the other declared himself a Calvinist. Eventually they agreed to divide the territories between them, and war was once more averted. But no one could doubt that another crisis would soon arise elsewhere.

That crisis seemed to be approaching in 1617, the centenary year of the Protestant Reformation, when, in an effort to increase religious ferment, the Archduke Ferdinand of Styria announced his claim to the Bohemian throne of his cousin, Emperor Matthias, who was dying without an heir in Vienna. Ferdinand, who had been brought up in a Jesuit college, was known to detest Protestants and to have done all he could to root them out of Styria. He was a friendly, fat, good-natured man with a red face and a passion for hunting—the most improbable of zealots. But a zealot he was, and a politician of both cunning and determination.

The elevation of this devout Catholic to the throne of Bohemia aroused the fear of every Protestant in the country. In 1609 a threatened uprising of Bohemian Protestants forced Ferdinand to grant them a measure of toleration, but they had reason to complain that the toleration accorded them in theory was denied them in practice, and that the disabilities from which they suffered under Matthias were becoming persecutions under Ferdinand. Led by Count Thurn—a nobleman who had been educated in Italy and who, having once been a Catholic, was now more Calvinist than Lutheran—they decided on rebellion. They demanded the execution of two leading Catholic ministers, Jaroslav Martinitz and William Slavata, and called for the immediate establishment of an emergency Protestant committee.

Martinitz and Slavata sent an urgent appeal to Vienna for help, but before their messenger reached the capital the Protestants seized control of Prague. A mob marched on the Hradshin palace, seized the two ministers, dragged them toward a high window, and threw them down into the palace courtyard. With the "Defenestration of Prague," the Thirty Years' War began.

The siege of the Huguenot city of La Rochelle by the French fleet in 1627.

Frederick of Bohemia and Elizabeth: "the Winter King and Queen."

The Rape of Magdeburg

Defying their Catholic Emperor's edict of 1629, the Protestant residents of the fortified Prussian city of Magdeburg refused to cede control of their community to Ferdinand II's son, Leopold. The enraged Emperor promptly laid siege to his arrogant fief, hoping to take by force what he had been unable to win by fiat. His actions provoked a Continental religious war that ultimately involved Sweden, France and Bohemia, as well as the German princes of Hesse, Saxony and Brandenburg. England, Denmark, Spain and the Netherlands were eventually drawn into the struggle—and long after Magdeburg fell, the political conflagration that had been kindled there was still raging. The religious antagonisms that the struggle provoked ended all hopes for a wider Counter-Reformation, divided Germany for decades and shifted the European balance of power.

A German soldier of the mid-seventeenth century.

Opposite Gustavus Adolphus, "the Lion of the North." German Protestants came to rely increasingly on Swedish armies to help them against their Catholic rivals during the Thirty Years' War.

The attack by the imperial German army on the Prussian city of Magdeburg began in the last days of March, 1631. The city, which guarded a crossing point on the river Elbe, was strongly fortified on its land side and was further protected by islets in the river. As one of the richest cities in Prussia, it was believed to be adequately supplied with gunpowder and generously provided with food.

Originally, Magdeburg had been a Roman Catholic archbishopric, but during the Reformation it had fallen into the hands of Lutherans and had acquired a Protestant administrator (or bishop). In 1629 the Catholic Emperor Ferdinand II—victor of the German civil war that began in 1618—issued an imperial edict calling for the restitution of former Roman Catholic properties. The wealthy archbishopric of Magdeburg was assigned to Ferdinand's young son, Leopold. When the city refused to accept the edict, Albrecht von Wallenstein, then the imperial commander-in-chief and an extraordinary soldier and Bohemian tycoon, received orders to occupy Magdeburg on Leopold's behalf.

For seven months in 1629 Count Wallenstein, leading six thousand men, laid siege to the city. His efforts were in vain; the 30,000 citizens of Magdeburg successfully defied their Emperor. Wallenstein, unpopular because of the independent attitude he adopted toward the Emperor, withdrew and was later dismissed. Johan Tserclaes, Count of Tilly, the septuagenarian general of the army of the Duke of Bavaria, took over the command of all the imperial armies. He was an experienced and victorious general who had not only defeated the Elector Palatine at the battle of White Mountain in 1620 at the outset of the German civil war, but had also easily defeated the King of Denmark, Christian IV, when the King came to the aid of the German Lutherans. As a boy, Tilly had been intended for the priesthood, but he had elected to become a professional soldier instead.

In the decade after White Mountain the military scene changed completely. By 1630, peace no longer reigned in Germany; the siege of Magdeburg rapidly ceased to be an isolated military operation and became part of a general war. On June 26, 1630, King Gustavus Adolphus of Sweden landed in Pomerania and announced that he was coming to the rescue of his fellow Protestants. While Gustavus Adolphus strengthened his base on the Oder River in northern Germany and reinforced his troops, Christian William, the Protestant administrator of Magdeburg who had temporarily taken refuge in Sweden, reentered the city at the end of July, 1630. Supported by Swedish soldiers, he declared that he would defend the archbishopric with the help of God—and the King of Sweden—against all his enemies. But the ultimate safety of the city depended on the coming of the King of Sweden himself, since Magdeburg lay isolated among the neutral territories of John George, Elector of Saxony, and George William, Elector of Brandenburg. Although they were Protestants, these electors had never declared war on their Emperor.

Count Tilly was assigned the task of stopping the Swedish advance into Germany. The aging Field Marshal regarded it as important not merely to secure the strategic Elbe crossing at Magdeburg but, because his Roman Catholic army was short of supplies in this largely Protestant area of Germany, to lay hold of the ample provisions said to be stored in the city. Nevertheless, he was torn between concentrating on confining Gustavus Adolphus to his bridgehead on the Oder and storming the isolated fortress of Magdeburg, which had declared itself to be the first Swedish ally. Thus, in November, 1630, Count Gottfried zu Pappenheim, Tilly's second-in-command, began a renewed investment of Magdeburg, while the Field Marshal himself led darting attacks on the lines of the Swedish King.

Gustavus Adolphus recognized his responsibility for the safety of Magdeburg, but he believed (early in 1631) that the city could hold out without his army's assistance for several months. It was, after all, well fortified and well supplied, and the King had sent one of his ablest subordinates, the fanatical

Above The siege of the town of Bautzen in 1620.

Below The Battle of Lützen,
fought on November 6, 1632, where
Gustavus Adolphus was killed.

No eagerness among Magdeburg's defenders

Lutheran Dietrich von Falkenberg, and a garrison of 3,000 men to organize its defenses. Meanwhile Gustavus Adolphus himself, with a trained and equipped army of about 13,000, advanced up the Oder, assaulting the important city of Frankfurt and conquering the nearby town of Landsberg.

The burghers of Magdeburg were far from eager to defend their city to the death against the overwhelming forces now assembled before them. They had already withstood over a year's investment by the imperial armies, and they were not particularly loyal to their Protestant administrator from Brandenburg. (Indeed, the burghers had recently looked to the more powerful electorate of Saxony for a ruler.) But they were obliged to yield to the pressure of Dietrich von Falkenberg, who was utterly determined to hold the city until his Swedish master came to the rescue.

Pappenheim, however, was as determined to capture Magdeburg as Falkenberg was to defend it. On May 7, the islets having already been occupied by imperial forces, Pappenheim attempted to storm the city from the river side. By May 9 the situation had grown desperate for the defenders, and the burghers were clamoring for surrender. Early in the morning of Tuesday, May 10, Falkenberg addressed the city fathers, urging them to fight on. But it was too late: Pappenheim, without orders from Tilly, renewed the assault—and this time he was successful.

According to the laws of war in those days, a city that had refused a summons to surrender could be put to the sword—and some 25,000 citizens perished as Magdeburg was pillaged by the imperial soldiers. It was impossible for Tilly to restrain his mercenaries, but he did see to it that the cathedral itself—which harbored thousands of refugees including the wounded Protestant bishop Christian William—and five other city churches were preserved from destruction. The rest of the city caught fire—apparently by accident—and was burned to ashes. Four days after

Wallenstein, who began the siege of Magdeburg for the Emperor.

the assault Tilly was at last able to call off the plundering, and the bodies of the dead were thrown into the river to prevent plague. But whatever booty his men may have acquired amid the dreadful scenes of fire, rape, and slaughter, the immediate military object of the siege was not attained. For Tilly did not obtain the provisions he sought to feed his army.

Gustavus Adolphus and his army were sixty miles

The assassination of Wallenstein, which took place after he had been dismissed from the Emperor's service.

A thrill of horror sweeps Protestant Europe

A cavalryman of the seventeenth century, from a series of prints on equestrian exercises.

Above right A cartoon showing the "Lion of the North" scattering Tilly's "Jesuits" at the Battle of Leipzig, 1632.

The rewards of the defeated, from *Les Malheurs de la Guerre*.

away at Potsdam when word of the sack of Magdeburg reached him. After his successes on the Oder, he had gone to Berlin to compel his brother-in-law, George William, Elector of Brandenburg, to join him as an ally. With the help of Brandenburg he had hoped to save Magdeburg. Now it was too late.

The thrill of horror that swept through Protestant Europe at the news of the sack of Magdeburg was tempered by fear in Germany. Whereas those princes more distant from the scene were inclined to look upon the King of Sweden as their only savior, the neighbors of Magdeburg were impressed by the ruthless efficiency of the imperial army.

Tilly himself had misgivings about his success. "Our danger has no end, for the Protestant Estates will without doubt be only strengthened in their

hatred by this," he reported to one of his masters, the Duke of Bavaria. Gustavus Adolphus at once recognized the advantage of the situation. In January, while on his way to Frankfurt, he had signed an open treaty of alliance with Catholic France. The French government had agreed to subsidize the Swedish army; in return, Gustavus Adolphus promised to respect freedom of worship for Roman Catholics in Germany.

Meanwhile, the King—part dreamer, part astute statesman—was making up his mind about future policy. He aimed to create a league of German princes who would be politically and militarily subordinate to him. As the head of such a league he could dominate northern Germany and humiliate the Emperor. The immediate question, however, was

how to deal with the recalcitrant electors in the north.

John George of Saxony had been attempting for some time to create a third force in Germany—one capable of mediating between the Swedes and the Emperor—and early in 1631 he summoned a convention of Protestant rulers to his capital, Leipzig. The convention agreed to raise an army and issued a manifesto to the Emperor Ferdinand outlining the Protestant grievances.

John George, who possessed the only army of any size in northern Germany, had refused to go to the aid of Magdeburg or to ally himself with the Swedish King; George William of Brandenburg was not made of such stern stuff. Even before the fall of Magdeburg he had allowed the Swedes to encamp on his territory and had permitted them to use the fortress of Spandau. Now, within a month of the sack of Magdeburg, he submitted to a series of ultimatums from his brother-in-law, Gustavus Adolphus. On June 11, he signed a treaty placing the resources of Brandenburg and the fortresses of Spandau and Küstrin at the disposal of the Swedes.

Throughout the war in Germany the position of Saxony was of decisive importance. If Gustavus Adolphus could persuade John George to abandon his idea of becoming a third force, all the Protestants would enroll themselves in the Swedish camp. Gustavus Adolphus realized that in order to make the right impression and efface the memory of Magdeburg he must now move forward from his base and seek a victory. On June 24, he decided to advance from Spandau toward the Elbe. Pappenheim had 13,000 men at Magdeburg, but the Swedish army had been substantially reinforced. Gustavus Adolphus crossed the Elbe some fifty miles north of Magdeburg and took the town of Tangermünde; he then withdrew north along the Elbe, since he was not yet prepared to fight Tilly. A clash between the two armies took place in the neighborhood of Werben (north of Tangermünde) at the end of July. After the

two sides had engaged in a cannon duel, Tilly drew off. The Swedes had won a moral victory, and several more German Protestant princes hastened to ally themselves with the invader.

Tilly at the siege of Magdeburg.

The victory at Werben left John George, the great neutral, even more isolated, his electorate threatened by warring armies on two sides. In the middle of August Tilly sent the Elector an ultimatum ordering him to join the imperial army with his troops. Refusing those demands, John George reluctantly turned to Gustavus Adolphus for help, and on September 3, an alliance was signed. The Elector of Saxony promised to join Gustavus Adolphus on the Elbe, to provide food and quarters for the Swedish army in his territory, and to make no separate peace without him. The treaty was a compromise, for John George retained his political independence and promised to submit his army to the orders of the Swedish King only as long as the emergency continued. But whatever the reservations, the Saxon-Swedish alliance was decisive for the future of the war.

Two days after the signing of that treaty Tilly stormed Leipzig, the Saxon capital. Twenty-five miles to the north the armies of Gustavus Adolphus and John George joined forces for the march south, and on Wednesday, September 8, their troops engaged the imperial army in the battle of Breitenfeld. After two hours of thunderous struggle, the Saxons retreated, but the imperialists were annihilated by the Swedes. Nearly 20,000 of Tilly's men were killed or taken prisoner, and the Empire never recovered.

The destruction of Magdeburg was, therefore, a "milestone" in what modern historians call the Thirty Years' War. That war had begun in 1618 as a revolt of Protestant nobles in Bohemia against the Hapsburg crown: Ferdinand II had been ordered deposed, and Frederick V, the Elector Palatine, had been called to the throne of Bohemia. The Bohem-

Magdeburg under siege: the fall of the town heralded the great international wars that were to rend Europe and its colonies apart.

ians took this revolutionary step because they considered that their liberties—and in particular the freedom of the Protestant churches inside the kingdom—had been menaced. The Emperor Ferdinand II, who had been brought up by Jesuits and was determined to extend the influence of his Church throughout Germany, was undeterred. He expelled the Elector Palatine from Bohemia and deprived him of his hereditary lands, which were ultimately transferred to the Duke of Bavaria, the leader of the German Roman Catholics. Kings James I and Charles I of England and the King of Denmark were eventually dragged into the contest, but up to 1630 the struggle in Germany remained primarily a civil war. And by 1630 Ferdinand appeared to be winning. It seemed likely that a new Counter-Reformation, supported by the secular arm of the Holy Roman Emperor, would spread throughout Germany.

At this point, however, other European states became directly or indirectly involved. For over sixty years the United Netherlands had been struggling to secure its independence and religious freedom from the formerly formidable empire of the Spanish Hapsburgs, who were considered the senior branch of the Hapsburg family. Because Spain now reckoned that she was owed a debt by Ferdinand II, she pressed for German intervention on her behalf in northern Europe. If peace prevailed inside Germany, the Emperor's powerful army could strike northward and give his Spanish cousins the aid they needed.

After Christian William fled from Germany to seek succor from Stockholm, Sweden and France entered the scene. King Gustavus Adolphus had long contemplated intervention in Germany, although whether he was essentially a Protestant crusader or merely an ambitious king has been disputed by historians. Whatever his motives, he capitalized on the religious ardor kindled at Magdeburg.

As for France, for some thirty years—ever since

Below right Tilly, who succeeded Wallenstein as the leading imperial general.

A mid-seventeenth-century German gun.

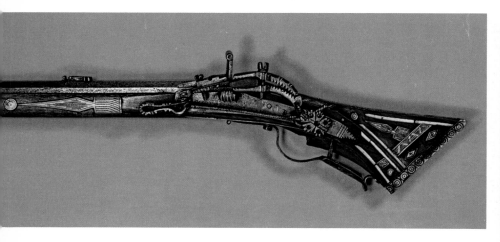

4/44

France supports the Protestants

the Bourbon Henry IV had succeeded to the throne of France—a tremendous struggle for power had been waged in Europe between the Bourbons and the Hapsburgs. Henry IV had been determined to end the stranglehold that the two Hapsburg dynasties had exerted over the French kingdom. His successor, King Louis XIII, sustained by his great minister, Cardinal Richelieu, had pursued this policy by every means at his disposal. But Louis was a Roman Catholic, and it was difficult to justify intervention against fellow Roman Catholics in Germany when they were being confronted by Protestant revolts. Richelieu attempted to bribe the Duke of Bavaria, head of the Catholic League in Germany, to fight against his Emperor, for the Bavarian dynasty had always been rivals of the Hapsburgs. But the Duke and his general, Count Tilly, had thrown in their lot with the Emperor and had been promised rich rewards, so Cardinal Richelieu reluctantly turned to the Lion of the North, the Protestant hero Gustavus Adolphus.

Gustavus Adolphus was no man's fool. He was not going to be Richelieu's pawn to humiliate the Holy Roman Emperor. He insisted that the Franco-Swedish treaty (signed at Bärwalde in January, 1631) should be an open treaty; the French were thus obliged to commit themselves in Germany. By the terms of the treaty they agreed only to become the paymaster of the Swedish armies, but after Gustavus Adolphus perished at the battle of Lützen the French were obliged to send an army into Germany.

The period that followed the fall of Magdeburg heralded the beginning of great international wars. At the same time the fall enflamed religious antagonisms in Germany. The signal humiliation of the German Protestants by Count Tilly rallied all the Protestants of northern and central Germany against their Emperor, enabled Gustavus Adolphus to claim to be their rescuer, and gave him the opportunity to advance from the Oder to the Elbe and to destroy the imperial cause at Breitenfeld and Lützen. Thus, the fall of Magdeburg created the conditions that led to a Protestant resurgence and ensured the division of Germany for many years to come. Protestant Brandenburg, the reluctant ally of the Swedes, was in fact to be the focus of a Lutheran-dominated German empire.

The siege of Magdeburg was significant because it helped bring Europe into Germany. In the end the Calvinists as well as the Lutherans achieved religious equality in those parts of Germany where they predominated. The prospect of a wider and fuller Counter-Reformation was brought to an end. Sweden and her paymaster, France, emerged victorious from the war, having inflicted terrible punishments upon the German people. Revolutions took place in England, France and Spain partly as the consequences of this long, expensive and grueling war. Franco-German enmity was ensured for hundreds of years, and the face of Europe was changed, with the center of power shifting to the west.

MAURICE ASHLEY

The Thirty Years War

1618-29

Frederick, the Elector Palatine and leader of the Protestant Union, was defeated by Bavaria and Austria in 1620 at the Battle of the White Mountain, having had no help from other Protestant states. The Bavarian army, under Tilly, and the Hapsburg army, under Wallenstein, were then supreme in Northern Germany.

- ⬤ Protestant Union of 1608
- ◯ Catholic League of 1609
- ◯ Hapsburg Territories
- — Boundary of Holy Roman Empire
- ▨ Intervention by Sweden
- ▨ Intervention by France

1631-47

The Protestant princes and France, alarmed at the Emperor's successes, persuaded Gustavus Adolphus, King of Sweden, to champion the Protestant cause. He defeated Tilly at Breitenfeld (1631) and Wallenstein at Lützen (1632). Gustavus Adolphus was killed at Lützen and without him the Swedish army was unsuccessful. It was finally routed at Nördlingen (1634).

France then declared war on the Austrian and Spanish Hapsburgs. Condé defeated the Spaniards at Rocroi (1643) and Turenne was victorious against the Emperor.

Treaty of Münster 1648

Germany was by now in ruins, with two-thirds of her population dead, and peace was finally made. The Treaty of Westphalia or Münster (1648) gave Eastern Pomerania, Minden and Magdeburg to Brandenburg; Western Pomerania to Sweden; the bishoprics of Metz, Toul and Verdun and parts of Alsace to France; and Bavaria gained the Upper Palatinate. The Holy Roman Empire was forced to acknowledge the independence of the United Provinces and Switzerland.

- ⬤ Gained by Brandenburg
- ⬤ Gained by Sweden
- ⬤ Gained by France
- ◯ Gained by Bavaria
- ⬤ Gained by Saxony

In February, 1613, King James I's pretty, high-spirited daughter Elizabeth married Frederick V, the Elector Palatine, one of the foremost Protestant princes of Germany. Two years later, in defiance of the Austrian Emperor, Frederick rashly accepted the crown of Bohemia from the Protestant rebels of Prague—and thereby involved England in the Continental dispute known as the Thirty Years' War.

Elizabeth, who was admired for her beauty and vitality and revered as the "Queen of Hearts," was extremely popular in England. And when the Emperor's troops marched against her husband's troops in Prague, her plight aroused the country's deepest sympathy and led to loud demands for her protection. The defeat of Frederick's troops at the Battle of White Mountain in winter, 1620, was followed by the fall of his former capital, Heidelberg, and he and Elizabeth were obliged to seek shelter in The Hague at the court of Prince Maurice of Orange. Demands for action on behalf of the Palatine's misused champion of Protestantism and his unfortunate young wife grew increasingly clamorous in England. There were demonstrations in favor of Elizabeth and against the Hapsburgs, and crowds marched through the streets calling for war against the Emperor. Parliament—when it was summoned in 1621 to provide funds for the government's foreign policy — urged a declaration of war against Spain, whose troops had joined forces with the Austrians.

Ignoring the saber rattling of Parliament and the warlike temper of his people, the English King — who had always turned in horror from the thought of war—persuaded himself that he could better serve his son-in-law by coming to terms with Spain. James was sure that he could restore order in Europe by marrying his son Charles to the Infanta Donna Maria of Spain and by inducing her brother Philip IV to use his influence to restore Frederick and Elizabeth to their palace at Heidelberg. The King's policy, unrealistic as it was and fruitless as it proved to be, was abhorrent to Parliament. The members wanted a Protestant alliance, not a Catholic one, a war against Spain and an immediate end to the marriage negotiations.

James, who had already dissolved a difficult Parliament in 1614—remarking as he did so that he was surprised that his "ancestors should

have permitted such an institution to come into existence"—thus came into direct conflict with the Commons once again. He refused to acknowledge their right to question his policy or to interfere with his inherited prerogative powers. "The state of monarchy," he told them, "is the supremest thing upon earth; for Kings are not only God's lieutenants upon earth, and sit upon God's throne, but even by God himself they are called gods. . . . Kings are justly called gods for that they exercise a manner or resemblance of divine power upon earth. … So it is sedition in subjects to dispute what a King may do in the height of his power."

In James' opinion, it was indeed seditious for Parliament to meddle in matters of State; foreign policy was the King's affair and upon the King's grace did their privileges depend. When the Members entered in their journal a protest that their privileges did not depend upon the King but were the "ancient and undoubted birthright of the subjects of England," James was so angry that he tore the protest from the book with his own hand, dissolved Parliament and ordered the arrest of those members whom he took to be the chief troublemakers. The long contest between the Stuart kings and their Parliaments had begun.

Buckingham

The failure of the negotiations for the Spanish match delighted the English people, and on the return of the Prince of Wales and his friend, the Duke of Buckingham, from the fiasco of their courtship of the Infanta in Madrid, the two young men found themselves suddenly and intoxicatingly popular. To consolidate his triumph, the Duke of Buckingham urged the King to call a Parliament to impeach the unpopular Earl of Middlesex who, as Lord Treasurer,

The Duke of Buckingham in his garter robes.

Henrietta Maria's entry into London.

was the most influential of Buckingham's critics and one of the leaders of the pro-Spanish party in the country.

"My God, Steenie, you are a fool and will shortly repent this folly," James told Buckingham—and added prophetically, "You are making a rod with which you will be scourged yourself." But James was old and ill, helplessly in love with Buckingham, and so delighted to have him back that he gave way. A Parliament was called; Middlesex was swept from power; the entire foreign policy of the country was reversed; and the principle that Parliament had no right to discuss foreign affairs—a principle that the King had vehemently defended three years before—was abandoned. The advice of the Commons was sought as to whether diplomatic relations with Madrid should be broken off.

With Buckingham, the Prince of Wales, Parliament and the country all demanding war, the King could no longer resist—and in preparation for the forthcoming war, alliances were negotiated with the Dutch and with France. (The young French princess, Henrietta Maria, daughter of Henry IV and sister of Louis XIII, was now seen as a bride for Prince Charles.) But although the Commons declared themselves resolved on a campaign in Europe, they declined to vote the money necessary for its proper prosecution. Consequently, the Spanish war—which dragged on for four years and was waged by English rogues, vagabonds, drunkards and cripples—was a tragic disaster. By the time it was over King James was dead and his son, King Charles I, was showing himself to be a monarch ill-suited to meet the challenge that faced the royal house.

Ships of Buckingham's fleet, 1627.

Charles I

Exasperated by Charles' refusal to explain what his foreign policy was intended to achieve or how the money he demanded would be used, the Commons allowed the new King only a fraction of the funds he needed. To make matters even worse, Parliament refused to grant the King the lifetime right to collect customs duties. Charles' predecessors had been granted that right for life; he was obliged to reapply annually. The most formidable orator in the House, an emotional, excitable, vehement West Country squire, Sir John Eliot, protested in his loud, harsh voice that he and his fellow members were not creatures of the King, elected merely to grant him money and to approve his policies, but men with individual consciences and a duty to act only in accordance with what they knew to be right. He condemned the government's policies—and above all he condemned the Duke of Buckingham who, as Lord High Admiral, had sailed across the Channel in 1627 in command of a disastrous expedition intended to support the Huguenots of La Rochelle in their rebellion against the French King.

and civil war breaks out

Eliot demanded Buckingham's impeachment, just as Buckingham himself had demanded the impeachment of the Earl of Middlesex —and Charles panicked. He ordered Eliot arrested and imprisoned in the Tower, but when the unintimidated Commons refused to do any further business until their champion was released, the King capitulated. Eliot returned to the attack with increased invective, and in an attempt to spare his friend further humiliation, Charles dissolved Parliament. The impetuous young monarch decided to raise the money he so desperately needed without Parliament's help,

Sir John Eliot, leader of the parliamentary opposition to King Charles.

to collect the customs duties previously denied him and to impose a capital levy. Those who refused to pay that levy were imprisoned.

The Petition of Right

Yet for all his determination to exist without Parliament, Charles found it impossible to do so. The extraordinary expense of the war against France obliged him to summon Parliament once more. The King hoped the recalled Commons would prove more tractable; lamentably, they proved even less so. Led by Sir John Eliot, they strongly condemned taxation without parliamentary consent and imprisonment without due cause. In 1628 they set out their grievances in a Petition of Right, and they refused to discuss the matter of supplies until the Petition had achieved royal assent.

The period that followed the King's acceptance of the Petition of Right was but a truce in a continuing duel. In January, 1629, a new House of Commons changed the direction of its attack. The archenemy, Buckingham, had been

removed by an assassin's knife at Portsmouth a few months before, but Eliot saw that the general principle of the Commons' right to criticize the King's ministers might be gained if demands for political changes were allied to the growing force of Puritan enthusiasm in the country. He and his supporters therefore launched an attack on the King for having appointed various High Church clergymen to important livings, chaplaincies and bishoprics, and they refused to grant Charles his traditional customs duties until they had debated a resolution that "the affairs of the King of Earth must give way to the affairs of the King of Heaven." Parliament's move was too much for Charles, who was devoted to the Church of England and firmly convinced that the administration of its affairs had nothing to do with Parliament. He sent orders to the

John Pym, Parliamentary leader.

Speaker, commanding him to tell the House to adjourn, but its militant members refused to do so. Shouting "No! No!" in the Speaker's face, they passed resolutions against both the payment of the customs duties and the religious policy of the government.

Charles was appalled. Bursting out in indignation against the "undutiful and seditious" behavior of the Commons and those "vipers" chiefly responsible, he once again ordered Eliot's arrest. And this time he refused to release him. Even when Eliot became fatally ill, the King continued steadfast in his refusal, and upon the "viper's" death at the age of forty, Charles turned down Eliot's son's request that the corpse be laid to rest in the Cornish courtyard where his family and ancestors lay. "Let Sir John Eliot be buried in that parish wherein he died," Charles decreed.

For eight years after Eliot's death, Charles contrived to pay his way without calling a Parliament

The Earl of Strafford.

by restoring to a number of devices for raising money—some of doubtful legality, all of them unpopular. But when the people of Scotland took up arms in 1640 in defense of their Kirk against the Anglican innovations of Archbishop Laud, Charles was forced to recall Parliament. That Parliament proved no more willing to grant the King money for his war against the Scottish rebels than its predecessor had been to vote money for the war against France. Its members declined to vote any supplies until the country's complaints had been satisfied.

Charles responded, as he had done in the past, by dissolving Parliament—but the humiliating outcome of an attempt to subdue the Scots with an underpaid and ill-supplied army led to the assembly of yet another Parliament. That Parliament, the last of his reign, was to force the King to accept an act prohibiting its dissolution without its own consent.

The new Parliament lasted for twenty years. It began by impeaching the King's stern and gifted

minister, the Earl of Strafford, whose execution Charles tearfully accepted for the sake of his family and to avoid further bloodshed. Parliament went on, in increasing confusion and excitement, to impeach twelve bishops and to threaten to impeach the Queen. In his anger and alarm, Charles—who had previously attempted to stem the tide of Parliament's demands by promises and prevarications, by standing his ground as long as he could and then gracelessly giving way, and by alternating between compromise and fitful displays of determination—made a rash and disastrous move. On January 4, 1642, he marched to the Commons with a squad of soldiers, intending to arrest five of its leading members. Those members, warned in time of his approach, escaped from Westminster by boat down the Thames to the City, London's financial district. The King, whose personal courage was never in doubt, followed them there and demanded that they surrender to him. When they refused, he returned to his palace at Whitehall through streets filled with crowds shouting "Privileges of Parliament! Privileges of Parliament!"

A few days later the five members came out of hiding and proceeded in triumph up river to Westminster, where they were met by cheering citizens and beating drums. There were shouts for war against the King and his supporters, and as the placard-bearing crowds passed Whitehall they pointed with excitement and satisfaction to the curtained windows of the empty palace. The King had fled from London the day before. When he returned there it was to his death.

The execution of Strafford.

"A Cruel Necessity"

On January 27, 1649, "Charles Stuart, Tyrant, Traitor, Murderer and Public Enemy" was condemned to death by England's highest court. Oliver Cromwell, leader of the Puritan Revolution, labeled the execution of Charles I "a cruel necessity." Cruel it certainly was—but there were many who doubted its necessity. The King's death effectively terminated a long and bitter struggle between Cromwell and the Crown, but it did not solve the Protector's problems. In the decades before his trial, Charles had dissolved four Parliaments for refusing to grant him his legal revenues —and each time he had been forced to recall the Members. After eliminating the King, whom he called a meddlesome "Man of Blood," Cromwell discovered that Parliament could no more exist without the King than the King without Parliament. A decade after Charles' execution, his fugitive son returned to England to reclaim the throne.

"I fear not death," said Charles I, King of England, as he dressed on the morning of the day on which he was to die. "Death is not terrible to me. I bless my God I am prepared."

Throughout his trial, Charles' courage and his spirit had impressed all who had seen him. His sunken cheeks, shadowed eyes and gray hair had made the forty-eight-year-old monarch look tired, old and worn, but he had walked briskly into Westminster Hall, had sat quietly before the president of the court, and had gazed calmly, almost aloofly, at the judges in front of him and at the spectators behind him as counsel for the prosecution read out the crimes with which he stood charged. When instructed to answer the charges, he spoke with clarity and confidence—and quite without the stammer that normally hampered his tongue—insisting in his Scottish accent that the court had no right to try him. Neither on that day nor on the two following days of the trial could he be induced, by any manner of persuasion, to betray the trust committed to him by God—and "by old and lawful descent"—to make answer to this "unlawful authority."

He was their "*lawful*" King" he reminded his judges, and he demanded that they show him a "legal Authority warranted by the Word of God, the Scriptures, or warranted by the constitution of the Kingdom." Since they had no such legal authority, he could not and would not answer them. And he still had not answered them when, on January 27, 1649, as "Charles Stuart, Tyrant, Traitor, Murderer and Public Enemy," he was condemned to be put to death "by the severing of his head from his body."

Shocked by the abrupt ending of the trial, Charles called out, "Will you hear me a word, Sir?"

"You are not to be heard after the sentence," the president of the court insisted.

"No, Sir?"

"No, Sir, by your favor, Sir. Guard, withdraw your prisoner."

"I may speak after the sentence—by your favor,

Sir, I may speak after the sentence. By your favor, hold! The sentence, Sir—I say, Sir, I do—"

For the first time in the trial he was incoherent; but as the soldiers closed around him to withdraw him from the court, he regained his former composure. "I am not suffered for to speak," he said with resignation. "Expect what justice other people will have."

Only once during the few days he had left to live did Charles again seem on the verge of losing control of his emotions. That moment came when the doomed King said good-bye to the two of his children who still remained in England. Having blessed them both, he walked quickly away to his bedchamber and with trembling legs fell down upon his bed.

On his last morning he was tranquil, almost serene, assuring the attendant who brushed his hair and fixed the pearl earrings in his ears that this was his second marriage day, that by nightfall he would be espoused to his blessed Jesus. When an army officer came to inform the King that it was time for him to leave, he knelt for a few moments in prayer and then, taking the hand of Bishop Juxon, who had been allowed to stay with him to the end, Charles said in a firm voice, "Come, let us go." As he walked out of Whitehall Palace toward the Banqueting House, his faithful dog Rogue gamboled after him.

The scaffold had been draped in black, and on it, surrounded by lines of helmeted soldiers with pikes and halberds, stood two army colonels, a group of reporters and the executioner and his assistant, both of them masked and disguised with false hair and beards. The King spoke to them all briefly. Then, tucking his long hair up into his white satin nightcap so that it would not deflect the edge of the executioner's blade, he looked up at the sky, said his last prayers, and lay down with his neck on the block.

The axe fell; the head was severed in a single stroke; and "at the instant whereof," said a young spectator, "I remember well there was such a grone by the Thousands then present as I never heard

Charles I's wife, the French princess, Henrietta Maria, whose Catholicism made her unpopular in England.

Opposite A memorial locket of Charles I, containing a piece of linen stained with the King's blood.

The final breach between King and Parliament

The execution on Tower Hill, London, in 1643 of William Laud, Archbishop of Canterbury, the King's most able supporter.

Charles I's family, with the future Charles II in the center.

before and desire I may never hear again."

Curiously enough, there were no disturbances. The execution had taken place outside the Banqueting House instead of on Tower Hill, for the square in front of Inigo Jones' imposing building was small and easily guarded. But the guards were scarcely needed, and although there was a scramble around the scaffold as men and women ran forward to dip handkerchiefs in the spilled blood, the square was soon cleared by mounted troops and London fell into silence.

To Oliver Cromwell, an East Anglian farmer of modest estate who had become the most influential man in England in the years following the civil war, the execution of Charles I in January, 1649, was a cruel necessity. Cromwell had been a member of Parliament during much of the long conflict between that body and the King that is known as the Puritan Revolution. Although it derived its name from the fact that the King and his followers supported the

Church of England while his opponents were on the whole Puritan, the Revolution involved much more than religion. Part of the conflict was constitutional—a dispute between a King who believed in his divine right to rule and a Parliament that wanted a constitutional monarchy. There were also economic issues, for the middle-class gentry and merchants who made up the bulk of the parliamentarian party were fighting for a greater role in determining financial and commercial policies.

The struggle intensified as Parliament sought to find new ways to limit the King's power. In retaliation, Charles tried to rule without a Parliament, but he found that he could not raise money by himself, and financial pressures forced him to reconvene Parliament several times. In 1640 the so-called Long Parliament began its session. Its demands, and the King's rejection of them, ultimately led to civil war.

When the final breach with the King came in 1642, Cromwell, who had been active in the Puritan cause, rushed home from Westminster. Out of his slender resources he equipped and paid a troop of horsemen to fight for the "preservation of the true religion, the laws, liberty and peace of the Kingdom." After the battle of Edgehill—in which Parliament's cavalry were driven from the field by Prince Rupert's Cavaliers (as the King's supporters were called)—Cromwell raised and trained a far larger force of cavalry. His new troops scattered the royalists on Marston Moor "like a little dust," securing the north for the Roundheads (the name given the supporters of Parliament). At Naseby, Cromwell's cavalry, which formed part of Parliament's professional, regularly paid and well-disciplined New Model Army, once again proved its sterling quality. And at Stow-on-the-Wold, on March 21, 1646, Charles' last army in the field was defeated.

Parliament and the army soon fell out among themselves, however, and in their quarrel the captured King sought and failed to find his own salvation. The quarrel began in a religious dispute. Cromwell had urged Parliament, after both Marston

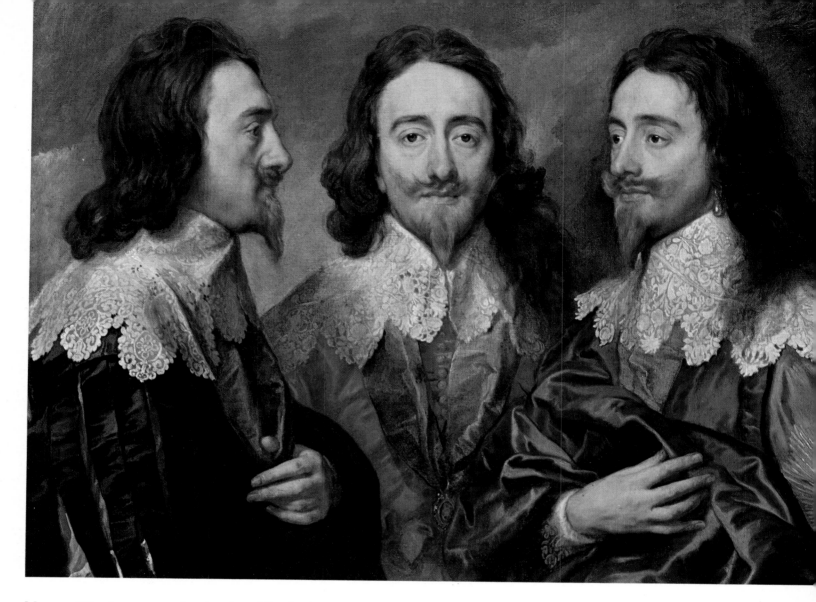

Moor and Naseby, to remember that the soldiers had risked their lives not only for the political liberty of their country but for religious toleration as well. The one cause was, after all, just as fundamental to the issues over which the civil war had been fought as the other. But the Presbyterians in Parliament, rigid in their orthodoxy and not content with persecuting those who, like the King, were devout members of the established Church of England, were insisting that Baptists should be subjected to life imprisonment, that laymen should be prohibited from preaching in public, and that all Independents should be dismissed from the New Model Army. Further, they attempted to disband the army without back pay.

Cromwell attempted to act as mediator in the increasingly bitter quarrel between Parliament and the army. He urged Parliament to be more tolerant and attempted to dissuade the army from falling under the influence of those wilder spirits who were preaching universal suffrage and radical reform. Cromwell himself was far from being a radical. He had nothing against the monarchy as an institution and earnestly desired to come to terms with the King. With the idea of a settlement in mind, he begged Charles to consider the "Heads of the Proposals," a moderate offer based on wide toleration.

Van Dyck's triple portrait of Charles I, designed to help the Italian sculptor Bernini execute a bust of the King. On seeing the portrait Bernini said that the features were those of a doomed man.

Prince Rupert of the Rhine, a brilliant but erratic general, whose undisciplined enthusiasm cost the King dear.

"Heads of the Proposals"

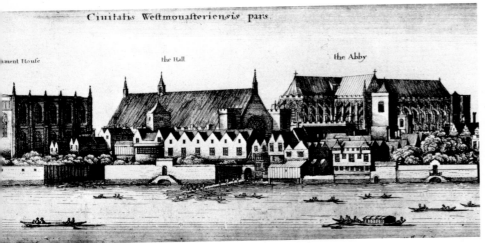

Civitatis Westmonasteriensis pars.

...ment House   the Hall   the Abby

The proposals envisaged the use of the English Book of Common Prayer for those who wanted it, a limited form of episcopacy, and an end to Parliament's sequestration of the estates of Cavaliers—a punitive measure that eventually caused the royalist squires to develop an irreconcilable hatred of Puritanism.

There was nothing in these proposals that Charles could not in all honor have accepted, and his more sensible advisers strongly urged him to agree to them. "A crown so near lost was never recovered so easily as this would be," one of them informed him. But Charles believed that by playing off one side against the other he could solve all his difficulties and return to Whitehall in triumph. And thus he preferred to dissemble, prevaricate and intrigue. Although he was a man of high moral character, Charles had no

A view of Westminster in the mid-seventeenth century, by Wenceslas Hollar. One of the centers of opposition to the royal government was the House of Commons.

Below A playing card attacking the "rump Parliament," a small group of militant members of the House of Commons who refused to allow Parliament to be dissolved.

The Rump and dreggs of the house of Com remaining after the good members were purged out.

Right Oliver Cromwell, the Lord Protector, as the Savior of England.

political scruples—and although he was in some respects a learned man, he was not an intelligent one. He was a fine judge of art and horses, but he had little understanding of the human character. He tried to deceive the army, he intrigued with Parliament, and he came to a secret understanding with the Scots that led to a brief new outbreak of the war.

By this time Cromwell had completely reversed his attitude toward the King. He had become convinced that Charles Stuart must be regarded as "a Man of Blood," and that the only hope for peace and order in the country was to bring the King to that justice which his underhanded and traitorous dealings so richly deserved. "I tell you," Cromwell cried out to the hesitant commissioners appointed to try the King, "I tell you, we will cut off the King's head with the crown on it."

Cromwell, his clever, earnest son-in-law, Henry Ireton, and those other regicides whose actions were not prompted by malice or desire for personal gain were all sincerely convinced that the execution of the King could alone prevent the country from falling into anarchy. So long as Charles lived, it was impossible to carry on government by consent; with his death it would become possible to rule by force. And by force they had to rule, or they too would perish.

Although there had been no disturbances in London after the execution, the mood of the country at large was alarming. To many Englishmen, the killing of the King was a sacrilege that God would surely punish, and republicanism was an evil system of government that would arouse His deepest wrath. To others, the new leaders of the country were as unworthy of trust and respect as the dead King himself had been—"silken gentlemen" who would soon prove their fundamentally conservative, not to say reactionary, nature.

Royalists who had fought for the King and Presbyterians who had fought against him joined in condemning the new government. The domestic situation deteriorated rapidly, as economic distress and social unrest were added to political uproar and religious dissent. Beggars roamed the streets; highwaymen by the hundreds infested the roads; the navy, grown mutinous, abandoned the control of

the seas to royalist privateers under the direction of Prince Rupert; Scotland and Ireland looked eagerly to the day when Prince Charles would return in triumph to his father's throne; and the monarchies of the Continent looked upon England as a country beyond the pale—convicted and doomed.

Yet the rulers of the country were at first inspired rather than intimidated by the problems that beset them on every hand. Once the new republic, known as the Commonwealth, was established in 1649, they acted quickly to abolish both the office of King and the House of Lords, thus giving to the House of Commons the supreme legislative and executive power in the state. Very soon afterwards they set up a council of state of forty-one members whose duty it was to administer the country's affairs.

Within four years of its establishment, this council

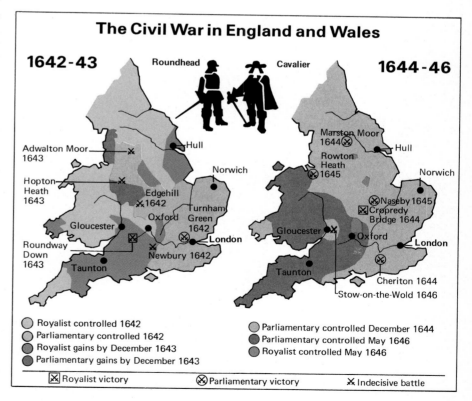

The Civil War in England and Wales

1642-43

Roundhead · Cavalier

1644-46

Adwalton Moor 1643
Hull
Norwich
Hopton Heath 1643
Edgehill ✕1642
Turnham Green 1642
Oxford
Gloucester
Roundway Down 1643
Newbury 1642
London
Taunton

Marston Moor 1644 ⊗
Hull
Rowton Heath 1645
Norwich
⊗ Naseby 1645
⊠ Cropredy Bridge 1644
Gloucester
Oxford
London
Taunton
Cheriton 1644
Stow-on-the-Wold 1646

○ Royalist controlled 1642
○ Parliamentary controlled 1642
○ Royalist gains by December 1643
○ Parliamentary gains by December 1643

○ Parliamentary controlled December 1644
○ Parliamentary controlled May 1646
○ Royalist controlled May 1646

⊠ Royalist victory   ⊗ Parliamentary victory   ✕ Indecisive battle

Dissolution of the Rump Parliament

had overwhelmed its enemies. Ireland was subjugated with exceptional ferocity—the garrisons of Drogheda and Wexford were slaughtered without mercy at Cromwell's orders—and two-thirds of the Irish lands were transferred to English ownership.

The council next turned its attention to Scotland. On September 3, 1650, Cromwell destroyed a Scottish army at Dunbar, and thus united Scotland to England in a single British Commonwealth.

Overseas, an overhauled, strong and efficient navy and the talents of Admiral Robert Blake, a seaman of genius, combined to make England the greatest naval power in the world. Prince Rupert's privateers and the Barbary pirates of the Mediterranean were attacked and defeated; war was waged against England's leading commercial and naval rivals; Jamaica was captured; and the Spanish fleet was crippled at Tenerife.

The cost of those wars led to heavier and heavier taxation and to the disruption of trade, and consequently to the increased unpopularity of Cromwell's government. Despite the benefits that its advocates prophesied, the kind of republicanism that

Cromwell's council imposed upon the nation did not recommend itself to the people; the majority of them were pleased when, in 1653, Cromwell forcibly dissolved the Rump Parliament (a group composed of those who had survived Colonel Thomas Pride's 1648 purge of unsympathetic, anti-military members). The members of the Rump Parliament had shown themselves jealous of their powers, addicted to interminable debate, and capable of enacting a statute that made adultery punishable by death. But the Nominated Parliament that followed it—and that in turn persuaded Cromwell to assume the title of Lord Protector—was no more capable of winning the people's trust than its predecessor had been.

The division of the country into eleven districts, each commanded by a major general, contributed more than any other factor to the disesteem in which the people held Cromwell's government, for these major generals were required to assume the duties of guardians of public morality as well as those of tax collectors and policemen. They suppressed horse races and cock fights, prohibited the performance of plays, closed brothels and gambling dens, enforced

The Royal Martyr; the frontispiece of *Eikon Basilike* (Image of a King). Charles' ineptitude as a ruler was only equaled by his piety as a man.

the laws against drunkenness and blasphemy and closed down numerous alehouses.

Aware that the only hope for the future lay in a return to the constitutional rule that he had unwillingly abandoned and to the civil legality that had been suppressed, Cromwell turned to the constitutionalists and legalists in an attempt to release himself from his dependence upon the army. Some of his advisers suggested that he take up the Crown of England and restore to the country the benefits of monarchy. Although at first inclined to do so, Cromwell ultimately rejected the suggestion in deference to the views of those Puritans he most admired. But by the time of Cromwell's death in September, 1658, there was no doubt that most Englishmen longed for a return to the traditions of monarchy—and so it was that, eighteen months later, the return of Charles' son as King Charles II was achieved not merely without bloodshed but with acclamation.

The Great Rebellion had not, however, been in vain. The period of the Commonwealth and of the Protectorate (the years from 1653 to 1659 when England was ruled by a Lord Protector), though rich in political debate and constitutional experiment, has been described as "an interlude in the domestic history of the British people." But it was more than that. It is true that most of what was achieved in the interregnum did not survive the Restoration, and it is true that Cromwell was unable to rule either with parliaments or without them, being compelled by the force of events to carry on a military government that flouted the sentiments of the British people as well as his own conservative instincts and preferences for constitutional rule. Yet it is also true that the experiences that the English people underwent in that era confirmed their hatred of military rule and of the kind of stark Puritanism with which it was associated. In the next decades Parliament suppressed Puritanism with vigor.

For the future, the English monarchy was to develop along peaceful and constitutional lines. In 1688, Charles II's brother and successor, the Roman Catholic James II, attempted to coerce the nation and he was replaced by his Protestant nephew, Prince William III of Orange, in a Glorious Revolution that was bloodless and quick. The power of Parliament, asserted by the execution of Charles I, was finally confirmed.

Henceforward, the English were to experience nothing to correspond with the absolutism prevalent on the Continent in the eighteenth century. Having undergone their Reformation in the sixteenth century and their Revolution in the seventeenth, the English were finished with much of the work that elsewhere remained to be done.

Nevertheless there was still a great deal to do in England: despite local regulation and private philanthropy, social conditions in many areas were appalling; the penal code was ferocious; nonconformists were discriminated against—although not so fiercely that they lived without hope of amelioration or that they emigrated to America in the numbers that had left under the persecution of the High-Church Archbishop Laud in the 1620s and 1630s—and Roman Catholics were subjected to unjust discrimination. Nonetheless, foreigners felt that the English were the most enviable of people and that their government and institutions were worthy of the highest praise and the closest imitation. Montesquieu pointed to their system of government as a model; and in his *Philosophical Letters* Voltaire expressed a widespread opinion when he wrote, "The English nation is the only one on earth which has succeeded in regulating the power of its kings by resisting them; and which after repeated efforts has established that wise government under which the prince, all powerful for good, is restrained from doing ill."

CHRISTOPHER HIBBERT

The execution of the King: an imaginary reconstruction.

The Juxon Medal, the gold medal that Charles gave Bishop Juxon (later Archbishop of Canterbury), just before his execution.

A centralized monarchy is created in France

The rule of Mazarin

The day after Cardinal Richelieu died, on December 5, 1642, King Louis XIII issued a circular-letter to France's leading officials, ordering them to send their future reports to another cardinal, Jules Mazarin. Mazarin, who was originally Giulio Mazarini, was the son of a Sicilian father and a mother who was related to the ancient Roman family of the Colonnas. He was born in the Abruzzi in 1602, educated by the Jesuits in Rome and at the University of Alcala in Spain, and before he reached the age of thirty he had distinguished himself as a diplomat in the service of Pope Urban VIII. In 1634 Mazarin became papal nuncio at the French Court, where his ingratiating charm and brilliant intellectual attainments so recommended themselves to Cardinal Richelieu that he was persuaded to

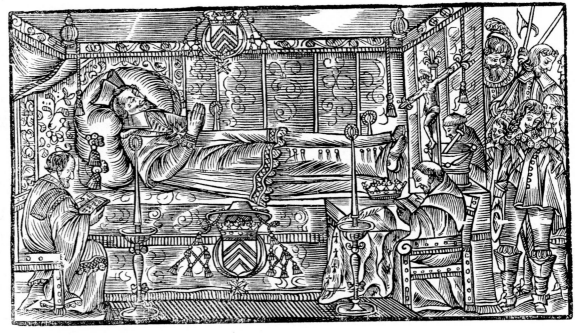

The death of Cardinal Richelieu.

Anne of Austria, Regent of France, by Rubens.

enter the service of Louis XIII and to become a naturalized Frenchman. He was elevated to a cardinalate in 1641 (after his triumphant success in establishing Louis XIII's sister, the Duchess of Savoy, in the regency of Savoy after the death of her husband), and a year later, at the age of thirty-nine, he succeeded Richelieu as chief minister of France.

Mazarin was an ambitious, avaricious man—cunning, devious and intuitive. Well aware that the sickly and lethargic Louis XIII did not have long to live, the Cardinal concentrated on winning the trust and affection of the King's wife, Anne, daughter of Philip III of Spain. Anne was a neglected wife as well as an attractive and responsive

woman, and Mazarin had no difficulty in winning her trust and, indeed, her devotion. Upon her husband's death in 1643 she was appointed Regent, and Mazarin's position as supreme minister remained secure.

Mazarin continued Richelieu's policies with skill and determination. He maintained the campaign against Austria and guided France expertly through the Thirty Years' War, avoiding its worst dangers and profiting by the opportunities it presented. And when the War ended in 1648, he was able to negotiate a settlement that could scarcely have been more favorable to French aspirations in Europe.

Yet Mazarin was distrusted and hated in France, where he was vilified as a foreigner, condemned as a profligate and gambler, censured as the new and evil power-behind-the-throne (his influence over the unpopular Queen Anne was purportedly due to his gratification of her unnatural physical passions), detested by the nobles—who could gain places at Court only through his influence—and above all, execrated by every class as the man responsible for insupportable war taxes. When the Thirty Years' War drew to an end, France was on the verge of revolution—and in their universal condemnation of Mazarin's financial policies the nobles, the people and the *parlement* of Paris united in an attempt to overthrow the Cardinal and destroy his autocratic power in France.

Mazarin provoked that outburst by levying a tax on the judicial officers of the *parlement* of Paris. When his demand was met by blank refusal—and by counterdemands for constitutional reforms—he ordered the leaders of *parlement* to be arrested. Parisians rushed out into the streets, built hundreds of barricades, and—by slinging stones

Cardinal Mazarin: hated in France.

by Cardinal Mazarin

through the windows of known supporters of Mazarin—gave the incipient civil war its name—the *Fronde* ("sling").

Condé and the court

These events took place in August, 1648. The Treaty of Westphalia had not yet been signed, and the government's troops, commanded by the Prince of Condé, had not yet returned home from their recent victory at Lens. The Court was therefore powerless to meet the

Prince de Condé: his arrogance and mannerlessness matched his ability as a military leader.

threat of the *frondeurs*. Releasing prisoners and promising reforms, Mazarin and the Queen fled from Paris. Two months later, Condé's troops were released from further operations by the signing of the Treaty. They promptly marched home and laid siege to Paris—and on March 11, 1649, they imposed the Treaty of Rueil upon the *frondeurs*.

Although he had saved the Court, the Prince of Condé soon became estranged from it. Condé—a man of enormous wealth and proven military ability, the acknowledged head of the French nobility and the owner of vast estates—was at the same time utterly unlikable and intolerably arrogant. He was equally contemptuous toward the Queen and toward the low-born Mazarin, who deeply regretted the necessity of having to call upon the Prince for help against his enemies.

Part of a satirical series attacking Mazarin.

The Second Fronde

In an action that was every bit as daring as sudden and as provocative as his arrest of the leaders of the *parlement* of Paris, Mazarin ordered the arrest of the proud and famous Prince and his leading supporters (who included the Prince's brother, Conti, and his brother-in-law, the Duke of Longueville). The country was immediately plunged into the Second *Fronde*, a period of tumult, discreditable intrigues, and disgraceful humiliations. The Prince's supporters attempted to release the captives from their prison at Havre; the Duchess of Longueville entered into negotiations to secure military help from Spain; and Marshal Turenne, whose successes in the recent war had rivaled those of Condé himself, invaded Picardy at the head of a Spanish army—a move prompted as much by the Marshal's desperate love for the Duchess of Longueville as by his support of the revolt.

The history of the Second *Fronde* was one of plots and counterplots, deceptions, conspiracies and betrayals. It was at once a tragedy and a farce, for there were no heroes, merely characters who did not themselves understand the succession of events in which they had become involved. For a time it appeared that the rabble-rousing priest Paul de Gondi would overthrow the government, but de Gondi was won over to Mazarin's side by the promise of a red hat and the bellicose Cardinal de Retz took his place. Marshal Turenne's invading army was defeated at Rethel, and Turenne also succumbed to a bribe (only to emerge as the commander of the government's forces some months later). Cardinal Mazarin, living in exile at Brühl, appeared at one point to have lost his influence—but by January of 1652 he was back at Court, his power confirmed and his confidence increased.

When Mazarin returned to Court, his enemy, Condé, was still rampaging about the countryside with a motley band of disaffected nobles and an army of recruits, half of whom were French and half of whom were Spanish. In July, 1652, the tiresome Prince reappeared at the gates of Paris, and once again Mazarin wisely withdrew into exile for a short time.

Although Condé entered Paris in triumph, Mazarin knew that the victory was really his, for the people were exasperated by the antics of the rebellious nobles, by the continual disruptions of trade, and by Condé's effrontery in having brought in Spanish soldiers to patrol the streets of Paris. Realizing that the tide of opinion was running against him, Condé withdrew from the capital at the end of that summer and accepted a high command in the Spanish army.

A new enemy

The Second *Fronde* was over. Mazarin could now concentrate on the destruction of Condé and the defeat of Spain. Like his mentor Richelieu, who had been willing to accept allies wherever allies could be found, Mazarin joined forces with Cromwell's Republic in a war against their common enemy, Spain. In 1658 an English army

Marshal Turenne: admirer of Cromwell.

landed in Normandy to fight with the French—led by Turenne—against the Spaniards who were led by Condé. Turenne soon developed a deep respect for the discipline and bearing of the English troops, and he reassured Mazarin that they were "the finest soldiers possible." The Marshal was confident of victory, and his confidence was not misplaced. At the Battle of the Dunes in July, 1658, the Spaniards were soundly defeated. And by the Peace of the Pyrenees, signed in November, 1659, they were obliged to abandon Dunkirk to the English and large tracts of lands in the southeast and along the Netherlands frontier to the French.

Condé, no longer a threat to the French throne, was granted a pardon and withdrew into a quiet retirement that lasted for the rest of the Cardinal's life. Mazarin concentrated his remaining energies upon winning the Spanish Netherlands for France by arranging a marriage between Maria Theresa, the eldest daughter of Philip IV, and her cousin Louis XIV, who celebrated his twenty-first birthday on September 5, 1659.

Louis XIV

Louis married Maria Theresa in June, 1660, and made his state entry into Paris at the end of August. As he rode past the balcony where Cardinal Mazarin stood watching the procession with the Queen Mother, he raised his white plumed hat and bowed low in his saddle to them both.

Mazarin, who was not yet sixty, was a dying man. In constant pain from gout and gallstones, he existed on a diet of milk, broth, game and opium. He had hoped to succeed Alexander VII as Pope, but it was too late for that ultimate ambition to be fulfilled. He was obliged to be content with having completed Richelieu's work, with having brought peace to France, with having accumulated both art and jewel collections of surpassing splendor and an immense fortune of incalculable millions of *livres*.

During his last illness he urgently advised the young King: "Govern. . . . Let the politician be a servant, never a master. . . . If you take the Government into your own hands you will do more in a single day than a minister cleverer than I could do in six months."

It was advice that Louis willingly accepted.

"L'état c'est moi"

With the death of Cardinal Mazarin—who was officially the godfather of Louis XIV and actually the ruler of France during the Sun King's minority—the full power of the state passed to the untested twenty-two-year-old monarch. Acting with astonishing self-assurance, Louis ordered his court into full mourning for the Cardinal, summoned a meeting of his highest ministers—and bluntly informed them that he wanted the benefit of their advice only when he asked for it. Mazarin's pupil had learned his lessons well: the country, threatened by internal rebellion and foreign intrigues, needed an absolute ruler and the young King was determined to be precisely that. Insisting that he **was** *the state, Louis XIV lifted France to the apogee of her glory and stamped his name on an age.*

In early February, 1661, an outbreak of fire at the Louvre Palace forced the seriously ill Cardinal Mazarin to leave for Vincennes. There he continued to meet frequently with his godson and disciple, Louis XIV, the young King of France. On March 3, the First Minister's condition grew more grave, and the disconsolate young monarch was seen weeping as he left Mazarin's room. That evening Louis convened the Council for the first time since the Cardinal's illness, but he hardly spoke during the meeting.

On March 8 it was clear that the Cardinal was dying, and that night a watch was kept over him by Pierrette Dufour, Louis' former nurse. Early the next morning Pierrette informed Louis that Mazarin had died sometime between two and three o'clock.

Louis ordered the Court to go into full mourning, an honor usually reserved only for members of the royal family. (Some historians claim that Louis' action was proof of a secret marriage between Mazarin and the Queen Mother. It seems more likely, however, that the contrary was the case; if a marriage had taken place, the King certainly would not have advertised it in this way.)

On the following day, March 10, at seven o'clock in the morning, Chancellor Séguier, the ministers and the secretaries of state assembled in the Louvre Palace. The eight politicians gathered dutifully around the King, and with a mixture of fear and curiosity they studied the face of that twenty-two-year-old man whose expression reflected his cold, enigmatic and determined personality.

The King addressed the Chancellor in the tone of a man who was "master of himself and of the universe"—a manner he was to maintain throughout his life:

Sir, ... up to the present time, I have been content to leave the governing of my affairs in the hands of the late Cardinal Mazarin. However, the time has now come for me to take over the reins of government myself. You will kindly assist me by giving me the benefit of your advice *when I ask you for it* ... From now on, Mr. Chancellor, you will not make any decision or sign any paper except on my orders and not before having discussed the matter with me, unless, of course, you are brought these orders directly from me by one of my secretaries of state. As for you, sirs, as my secretaries of state, I forbid you to sign anything at all, not even a safe-conduct pass or a passport, without my prior approval.

Louis' words were received in stunned silence. Yet even those seasoned politicians did not realize that the King's speech ushered in a new and revolutionary phase in the history of France and of the world.

What led this seemingly timid, inexperienced young man to make such a momentous decision— a decision that amounted to a coup d'état? Fortunately, Louis' *Mémoires* provide much of the answer: Mazarin had advised him "not to appoint a First Minister," and Louis had decided to follow his advice "since nothing is more shameful than to see all the functions of the state collected together on the one side while, on the other, there is only the title of king." Louis was devoured by a passion for glory: "In my heart, I desire, more than anything else, more than life itself, an illustrious reputation.... The one emotion which overpowers all others in the minds of kings is the sense of their own greatness and glory."

France in 1661 required strong leadership. The country was exhausted by the excesses of the Fronde, the armed rebellion of the nobility that had lasted from 1648 to 1653. Louis recognized that fifty years of civil and foreign wars, financial chaos and court intrigue had left France in a deplorably weakened state. He was conscious of the weight of his new responsibility, for "when one holds such a high rank, the slightest error of judgment can lead to the most unfortunate consequences." Yet an unshakable belief in his own divine authority gave him complete self-assurance. That belief was to be the cornerstone of his government: "When God appointed kings to rule over men, He expected them, as His lieutenants, to be shown the respect due to them. Only He has the right to question the conduct of kings."

It was only after 1789 that revolutions were

Cardinal Mazarin, who built up the power of the throne which Louis XIV inherited.

Opposite Louis XIV, the Sun King: he said "L'état c'est moi."

Louis XIV visiting the tapestry factory of Les Gobelins. Louis was a patron of the arts.

associated with movements whose aim, at least in theory, was to further the interests of the masses. Therefore, the sudden change in government that Louis XIV inaugurated after the death of Mazarin was not fully appreciated by his contemporaries. A conventional monarch who respected ancient traditions would not have behaved as Louis did. He was acting on his own initiative, in the style of a Julius Caesar. Although his conception of kingship had its roots in Mazarin's theories, Louis himself developed it into a new and original philosophy. According to his view, a monarch should possess virtually dictatorial powers, the like of which had never previously been seen in France.

Unlike a twentieth-century dictator, who has to maintain his position of power through frequent, spectacular achievements, an absolute ruler such as Louis had nothing to fear from the fickleness of public opinion. Therefore he could rule with the serene self-assurance of one who knows that he is part of a divine, eternal pattern of life.

Like Napoleon, Louis XIV tried to impose his will not only on the French government but on every aspect of national life. He controlled everything—from the order of precedence at Court to troop movements and theological controversies. Nothing—from an important marriage to the building of a road—could be arranged without his approval. King and country eventually became synonymous, and it was no longer possible for Frenchmen to imagine the separation of the two without a sense of anguish and

disorientation. In fact, it was unthinkable that anyone should dare to replace Louis—the divine king who had been empowered by God to rule over his people. Louis created an excellent intelligence service and founded the modern police force, but his authority was never based on a system of police terror. He succeeded in stifling the various factions, destroying the parties and wiping out ideological divisions with the general approval of the people and without resorting to violence.

The France of Louis' time, like the France of today, was a mass of contradictions. Theoretically, there were no limits to Louis' authority, but in practice he was continually confounded by traditional customs and franchises. Feudalism survived in many forms throughout the country, and the *parlements* still claimed to be the arbiters of power. Although individual liberty was unknown, various groups possessed collective liberties and privileges that obstructed the work of the central government. Even civil servants were not directly answerable to the state—having purchased their positions, they were immune from transfer or dismissal. The King had no control over education, and the economy was in a complete state of chaos, hemmed in by a mass of restrictions and anomalies.

Louis set out to correct these deficiencies with a tenacious will and determination. The people were clamoring for law and order, and he intended to give it to them. But he had something even more precious to offer them: he was the personification of a nation

France: a mass of contradictions

Far left Colbert, Louis XIV's brilliant financial minister, who provided most of the funds for Louis' ambitious building programs, patronage of the arts and war making.

Louis XIV, a bust by Bernini at Versailles; Louis' ambition expressed itself in wars against his neighbors, and in an attempt to secure the throne of Spain for his heirs.

The appointment in 1699 of The Comte de Pontchartrain as Chancellor.

at the height of its powers, overflowing with vitality and health, a nation that longed for magnificence.

Louis XIII, an austere, reserved monarch, had been respected from a distance by his subjects, while they had loathed Richelieu and despised Mazarin. Their joy and relief were unbounded when they discovered that their new King was a proud, handsome young man, as yet untarnished by corruption and dishonesty. France was soon infatuated with Louis. The nobles, fresh from their rebellion, and the masses, including the forerunners of the angry revolutionaries of 1789, did not submit passively to absolute rule—they were carried away on a wave of enthusiasm for and devotion to Louis. Their obedience was not forced on them but grew out of their state of mind and the particular needs of the moment.

Voltaire commented that during the first half of Louis XIV's reign, he had proved "that when an absolute monarch wants to do good, he can achieve anything he sets out to do." Indeed, with the support of both nobles and commoners, Louis' untried government was able to transform the country in an astonishingly short space of time.

Jean Baptiste Colbert, Louis' Finance Minister, embarked on a systematic economic policy of mercantilism with the object of promoting France's industrial and commercial prosperity. He created new manufactures, encouraged a higher birth rate and methodically set about mobilizing the labor force. During his ten-year term of office, he supervised a major reorganization of the economy: new

Genius at its peak of brilliance

roads were built, canals dug and abandoned ports reconstructed. Colbert created a merchant marine and increased the number of warships from a mere twenty to three hundred. The army was modernized, while the administration was streamlined and carried on with a high degree of efficiency.

Culturally, Louis' reign marked a new high for France. Paris was transformed and monuments were built in every major city. The Louvre, the Tuileries and Saint-Germain were given a new look, and masterpieces of architecture were created: Versailles, the Trianon, Marly. The French genius was at the peak of its brilliance.

Louis XIV cannot be personally credited with these extraordinary achievements. Yet he did preside over a galaxy of talented men—statesmen, generals, engineers, artists, writers, preachers and philosophers, who were the envy of Europe—like an orchestra conductor, carefully controlling them, maintaining harmonious relations among them and, when necessary, manipulating them to serve his own ends.

At the end of twenty years, France, the absolute monarchy and Louis XIV himself were at the height of their glory. The palace of Versailles epitomized the splendor of France and served as a magnificent setting for a king who was universally acclaimed as the greatest monarch of the day and who fully justified the title "The Sun King." No European state dared to fire a gun or make a move without first consulting Louis. Virtually singlehandedly, France under Louis' rule had held the powerful coalition of European powers that opposed her in check, had been victorious on both sea and land, had annexed Flanders, Franche-Comté and Strasbourg, occupied Lorraine and dictated terms to her defeated enemies. Overseas, the French flag was flying in Africa and America.

Other monarchs were quick to appreciate and profit from Louis' example. Since the Renaissance and the Reformation, two distinct currents of political thought had developed in Europe. Catholicism and autocratic centralized monarchy had prospered in the Mediterranean countries. (Long before the accession of Louis XIV, Philip II ruled as absolute monarch over Spain's vast empire.) The political life of the northern regions, on the other hand, had moved in various directions: in England, a constitutional monarchy had been established; in the Netherlands, democracy. Germany, in a state of anarchy, was broken up into a number of small states. Some of these states were ruled by an autocratic monarch, notably the newly created state of Prussia which the Hohenzollerns governed despotically. In the same way, in Russia, Peter the Great had established an autocracy after crushing the boyars, while Catholic Austria was ruled by the Hapsburg dynasty.

A similar situation might easily have arisen in Great Britain, for the Stuarts were only too eager to

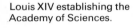

Louis XIV establishing the Academy of Sciences.

rule as absolute monarchs in spite of the unfortunate fate of their predecessor, Charles I. The Stuarts' designs were thwarted by the simultaneous growth of commercial capitalism and utilitarian individualism, which eliminated governmental control over private property—a control that was considered a natural and essential function of absolute monarchy. When William of Orange landed in Great Britain in 1688, he brought with him not only 15,000 soldiers—symbolizing protesting, Protestant Europe—but also the English philosopher, John Locke, who had been in exile in the Netherlands. Locke believed that absolute power was incompatible with civil society. "The law of nature," wrote that philosopher of the new thinking, "has instituted political law in order to prevent the natural rights of man from being threatened in the course of his daily life." Locke's political theories triumphed in 1697: Louis XIV was forced to recognize William as King of England and, for the first time, "divine right" gave way to the "natural rights of the people." Divine right was again discredited in 1713 after the War of the Spanish Succession, when Philip V was forced to relinquish all rights to the French throne.

Meanwhile, the absolutist system had already revealed some grave weaknesses. The most serious—the fundamental mistake of Louis XIV—was the expectation that an absolute monarch could successfully shoulder responsibilities beyond the capacity and endurance of a single individual. By vesting all the powers of the state within himself, Louis had exposed absolutist monarchy to the frailties of nature. As he grew older and his faculties began to fail him, so France gradually and simultaneously declined.

The successors of the Sun King were not equal to the task he left them. Louis XV, contrary to general belief, was an extremely lucid, intelligent and hardworking man, and would have probably made an excellent constitutional monarch. Because of his timidity and lack of decisiveness, however, two

Above The Battle of Rocroi, 1643, at which the Duc de Enghein, who was to be better known later as the Prince de Condé, won a great victory over the Spanish army.

Below A corner of the Throne Room at Versailles, Louis' great palace fifteen miles from Paris.

Versailles under construction.

Below A symbolic drawing showing how heretics will be driven from France by the Sun King.

opposing protest movements developed during his reign, both in revolt against the concept of absolutism: the popular movement, based on the ideas of the *philosophes*, and the revolt of the privileged classes, which, from generation to generation, fundamentally opposed the power of the monarchy. The clash of these two revolutionary movements eventually produced the final explosion that became the French Revolution.

Louis XVI, on the other hand, committed a fatal error of judgment when he tried to extricate himself from chaos and confusion by attempting to preserve an obsolete system. He was a scrupulous and virtuous man, but he totally lacked the qualities of leadership. It is said that when he succeeded to the throne, he cried out in desperation: "What a responsibility! I have the feeling that the whole world is going to topple over on top of me!" These prophetic words were to come true in 1789.

Before the final collapse of the absolute monarchy, however—while it was being attacked on all sides, by the *philosophes*, by the *parlements* and by a large

Louis XVI supports the American colonists

number of the aristocrats—France enjoyed an unparalleled success in Europe. Paradoxically, the European nations that had been at loggerheads with Louis XIV during his lifetime began to emulate him after his death. Now that he could no longer dictate to and control them, the European monarchs began to adopt the French way of life with mounting enthusiasm. Every king and prince had to have his own palace of Versailles and his own court etiquette modeled after that of the Sun King. French became the language of diplomacy and was adopted by the world of culture. Thus, absolutist monarchy had not only transformed France into a modern, prosperous country but had also served as a model for Western civilization.

Louis XVI supported the American colonists in their fight for independence, and in so doing, he bankrupted the French treasury. Thus, ironically, the American colonists may be held largely responsible for the downfall of the monarchy in France and for the preservation of the monarchy in England. If the Americans had lost the war, the trend toward

authoritarianism in England would inevitably have been accelerated and the English would most likely have reacted violently against it, as they did at the time of the Stuarts. Because George III was defeated, however, he had no choice but to revert to constitutional and parliamentary rule.

The revolution of 1789 swept away the absolutist monarchy in France, but it was a long time before absolutism disappeared from the rest of Europe. In Austria, Germany and Spain, the ruling monarchs reluctantly accepted constitutions, although the rulers managed to retain quite a large share of power —the power that had formerly been theirs by "Divine Right."

Up to 1914, Kaiser Wilhelm II of Germany, Franz Josef of Austria and Tsar Nicholas I of Russia ruled over their empires despotically. It was the disruptions of World War I and the revolutionary movements that developed out of it that finally put an end to the system of absolute monarchy conceived by the young King Louis XIV at the deathbed of Mazarin.   PHILIPPE ERLANGER

Louis XIV and his family : the King's ambitions for his relations were the cause of struggles that involved most of the countries of Europe.

The golden age of Dutch military and naval

A naval nation

When Louis XIV assumed absolute power in France, William, Prince of Orange, who was to become one of Louis' most formidable enemies, was still a boy at school. Twenty years earlier, William's father, the Dutch Stadtholder, had married Mary, eldest daughter of Charles I of England and his French wife Henrietta Maria. The fourteen-year-old bridegroom died ten years later, in 1650; his son Prince William was born a week later.

William grew up in a world dominated by the rivalry between England and Holland, the two great maritime powers of northern Europe. From the earliest days of the Republic, the energy and expertise of Dutch seamen, shipbuilders and merchants had won the Dutch Republic international renown. In Asia the successes of Dutch

St. Paul's Cathedral, rebuilt by Sir Christopher Wren after the Fire of London.

their shared Protestantism united the English and Dutch. In 1588, for example, a Dutch fleet lying off Dunkirk had prevented the Duke of Parma from joining the Spanish Armada's final assault on Elizabeth's England. Since that time, the Dutch had twice demonstrated

The scandal of the Downs

Although they did not regret Spain's collapse, the English viewed the rise of Dutch naval power with concern. The Battle of the Downs

had actually been fought in English waters, and Tromp had arrogantly used those waters as his own. As a result, outraged Britons referred to the sea clash as "the scandal of the Downs." Fortunately for the Dutch, the English, who were on the verge of civil war, were in no state to punish the pretensions of "the damnable Dutchmen." While an irate but impotent England watched, Dutch seamen pushed their way into overseas markets that had formerly been English preserves.

The end of the English civil war, the execution of the English King and the rise to power of Oliver Cromwell, England's energetic and patriotic Protector, opened the way for English resentments to find expression in war. To British regicides, war with the Dutch seemed additionally appropriate, for the young Prince of Orange was the grandson of the traitor they had put to death in 1649.

William of Orange and Mary, daughter of England's Charles I : parents of William III, who later became King of England.

traders and of their East India Company were the envy of the commercial nations of the West; in Australasia, Dutch explorers opened up vast tracts of territory to settlement and exploitation; and in Europe Dutch engineering skills, administration and economy were much admired.

The hustling, aggressive, sometimes ruthless enterprise of the Dutch naturally brought them into conflict with Britain and Spain, and much of what happened in Europe before the Dutch economy began to decline can be seen in terms of the conflict between these great rivals.

There had been a time when

their prowess at sea in brilliant style. In the 1639 Battle of the Downs, Marten Harpertszoon Tromp, a native of Brill, had roundly defeated a strong Spanish fleet under Admiral Oquendo in a naval engagement that confirmed the eclipse of Spanish power in Europe and dealt a blow to the Spanish navy from which it never recovered. And in 1640, at Itamarca (off the coast of Brazil), another Dutch fleet decisively disposed of a Hispano-Portuguese armada that had crossed the Atlantic in a last desperate bid to remove the upstart Protestants from their South American empire.

VILLAGE FLOTTANT. DRYVEND-DORP.

Pêche a l'oiseau Vissery met Vogels

VILLE DE PAU ING HYEN AVEC SES MOULINS A VENT.

Dutch commercial enterprise in the Far East.

strength and commercial enterprise

Anglo-Dutch wars

The opening shots in the Anglo-Dutch wars were fired by the English, whose Navigation Act of 1651 had forbidden the importation of all Asian, African and American goods in non-British ships. (The Act also forbade imports from Europe that did not arrive in British ships or in ships belonging to the country of origin.) Since the English did not have enough ships to break the Dutch monopoly themselves, the Navigation Act was more of a petulant

Admiral de Ruyter led Dutch attacks on the English fleet.

challenge to the Dutch than a real threat to their carrying trade. But when the English backed up their challenge by asserting their right to board Dutch ships and to search them for French goods, war was inevitable. For fifty years the Dutch

had ruled the northern seas, and they could see no reason to observe the outmoded practice of saluting the British flag. They refused to do so, and they opened fire on the English.

It was a bitter and costly war in which first one side and then the other seemed to have the advantage, a war in which the British admiral Robert Blake and the Dutchman Tromp proved themselves to be among the greatest commanders in the history of naval warfare. And when the war ended in 1654, the rivalry was not yet settled; the English continued to regard the Dutch with that mixture of envy, admiration and distaste which they generally reserved for the French.

Open war was touched off again in 1663, when a British squadron sailed to West Africa to support the Royal Africa Company in their quarrel with Dutch West African merchants. The fleet seized various Dutch possessions—all of which the Dutch admiral Michiel de Ruyter immediately recaptured—and the ensuing years of war were as costly and indecisive as those of the 1650s had been. The continuing power of the Dutch Navy was forcefully demonstrated in 1666, the year of London's Great Fire when Admiral de Ruyter trounced the English in the Channel, inflicting nearly eight thousand casualties. (The corpses of countless English sailors were left floating in the sea, clad in the civilian clothes that they had been wearing when the press gangs marched them off.) The next year the Dutch barged through the boom and into Chatham harbor in Kent, burned

Catherine of Braganza, wife of Charles II of England.

four ships of the line, bombarded the docks and crowned their achievement by towing away the largest vessel in the English fleet.

On July 31, 1668, a treaty was signed at Breda, and the second Dutch war came to an end. This treaty settled some vital differences between the two nations, but their quarrels were not yet over. Although mutual fear of the ambitions of Louis xiv brought England and the Netherlands into temporary alliance against France, Louis had little difficulty in persuading Charles ii that the Dutch, not the French, were his real enemies—and in 1670 an alliance was signed between England and France that provided for an attack upon Holland, the destruction of its commercial power and the partition of the country.

The Republic alone

The Dutch Republic displayed remarkable resilience and resource in the face of such formidable opposition. The English again failed to defeat the Dutch navy, and the French failed to reach Amsterdam when the Dutch opened the dikes and flooded the countryside. The war continued for six years, and at its end Holland remained as real a commercial rival to England as she had been before it began. During that period she became a dangerous rival to France as well, for her new ruler, William, Prince of Orange, a harsh, brilliant, unattractive, asthmatic soldier, was the leading opponent of Louis xiv's aspirations and the chief architect of the European alliances against him. By the time the European wars were finally over, England had achieved most of her ambitions and had greatly increased both her share of world trade and the power of her navy. Holland emerged from the conflict immeasurably weakened; she was never able to regain her former position as a world power.

The Scientific Revolution

In the course of Holland's economic decline, her people lost nothing of their earlier genius. Her artists continued to guide European trends in art and her universities continued to make their own distinctive contribution to what was to become known as the Scientific Revolution. One of the precursors of this Revolution, a leading pioneer of the scientific method, was

René Descartes, "the father of modern philosophy."

Francis Bacon. Bacon's *Advancement of Learning* was published in 1605, his *New Atlantis* appeared in 1627, and his reiterated call for "minds washed clear of opinions" became the rallying cry of the age. Ten years after the appearance of *The New Atlantis*, René Descartes—the rationalist philosopher, mathematician and inventor of coordinate geometry who has become known as "the father of modern philosophy"—published his *Discours de la méthode*, in which the celebrated Cartesian principle of "systematic" doubt was propounded. The age of Bacon and Descartes was also the age of Johannes Kepler, the German astronomer and mathematician, and of Galileo Galilei, the marvelously versatile Italian astronomer, lecturer and inventor, who perfected the refracting telescope (which had been invented by the Dutch in 1608). With the help of that telescope Galileo was able to demonstrate the essential truth of the Copernican theory.

In 1666 the scientific discoveries of the first half of the seventeenth century were given a deeper meaning when a Cambridge scholar, Isaac Newton, discovered the law of universal gravitation.

A Dutch attack on Sheerness, 1667.

Cambridge's Young Genius

In the same year—1665—that Isaac Newton graduated without distinction from Trinity College, Cambridge, the Great Plague struck England. The colleges at Cambridge closed, both scholars and faculty dispersed, and Newton went home to Woolsthorpe. Two years later, mathematician Isaac Barrow's shy and unpromising protégé returned to Trinity—where he promptly astounded his master with the results of his independent experiments. In two short years, Newton had laid the groundwork for discoveries in the fields of geometry, optics and planetary motion that were to revolutionize those disciplines and radically alter man's conception of his universe. Indeed, Newton's studies of motion and gravitation—summarized in his monumental 1687 work, Principia Mathematica—*and his experiments with light and color—detailed in* Opticks, *which Newton published some seventeen years later—are the basis for modern physics.*

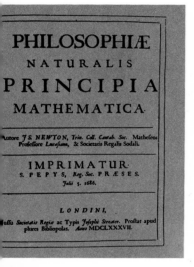

The title page of the first edition of Newton's revolutionary work, *Principia Mathematica*, with Pepys' *imprimateur* on behalf of the Royal Society. The *Principia* explained Newton's ideas about gravity.

Opposite Newton's reflecting telescope: until the development of radio astronomy in the mid-twentieth century, the reflecting telescope remained the usual design for large telescopes, such as that at Mount Palomar, in California.

Isaac Newton, perhaps the greatest intellectual giant among scientific men, is remembered primarily for his theory of universal gravitation, which was published in 1687 and which opened a new chapter in the scientific revolution. Newton demonstrated that the force of gravity could account precisely for the motions of bodies on earth and in space—motions that had previously been considered essentially different, and that had defied mathematical analysis. Newton also developed novel mathematical techniques—particularly the calculus—discovered the nature of white light and colors and designed and built the first practical reflecting telescope.

Newton was born at the small manor house in the village of Woolsthorpe in Lincolnshire on Christmas Day, 1642. Although sickly as an infant, Isaac grew sturdier each year. He was enrolled at a local grammar school to prepare him to manage the small family estate, but Newton was no farmer. He was more interested in making model waterwheels than in minding sheep, and his mother was persuaded by the headmaster of the grammar school to allow her son to attend a university. Newton went to Cambridge in June, 1661. The family finances were limited, however, and he entered Trinity College as a subsizar—which meant that he would pay his own way by waiting on his tutor and doing other tasks.

Neither at grammar school nor at the university did Newton show any particular intellectual brilliance, but in 1663 he came under the influence of the remarkable scholar and mathematician, Isaac Barrow. Barrow recognized something of Newton's abilities, although when he examined the young man in 1664 he found that his young protégé's knowledge of geometry—in those days one of the most important of mathematical studies—was poor. Under Barrow's guidance Newton began to develop and to take an increasing interest in light and the behavior of lenses. When he took his B.A. in 1665, however, he passed without any distinction.

The year 1665 saw the advent of the Great Plague,

first in London and then, less virulently, at Cambridge. The university closed and the scholars dispersed to their homes. Newton returned to Woolsthorpe, and there, in the quiet and isolation of his home, he began to make the first attacks on the problems that he was later to solve so brilliantly. He developed his mathematical skills and began to lay the foundations of a method for calculating quantities that depend upon one another in ways that are never the same from one moment to the next—what has since become known as the calculus. His optical work was concerned first with grinding glass lenses and experimenting with them to try to improve the telescope, and second with investigating the way in which sunlight ("white" light) is broken up into colors by a prism. The latter led him to devise crucial experiments which showed that while white light could be dispersed into colors by one prism, a second prism would disperse each color no further but, if turned upside down, could cause the colors to recombine to form white light. Newton therefore decided that white light was really a mixture of the light of all colors, a view different from those then in general currency, which supposed each color to be a mixture of white light and darkness in different proportions.

The idea of gravity—the attractive power of the earth on objects—was much discussed at this time, and also the behavior of the planets as they orbited the sun. Newton was naturally intrigued by these problems. (His niece, Catherine Barton, first recounted the well-known story of how an apple fell at Newton's feet while he was sitting under a tree at Woolsthorpe, causing him to question whether the earth's gravity, which had pulled the apple downward extended out as far as the moon. Newton felt that without gravitational pull, there was nothing to keep the moon from moving straight out into space, and that only a "fall" toward the earth could change a straight path into a curved one centered on the earth. But although Newton at this point made some

A meeting of the Royal Society, with Newton in the chair.

Working at the Royal Mint. Newton became Warden of the Mint in 1696 and Master in 1701.

calculations—and although he said as an old man that they answered the facts "pretty nearly"— recent scholarship indicates that he was still very far from his final theory when he was at Woolsthorpe.

Using the extremely accurate observations of planetary positions made by the Danish nobleman Tycho Brahe between 1576 and 1597, the German astronomer Johannes Kepler had analyzed planetary motions and come to the conclusion that the planets orbited the sun in elliptical paths, not in circular orbits as hitherto believed. Kepler also found that the time taken to complete an orbit depended on a planet's average distance from the sun, and that the motion of a planet was not uniform but accelerated as the body approached the sun.

These three "laws" of planetary motion had been published between 1609 and 1621; there is evidence, however, that Newton did not know of the law of changing planetary velocities when he was at Woolsthorpe or, indeed, for some years later.

In addition to accepting Kepler's teaching on planetary motion, the scientific world of the 1660s much favored the general picture of the universe that René Descartes had published in 1644. This was particularly so at Cambridge, and there is no doubt that Newton was familiar with every detail of Descartes' theory; it seems certain that Descartes' ideas also exerted considerable influence on Newton during his first years of research. Descartes thought that the universe was completely filled with material that was collected together into giant vortexes. At the center of each vortex lay a star, and around it orbited planets carried by the whirling material of the vortex. The theory concerned itself too with the nature of matter and of other physical aspects of the universe, including light. It was broad in scope and exercised immense influence for a time, and when Newton was at Woolsthorpe turning the question of gravity over in his mind, it is almost certain that he was doing so within the context of Descartes' theory.

That context is especially significant, because although Newton later claimed that he reached his main conclusions about gravitation while at Woolsthorpe, he made no announcement of what he thought until almost twenty years later. It is usually accepted that during his Woolsthorpe years Newton did not know the size of the earth—and thus the moon's distance—with sufficient accuracy, nor could he prove that the earth attracted bodies in space as if its power of gravitation were concentrated

Newton constructs a new telescope

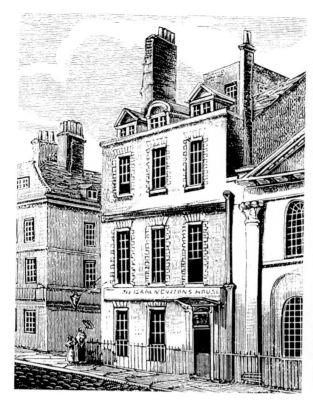

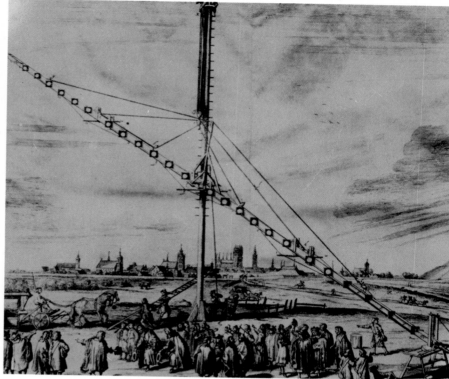

at its center. Scholars have always felt that neither of these difficulties would have prevented Newton from bringing his ideas to a reasonable state of completion. It seems highly probable, however, that Newton's acceptance of Descartes' idea of vortexes prevented him from being able to calculate his answers with complete precision.

Newton returned to Cambridge late in March, 1667, and received his M.A. a year later. He worked with Barrow, helping him to compile a book on optics, but made no reference to his own experiments at Woolsthorpe. Because Newton was shy and feared controversy, he never went out of his way to publicize his achievements. Indeed, Barrow might never have known of his pupil's independent work had he not mentioned Nicholas Mercator's success in calculating the area under a hyperbola. Newton replied that he himself had already done that, and he showed Barrow his notes. It was clear that he had indeed done so—and before Mercator. Barrow soon made Newton's mathematical genius known, and in 1669 he resigned his chair at Trinity in favor of his protégé.

In the seventeenth century a professor of mathematics included in his purview such physical subjects as light and optics, and Newton frequently lectured on those topics. The lectures appear to have created no great stir, but Newton also spent some time constructing a reflecting telescope, and rumors about his work in that area did move outside his immediate circle. Contemporary telescopes were of one type: refracting instruments that consisted of a large lens at the front and a small eye lens at the rear. Such telescopes had several notable defects: they displayed colored fringes around objects and they had a very small area of sharp focus. To obtain even

limited results, telescopes had to be as much as 150 to 200 feet in length. Newton's Woolsthorpe experiments had convinced him that a refractor could never be cleared of its colored fringe images. In this he was wrong, but the mistake led him to consider the construction of reflectors, in which a curved mirror at the back replaced the lens at the front. James Gregory, a Scottish mathematician, had published a design for a reflecting telescope in 1663, but no one had constructed the instrument, which Newton felt had many faults. He therefore designed his own instrument and built a small model, which, although no more than six-and-one-quarter inches long, was as good as any refractor a dozen times larger.

For some years Newton remained at Cambridge, but in 1677 Robert Hooke—one of his sternest critics —became an honorary secretary of the Royal Society and wrote to try to mollify Newton. After Newton agreed to discuss scientific matters again, Hooke began trying to draw him out on the still unsolved question of planetary motions.

Hooke was not alone in trying to find a solution to the movements of the planets. In London Sir Christopher Wren, architect and onetime astronomer, and the astronomer Edmond Halley also discussed the question with Hooke. But although they were all convinced that the planets kept in their paths because the sun attracted them, and that the force of this attraction became less with distance in a particular way, they could not prove their point. The mathematics defeated them. Halley decided to consult Newton and in August, 1684, visited him at Cambridge. Newton agreed that Hooke, Halley and Wren were correct in their surmise about the law of

A refractor telescope made by Hevelius in 1673. Newton's invention of a reflector telescope meant that more satisfactory results could be obtained from a far smaller telescope than was previously possible.

Above left Newton's house in London, off Leicester Square.

John Flamsteed, Astronomer Royal. Newton's insistance that Flamsteed should publish the results of his work as soon as possible led to a quarrel between the two men.

Newton by Kneller, painted in 1702.

Right The Cottage at Woolsthorpe where Newton was born.

of two printers to overcome any delay, and it was published in London in 1687, with the title *Philosophiae Naturalis Principia Mathematica (The Mathematical Principles of Natural Philosophy)*. Known ever since as the *Principia*, it ran to three editions in Newton's lifetime and brought its author undying fame.

The book is amazingly comprehensive. It deals first with the motions of bodies, both on the earth and in space. Both are controlled, Newton shows, by the three laws of motion: first, a body is either at rest or moves forever in a straight line unless acted upon by external forces; second, the change in such motion is proportional to the external force and the direction in which it is applied; third, to every action there is always an equal and opposite reaction. Newton extends and develops these laws into a whole theory of planetary motion. He then considers the difficult problem of the motion of bodies in a resisting medium such as air or water. Finally he moves on to practical applications of his theoretical assertions.

Revolutionary though the *Principia* was, and widely read as it was, it took time before the teachings it contained were fully accepted. This was true especially in France, where it was primarily due to the efforts of Voltaire that opinion turned in favor of Newton's theory of universal gravitation. Further, writing the book had cost Newton much mental strain. After it was finished, he turned more to other interests, in particular to his studies in chemistry and alchemy. He also turned to theology, for Newton was a Unitarian who spent a great deal of effort on Biblical exegesis to support his views.

In 1693, the strain told: Newton suffered a nervous breakdown. After his recovery he spent very little time and concentrated effort on science, and when recoinage of the currency was agreed on by Parliament, Newton's friend and supporter Charles Montagu obtained the post of Warden of the Mint for him. Newton held the position from 1696 until he was appointed Master of the Mint three years later. During the recoinage the work of Warden was arduous.

In 1701 Newton resigned his chair at Cambridge.

attraction, because he had proved it. But he could not find his proof and promised to rework the mathematics and send the results to Halley. When Newton's proof arrived, Halley realized that the significance of what had been achieved was much broader than mere planetary motion. He therefore persuaded Newton to summarize his ideas of motion and gravitation in the form of a book and he obtained the Royal Society's agreement to act as publisher. As it turned out, the Society was unable to meet the publishing costs and Halley defrayed these out of his own pocket.

Halley had more than costs to worry about in getting the book published, for when Hooke raised a question of acknowledgment while Newton was writing, Newton decided to write no more. It took all Halley's powers of persuasion to make him continue. Halley nursed the volume through the hands

The discovery of the law of gravity

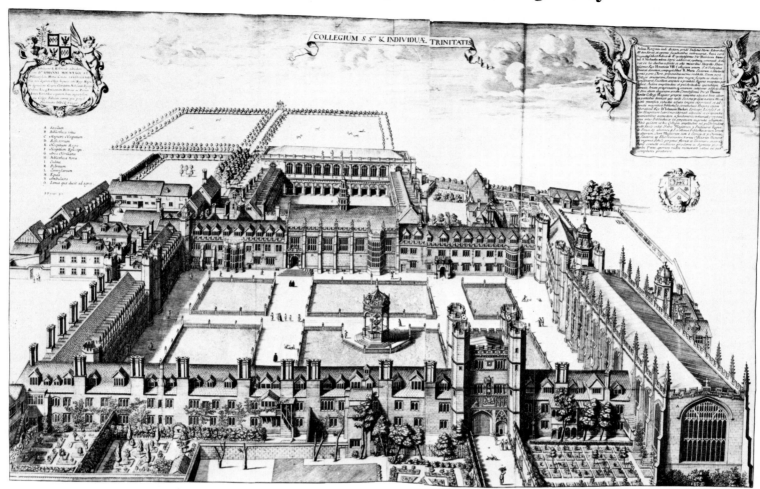

Two years later he was elected president of the Royal Society, an honorary position that he held for the rest of his life. It is unfortunate to record that during his presidency, Newton was the center of two bitter controversies, one with the first Astronomer Royal, John Flamsteed, the other with the German mathematician Gottfried Leibniz. The trouble with Flamsteed arose because, although he had been appointed Astronomer Royal in 1675, he had not published any observations. Since he had to supply his own observing instruments, Flamsteed claimed that the observations were his own property and that he would publish when he had them as correct as he could make them. Newton and many others disagreed, and in the end Newton obtained a royal grant for publication and placed Halley in charge of the material that Flamsteed deposited—under duress—with the Royal Society. In 1712 the results came out. Flamsteed had unquestionably been uncooperative and stubborn, but Newton himself behaved in a high-handed way throughout.

But if Newton had personal failings, his scientific contributions make these pale to insignificance. In 1704, after the death of Hooke, he allowed his book *Opticks* to be published. In it he set down not only his theory of colors, but also his view that light was caused by minute particles, a view that allowed him to explain all optical phenomena then known. In 1705 he received the first knighthood to be awarded for science. So immense was his reputation that when he died he was buried in Westminster Abbey.

Newton's greatest monument is his work. Vindicated time and again after his death, first by Halley and then by others, his theory of universal gravitation has acted as a foundation for vast areas of scientific development. It lies behind present space technology and has acted as a beacon to those who have followed his voyages into what he once called "the great ocean of truth."

COLIN RONAN

Above Trinity College, Cambridge. Newton's rooms are between the Chapel and the Gate: the Library is in the rear.

Below left Isaac Barrow, Master of Trinity, who gave up his Professorship so that Newton could succeed him, and who persuaded Wren (*below*) to design the Library without charge.

War and revolution plunge the states of

While central and northern Europe were fighting their religious, dynastic and civil wars, Europe south of the Po and the Danube remained relatively quiet—but not entirely at peace. Increasing numbers of travelers were crossing the Alps and sailing into ports on the coasts of the Adriatic and Tyrrhenian seas at that time, and those travelers returned home with ideas and tastes that were to have a profound effect on the character of the north in the next century. The Grand Tour had, in fact, already become an integral part of the seventeenth-century aristocratic culture. The tour was not without its dangers, however, and foreign travelers were often advised to alter their routes in order to avoid local insurrections.

Spain remained the dominant power in Italy until the beginning of the eighteenth century, when she was replaced by Austria. The Kingdom of Naples and Sicily—which comprised the whole of Italy south of the Abruzzi—was ruled by viceroys appointed by the Spanish King. The oppressive character of their government provoked repeated uprisings, among them the 1598 rebellion in Calabria that was led by the philosopher Tommaso Campanella. His unsuccessful attempt to free Naples from Spanish tyranny was put down with great severity, and

The Amalfian fisherman, Massaniello, who became Captain-General of the Neapolitan rebels, but was murdered in 1647.

Tommaso Campanella: imprisoned for twenty-seven years for attacking Spanish rule in Naples.

Campanella spent the next twenty-seven years of his life in prison.

In 1647 there were widespread riots in Sicily that forced the Spanish Viceroy to flee from Palermo, and that same year there was a revolution in Naples that obliged the Viceroy there to seek safety in Castelnuovo. The Neo-

politan rebels—who had been provoked to violence by a new tax on fruit, the staple food of the poor—elected a fisherman from Amalfi to be their captain-general. And when the tumult spread beyond the walls of the city and into the villages and towns of the hinterland, the Viceroy gave way and granted all of the rebels' demands. The fruit tax and all other oppressive taxes were removed, various concessions were granted and the citizens were given permission to remain in arms until the treaty was ratified by the King of Spain.

On July 16, 1647, however, the rebel leader was murdered while haranguing his followers in the marketplace. When the tumult broke out afresh, the Viceroy was again compelled to seek refuge in the Castelnuovo, and a new revolutionary leader was found in Gennaro Annese. When he learned that reinforcements had been dispatched from Spain, Annese appealed to France for help, and in response to the rebel's appeal, the Duke of Guise landed in Naples with an

expeditionary force. Following the unpopular Viceroy's recall, order was restored by his wily successor, Count d'Ognate, who promptly came to terms with Annese—and then had him and all the other ringleaders executed.

Revolt in Sicily

Thirteen years after this popular revolution had almost ended Spanish control over Naples, there was a similar uprising in Sicily. Like the Neapolitans before them, the Sicilians called upon the French to help them drive the Spanish out—and the Spanish, unable to quell the revolt, turned to the Dutch. Both countries responded: a French fleet commanded by the Duke of Vivonne and a Dutch fleet under de Ruyter both sailed for Sicily.

By the 1678 Peace of Nijmegen, Louis XIV abandoned the Sicilian rebels to the persecution of the Spaniards, however, and it was not until 1707 that the Spaniards were at last driven out of Naples.

Even then, it was an Austrian army, not a Neapolitan army, that drove the Spaniards off. By the terms of the Treaty of Utrecht, which was signed in 1713, the Spaniards were obliged to abandon Sicily, which was handed over to Duke Victor of Savoy. Five years later Sicily, like Naples, became an Austrian possession.

Northern Italy

North of the Kingdom of the Two Sicilies lay the Papal States, which had recently increased in size through the reversion of two important fiefs, Ferrara and Urbino, to papal jurisdiction. Urban VIII's attempt to expand his holdings further by attacking the Duchy of Parma was checked by Tuscany, Modena and Venice, and after the 1648 Treaty of Westphalia no hope of extending the papal territories could be entertained. They remained notoriously ill-governed and financially embarrassed until the advent of Napoleon.

The extensive Duchy of Milan had been a dependency of the Spanish Crown since the death of Francesco Sforza ended his family's reign in 1535. Like the Spanish possessions in the south, Milan was handed over to Austria at the close of the War of the Spanish Succession. Tuscany, a neighboring state, was ruled by a succession of grand dukes, all of whom were members of the Medici family and all of whom were incompetent. Upon the death of the last Medicean Grand Duke in 1737, it was agreed that the state should be given to Francis, Duke of Lorraine and husband of Maria Theresa of Austria.

Although repeatedly at odds with their more powerful neighbors, the dukes of Savoy managed to retain their independence. By the 1669 Treaty of the Pyrenees (which ended the war between Spain and France), Charles Emmanuel II was permitted to re-occupy most of the towns that the French had captured. And at the end of the War of the Spanish Succession—during which Prince Eugene of Savoy decisively defeated the French at the 1706 siege of Turin—the Duke of Savoy received the Kingdom of Sicily, which was exchanged for Sardinia in 1718. Thereafter, the rulers of Savoy became known as the kings of Sardinia.

The other principal states of

Italy into turmoil

The signing of the Treaty of Nijmegen, 1678, by which Louis XIV gave up his support for the rebels of Naples.

northern Italy were Modena and Parma. The former, governed by the Este family, was transformed by France into the Cispadine Republic during the reign of Hercules III and thereafter became a dependency of Austria. The Duchy of Parma remained in the possession of the Farnese family until 1731, when, upon the death of Duke Antonio, it too passed into the hands of the Austrians.

The Demise of Venice

By the turn of the century, the Republic of Venice had lost most of its former power and vitality—and after years of war with the Turks and repeated quarrels with its jealous neighbors, it had lost most of its overseas possessions as well. In 1570 a 60,000-man Turkish army led by Selim II had landed on the island of Cyprus, which the Venetians had held since 1489. The invaders soon occupied most of the

island, took the city of Nicosia and slaughtered over 20,000 of its inhabitants. Famagusta held out for nearly a year, but in August of 1571 it too was forced to capitulate. The Turks, breaking the terms of the capitulation, flayed the governor alive and dispatched his skin, stuffed with straw, to Constantinople.

A few months after the conquest of Cyprus, the Turkish navy was soundly defeated at Lepanto. The Venetians derived no lasting benefit from their triumph, however, for in 1645 the Turks turned their attention to Crete, which had been a Venetian possession for four centuries. In 1646 they landed an army of 50,000 men, occupied Canea and took Retimo, and two years later they laid siege to Candia. The siege lasted for more than twenty years, but Candia eventually fell—and in September, 1669, the whole island passed into the hands of the Turks.

There was a brief resurgence of

Venetian power under Francesco Morosini, who was appointed commander-in-chief of the Republic's army in 1684 amid renewed hostilities with Turkey. With the help of German mercenaries, Morosini reconquered Dalmatia and the region of southern Greece known as the Morea. The septuagenarian commander was elected Doge, but after his death, the territories that he had reclaimed reverted to the Turks and the Republic ceased to be a threat to the Turkish Empire.

Kitchen to Court

From 1648 to 1687 the Ottoman Empire was ruled by Mohammed IV. His Grand Vizier, an able and vastly energetic Albanian named Mohammed Kuprili who began his career as a scullion in the imperial kitchen, was largely responsible for the resurgence of the Empire's power. Kuprili restored the fleet, recaptured the islands that had been taken by the Venetians and put down revolts against his harsh regime with severity. In 1661 he was succeeded by his son, Fazil Ahmed Kuprili, a more humane

but equally able administrator.

In 1663 Ahmed Kuprili attacked Austria, which represented a far greater threat to Turkey than the Venetian Republic. Following a succession of victories, Ahmed's troops were overwhelmed at the Battle of St. Gotthard Abbey and he was forced to conclude the Treaty of Vasvar on August 10, 1664. A twenty-year truce was imposed—and for eight years the Sultan observed it. Then, in 1672, Turkey declared war on Poland's King Michael Wisniowiecki (who had set himself up as champion of the Sultan's rivals in the Ukraine). And this time Ahmed Kuprili was more successful: his army captured Kamenets, Lemberg and Lublin—and Podolia, the area between Moldavia and the Ukraine, was ceded to Turkey by the Treaty of Buczacs.

Led by John Sobieski, Poland set out to retrieve her fortunes: war against Turkey was resumed, and on November 11, 1673, John Sobieski won his first great victory at Choczim. He was soon to win another more momentous victory at Vienna, one that foreshadowed the collapse of the Turkish Empire.

John Sobieski: determined to revive the greatness of Poland.

Disposing of the dead and fumigating houses during a seventeenth-century cholera epidemic in Rome.

Vienna Under Siege

Vienna—capital of the Hapsburg Empire, cultural hub of Austria's golden age and gateway to the heart of Europe—became the object of an enormous Turkish siege operation in July of 1683. By August of that year the city appeared doomed: its bastions were in ruins, its garrison was decimated by dysentery and cannon fire, and its supply line to Poland was threatened by a Hungarian-Turkish army. Mustering a relief force of more than 60,000 Polish and German troops, John III Sobieski, King of Poland, marched south to save the embattled city. Sobieski's followers arrived in Vienna on September 7, and five days later they met the Turks at Nussdorf in a bitterly contested battle that turned back the "invincible" Ottoman armies. The Sultan's forces would not threaten Europe again.

Suleiman I, whose victory at the battle of Mohacs in 1526 created the threefold division of Hungary that still existed in 1683.

Opposite Mohammed IV's siege of Vienna: the high point of the Turks' advance into Europe.

At the battle of Mohacs in 1526, Suleiman the Magnificent, the most famous of the Ottoman sultans, crushed the medieval kingdom of Hungary. The King of Hungary was killed in that battle, and his country fell under Turkish domination. The Hapsburgs of Vienna laid claim to the slain King's crown, and a long contention between Austria and the Ottoman Empire ensued. During the reign of Sultan Suleiman, three distinct Hungaries emerged: Ottoman Hungary, centered around the great fortresses of Belgrade, Buda and Esztergom on the middle Danube; Transylvanian, to the east of the Tisza and under the control of a prince dependent on Istanbul; and Hapsburg, the territories located to the far north and west of the realm. This threefold division was to undergo little change after Suleiman's death.

In 1664 the forces of the Hapsburg Emperor Leopold I overcame the Ottomans at St. Gotthard on the river Raba. That campaign was the first major field battle that the Christians had ever won against the formidable might of the Ottoman Turks. Despite his victory, the Emperor made peace with the Sultan at Vasvar in 1664 on terms unfavorable to himself. He surrendered several fortresses and recognized an Ottoman nominee as Vaivode of Transylvania.

The situation prevailing in the Emperor's Hungarian territories led the statesmen at Vienna to accept the agreement made at Vasvar. The Hungarian magnates and nobles in Leopold's domain were divided into a pro-Hapsburg element and a faction suspicious of the policies emanating from Vienna. Many of the nobles feared that the Hapsburg desire to impose more centralized administrative and political control would mean the loss of their own large privileges. There was friction, too, on religious grounds. Calvinism had won much success in Hungary, and the forces of the Counter-Reformation sought to end that Calvinist allegiance.

In 1678 Imre Thököly, who was to become a leader of Hungarian resistance to the Hapsburg regime, assumed command of a rebel army.

Thököly turned to Istanbul for aid, and the Grand Vizier Kara Mustafa Pasha sent some assistance to the Hungarian rebels in 1681. At this same time the Emperor, hoping to placate the malcontents, summoned a Hungarian Diet to meet at Sopron. But Kara Mustafa Pasha induced Thököly to repudiate Leopold's concessions and began to give the rebels much more active support.

Leopold I and his ministers, who seemed to be listening to the latter group, concentrated on the activities of Louis XIV. To the government in Vienna, nothing was more unwelcome than a renewal of conflict with the Ottoman Turks—and it was this outlook that led the Emperor to seek from the Sultan a prolongation of the Vasvar settlement, due to expire in 1684. The Austrian ambassador at Istanbul sought to achieve this aim in 1681, but without success. Nor was Albert Caprara, a special envoy sent from Vienna in 1682, able to secure a continuation of the peace. Kara Mustafa Pasha, the Grand Vizier, had now in fact reached the moment of decision. In August, 1682, Thököly received the title of King from Sultan Mohammed IV—a clear indication that the Grand Vizier had chosen war, not peace.

In October, 1682, the Grand Vizier left Istanbul for Edirne (Adrianople). The preparations for a great campaign continued throughout the ensuing winter. At the end of March, 1683, the Ottoman forces set off from Edirne for Belgrade, arriving there at the beginning of May and encamping at Zemun on the northern bank of the Sava. Rain and the need to repair the great bridge across the marshes at Osijek hindered their subsequent advance; not until late in June did the Ottomans reach Szekesfehervar. There the Grand Vizier revealed to a council of war his determination to attack Vienna; there, too, Tartar horsemen from the Crimea joined the army. By the beginning of July, Kara Mustafa had reached Raab, one of the few Hungarian fortresses still under Hapsburg control.

No effort was spared to secure aid from abroad. In January, 1683, the Elector of Bavaria agreed to

Vienna during the siege.

Right An allegorical picture of the Emperor Leopold, who had reduced Ottoman pressure on Europe by his victory at St. Gotthard in 1664.

Atti Bassa, the Governor of Buda, who was to be killed when the Christians recaptured the city, 1686.

send troops to assist the Emperor. More important still was the compact negotiated with Poland. The activities of Thököly and his rebels in the Carpathians, and the resulting suspicion that the Ottomans might be contemplating an attack on the lands around Cracow, induced the Polish King, John III Sobieski, to reach an agreement with Emperor Leopold in the autumn of 1682. The terms of the agreement were clear and simple: Austria would seek to hold the Ottomans on the Danube, and Poland would attack them in the Ukraine. If the Ottomans moved against Cracow, the Emperor would send troops to its assistance; the Polish King would perform a like service should the Ottomans decide to besiege Vienna.

In the spring of 1683 Charles of Lorraine concentrated his forces at Pressburg, and then moved down the Danube to the region of Raab and Komarno. He hoped to reach either Nove Zamky or Esztergom, two important fortresses under Ottoman control, but a divided high command, inexplicit orders from Vienna and a shortage of supplies and fodder doomed his campaign. Lorraine had to fall back toward Raab, and then still farther in the direction of Pressburg. Soon all prospect of holding back the Ottoman advance was gone. A messenger

Poland attacks the Ottomans

was sent to Sobieski on July 5, telling him that Vienna was beyond all doubt the objective that Kara Mustafa Pasha had set for himself.

On July 7, the Emperor and his court withdrew westward to Linz and thence to Passau, leaving Commandant Ernst von Starhemberg to hold Vienna. Lorraine, with his cavalry, reached the capital on July 8 and most of his men encamped in the suburb of Leopoldstadt or on the islands in the Danube. His infantry, under General Leslie, began to arrive in Vienna on July 10. To defend the capital, Starhemberg would have eleven thousand regular troops and a number of civilian auxiliaries, amounting to perhaps five thousand additional men. On July 13 the embankment before the walls of Vienna was cleared of buildings that might give protection to the Ottomans. On the following day, Lorraine began to pull his cavalry out of Leopoldstadt, breaking down the bridges across the Danube and retiring to a new position north of the river. On that same day Grand Vizier Kara Mustafa Pasha reached Vienna. The long siege was about to begin.

The defenses of Vienna comprised a banked earthen grade behind which was a counterscarp with palisades and a covered road along its summit. That road was divided into sections, each defensible as a self-contained unit. To the rear of the counterscarp was a dry moat. Additional defenses—in the form of entrenchments and blockhouses—had been erected on its floor. Behind the moat lay the actual walls of Vienna, strengthened with large and formidable bastions. The main Ottoman assault was to be launched against the southern flank of the fortress. On their right wing the Ottomans faced the Burg bastion; their center stood opposite the Burg ravelin, located within the moat; and their left was over against the Löbel bastion.

The Ottoman siege works—an elaborate system of deep trenches covered with timber roofing and provided with gun emplacements—would later receive high praise from the Christians. Kara Mustafa had brought a considerable number of medium- and light-caliber cannon with him, but no large siege guns. The main instruments of attack would therefore be trenches and mines.

The Ottomans began digging their approach trenches on the night of July 14-15. Along the slopes behind these trenches the Ottoman batteries opened fire on the morning of the fifteenth. Kara Mustafa, eager to complete the encirclement of Vienna, sent a strong force across the "canal"—the southern arm of the Danube—with orders to seize Leopoldstadt and the islands in the river. From that vantage batteries soon came into action against the northern walls of the fortress. At the same time the Ottomans established bridges across the Danube, above and below the Viennese fortifications. It was now possible for the Turks to cut off the flow of supplies down the river.

On July 23 the first Ottoman mines exploded along the sector between the Burg bastion and the Löbel bastion. A whole series of assaults and counteroffensives followed thereafter. By August 3 the Turks

had broken through the counterscarp opposite the Burg ravelin.

The Ottomans next directed their attack downward against the entrenchments and blockhouses in the moat. After nine days of furious conflict the Turks reached the edge of the ravelin. Starhemberg was forced to withdraw his large guns from the threatened area to the actual walls and bastions of the fortress. On August 12 the Ottomans fired a mine of exceptional size and launched a violent assault that secured them a lodgment on the ravelin itself.

The fighting continued stubborn and bitter throughout the second half of August. Nothing that the Christians could do sufficed to halt for more than a brief interval the steady advance of their foe. On September 3 Starhemberg abandoned the ravelin. Worse was to follow: on September 4 a great mine brought down some of the Burg bastion, and on September 8 two more mines inflicted serious damage on the Löbel bastion. Dysentery and battle wounds reduced the Viennese garrison to perhaps four thousand effective soldiers. If help did not come soon, the city would fall to the Ottomans.

Meanwhile, events of importance had been taking place outside the fortress. Upon the arrival of the Ottomans, Charles of Lorraine had left Leopoldstadt and withdrawn to Jedlesee. There news reached him that Imre Thököly and a mixed force of Hungarians and Turks were thrusting westward along the north bank of the river. That movement, if unchecked, might cut the lines of communication linking Vienna with Poland. It would also diminish the area still capable of providing supplies and forage for the Hapsburg troops in the field. Lorraine, recognizing the danger, advanced eastward to Pressburg and there, on July 30, drove back Thököly and his

Charles of Lorraine, the leader of the Christian army which fought the Turks.

A view of the Siege of Vienna by de Hooghe.

The Siege of Belgrade, 1690. The defeat of the Turks at Vienna did not immediately shatter their hopes of making further conquests in Europe and they recovered much of the territory they had lost during the next few years, but the great threat to Europe was much diminished.

men. At Stammersdorf, on August 24, Lorraine was able to repel a second Turkish-Hungarian advance. The routes along which aid might come from Poland and the German lands remained free.

And at last help was indeed arriving for the relief of Vienna. Toward the middle of August some 11,000 Bavarian troops reached the area south of Krems. Soon about eight thousand soldiers from Franconia and Thuringia joined them. At the same time regiments that had hitherto been serving the Emperor

on the Rhine began to appear at Krems.

Meanwhile, the news had reached John Sobieski on July 15 that Kara Mustafa was moving against Vienna. Orders went out for troops from northern Poland to concentrate at Cracow, as well as forces from the Ukraine, experienced in warfare against the Turks from their service in the Podolian War. The Polish King entered Cracow on July 29; the Podolians, led by Nicholas Sienawski, arrived there on August 2, and the contingents from the north, under Stanislas Jablonowski, on August 8. Time was needed at this juncture to decide which routes should be followed through Silesia, Moravia and Austria, and to arrange with the representatives of Emperor Leopold for the procurement of supplies adequate to maintain the Poles during their advance toward Vienna. But by August 20 all the Polish forces stood waiting at Tarnowski to begin the great campaign. The march southward began on August 22. Nine days later, on August 31, Sobieski met Charles of Lorraine at Oberhollabrunn. Here the German troops also had been brought together—Bavarian, Hapsburg and Franconian, soon to be strengthened through the arrival, on September 6, of a Saxon contingent over 10,000 strong.

By September 7, all the relief forces (numbering more than 60,000 men) were concentrated south of the river near Tulln. On September 9 the fateful advance began eastward across the Wienerwald. On the Christian left stood the Hapsburg troops and the Saxons; the Bavarians and other German contingents held the center; on the right wing rode Sobieski with the Polish forces. By September 11 the army was on the Kahlenberg ridge, only five miles from Vienna.

Kara Mustafa Pasha had begun to suspect that all was not well on his western flank. On September 8-9 he held two councils of war, at which he decided to withdraw from the siege about six thousand infantry and a considerable number of guns. To these troops he added some 20,000 horsemen. It was a belated measure designed to make good a situation

The Decline of Turkey's European Empire

🔴 Hapsburg Empire in 1683
— Frontier of Ottoman Empire in 1683
🔴 Poland in 1683
🔵 Acquired by Hapsburg Empire in 1699
▪▪ Frontier of Ottoman Empire in 1699
⚪ Acquired by Poland in 1699
⚪ Acquired by Venice in 1699
⚪ Acquired by Hapsburg Empire in 1718

SILESIA
POLAND
Cracow
MORAVIA
RUSSIA
AUSTRIA
PODOLIA
Pressburg
HAPSBURG
Linz
HUNGARY
Krems
Vienna
Raab
River Tisza
Heiligenstadt
Budapest
Esztergom
TRANSYLVANIA
OTTOMAN HUNGARY
Mohacs
Karlowitz
Belgrade
Passau
River Danube
Adrianople
Istanbul

Vienna saved from the Turks

now becoming critical. For Kara Mustafa had committed a number of grave errors in the deployment and use of his forces. He had neglected patrols in the Krems-Tulln area, watches over the routes across the Wienerwald, occupation of the Kahlenberg and adequate defenses for the protection of the Ottoman encampments before Vienna. The price demanded for this negligence was high.

Vienna was saved on September 12, 1683. An Ottoman attack in the region of Nussdorf, below the Kahlenberg ridge, led to a stubborn and complicated battle in broken terrain. Most of the fighting, until noon, was on the left of the Christian line. The Ottomans at length withdrew from Nussdorf, leaving the road toward Heiligenstadt open. On the right the Polish advance was less rapid, but at last Sobieski and his men came out on the slopes above the Alsbach stream. Ahead was more level ground, not two miles distant from Vienna and from the headquarters of Kara Mustafa Pasha near St. Ulrich.

The Christian forces now formed themselves into two lines. It was the moment for a supreme effort. The Hapsburg and Bavarian troops, pushing forward on the left against a strong resistance, swung toward the right. So, too, did the Saxon and German troops attacking in the center. The whole tide of battle surged toward the south and east. And now Sobieski and his horsemen struck hard against the Ottoman center. The Turkish defense held out for a while, then weakened and degenerated almost at once into a total collapse.

Only a rapid pursuit would draw the fullest advantage from the new situation. The difficulties hindering such a pursuit were serious enough—the shortage of supplies at Vienna and the ravaged state of the lands lower down the Danube. Nonetheless, Lorraine and Sobieski wanted to press forward. On September 17 the campaign was once more in motion. By September 23 a bridge had been reconstructed over the Danube below Pressburg. Now the Christians would have access to the supplies and forage available in the district of Schütt. The advance continued thereafter toward Parkany, where a bridge to the great Ottoman fortress of Esztergom crossed the Danube. On October 9, at Parkany, the German and Polish troops, amounting perhaps to 25,000 men, confronted an Ottoman force some 16,000 strong. The Turks made a wild attack, failed to break through and found themselves driven to the bank of the river. A portion of the bridge over the Danube, weakened by the fire of the Christian guns, fell into the water. Unable to escape, about nine thousand Ottomans lost their lives. By October 19, pontoon bridges had been brought into position for a crossing of the Danube. On October 22 the Christians laid siege to Esztergom. The Turkish garrison, seeing no hope of relief, surrendered on October 27. This event brought to an end the operations of 1683.

The siege of Vienna was a great and famous event, celebrated throughout Europe. On the level of individual success or failure it raised men like Starhemberg, Charles of Lorraine and Sobieski to the summit of their personal fame, while to Kara Mustafa it

Turkish troops in the mid-seventeenth century.

brought death, at Belgrade, on the order of the Turkish Sultan.

Its consequences were more notable still in the realm of politics and war. At Linz, in March, 1684, a "Sacra Liga" was formed between Austria, Poland and Venice against the Ottoman Empire. The war thus begun was not to end until 1699, at the peace of Karlowitz. It brought to the Hapsburgs almost all the Hungarian lands; Venice received the Morea (only to lose it to the Ottomans in 1718); Poland acquired Podolia; and Russia, a late participant in the conflict, was given Azov.

It is debatable whether the relief of Vienna saved Europe from an Ottoman conquest. It can be argued that the last Turkish offensive that might perhaps have led to the subjugation of Austria occurred in the bitter conflict of 1593-1606, a war that underlined the fact that the Ottoman Empire had reached the viable limits of expansion. Now, problems of time and distance, of terrain, climate and logistics rendered dubious any enlargement of the already extended frontier.

Even in the realm of warfare, the tide of events was adverse to the Ottomans. Technological advance in Europe had brought about the elaboration of tactical systems which the Turks would find hard to meet. The Ottoman war machine might still be formidable in sieges—witness the assault on Candia in 1667-69 or even on Vienna itself in 1683. On the field of battle, however, the outlook for the Ottomans was grave. Further, the Austria of 1683 was not the Austria of 1526—it stood now on the verge of a golden age as one of the great powers in Europe.

Yet Kara Mustafa had almost achieved the conquest of Vienna. This simple fact will serve to explain how it was that Sobieski, only twenty-four hours after his cavalry had cut through the Ottoman defense, could write to Pope Innocent XI, on September 13, in a spirit of immense and pardonable jubilation, "we came, we saw and God conquered." So must other men have thought on that memorable September 12, 1683.

V. J. PARRY

Barbarossa, one of the most capable sixteenth-century Turkish generals, who led an earlier but also unsuccessful attack on Vienna, 1529.

Under Louis XIV France seeks—without

While the Holy Roman Emperor's attentions were diverted by the Turkish invasion of Austria, the French army was making inroads along his western frontier. Louis XIV had ample reason to be proud of this army: composed of 200,000 well-trained officers and men—mostly infantry armed with wheel muskets, bayonets and fourteen-foot pikes—it was well equipped and harshly disciplined. The name of one of its officers, Jean Martinet, a military engineer and renowned tactician, was to give a new word to the English language. The army's strength and efficiency was

Vauban, the most distinguished military architect of the seventeenth century, whose ideas formed the basis of fortifications for two hundred years.

the work of Louis' war ministers, Michel le Tellier and Tellier's son, François Michel le Tellier, the Marquis de Louvois. Marshal Vauban—whose fortresses, built as a cordon around France between 1678 and 1688, are masterpieces of the craft—was responsible for the army's outstanding skill in engineering and siege techniques.

The army had already captured Dunkirk, the Franche-Comté and extensive territories along France's disputed eastern border with the Low Countries—whose towns, Louis confessed, were ever before his eyes. Those victories were confirmed in the 1684 Truce of Regensburg. The Truce ratified French possession of a string of fortified Flemish towns—Luxembourg, Alsace and Strasbourg—as well as the Franche-Comté.

France under Louis XIV

The France of Louis XIV was at the height of its power, but the King had even greater ambitions. In 1683 death removed the restraining counsels of his great minister, Jean Baptiste Colbert, who had restored the country's finances and built up its powerful navy—and Louis' thoughts again turned to war. His opportunity came in 1685, when the Elector of the Palatinate died childless. Louis immediately claimed the country for France.

This claim aroused Europe against him and led to the formation of the League of Augsburg (an alliance composed of Austria, Sweden, Holland and several small German states) in 1686.

England did not join the League, for its Roman Catholic king, James II, was committed to continuing his brother Charles II's policy of maintaining good relations with France. That policy was so unpopular with the English people—indeed, the French ambassador informed Louis that Charles and James were his only English friends—that only French money enabled the last two Stuart kings to avoid war with France. Peace could be

kept only as long as James remained King, but in the Glorious Revolution of 1688 he lost his crown to his Protestant rival, William of Orange—largely because his determination to force Catholicism on his people by unconstitutional means forced his subjects to turn to William for protection.

William of Orange

William's claim to the English throne was twofold: he was the son of Charles I's eldest daughter Mary, and he was the husband of Princess Mary, daughter of James II. On November 5, 1688, William landed at Torbay in Devon with a combined English and Dutch army of 15,000 men. The people welcomed him, James fled to France, and Parliament declared the throne vacant. William and Mary were proclaimed King and Queen on February 13, 1689.

Louis might have prevented the accession of William, his most dangerous enemy, by attacking him in the Netherlands before he could sail across the Channel. Instead, Louis hurled his armies against the Palatinate, thus declaring war on the League of Augsburg. The members of the League were

joined in war against France by Spain, Savoy and, of course, England.

War of the League of Augsburg

Despite the number and strength of his enemies, the war went well for Louis. The Duke of Luxembourg, a worthy successor of Condé and Turenne, decisively defeated the allied armies under the Prince of Waldeck at Fleurus in 1690 and under William III of England at Leuze the next year. Mons was captured in 1691 and Namur was besieged and occupied in 1692. The Duke of Luxembourg won further victories over William at Steenkirk in 1692 and at Neerwinden in 1693. Meanwhile, Marshal Catinat captured Nice and overran Savoy, defeating Amadeus II, Duke of Savoy, at Staffarda and Marsaglia. At sea, the navy that Colbert had developed with such care forced the English and Dutch to retreat in disorder off Beachy Head in 1690—and although the French Admiral Tourville lost fifteen ships at the Battle of La Hogue, he inflicted a crushing defeat on the allies in the Mediterranean in 1693.

Despite these early victories, the war had so exhausted France's resources that Louis was compelled to bring it to an end in 1697. By the Treaty of Ryswick, he surrendered nearly all the German territories (except Strasbourg, which he had conquered earlier). Louis was compelled to allow the Dutch to garrison the frontier towns of the Spanish Netherlands and to recognize not only that William of Orange was King of England, but also that William's staunchly Protestant niece, Princess Anne, daughter of James II, should succeed him.

War on heresy

Louis had made another mistake in the 1680s—apart from his decision to go to war. His Queen, Marie Thérèse, had died in 1683, the year of Colbert's death, and left him free to marry Madame de Maintenon. The new Queen, granddaughter of the distinguished Huguenot, Théodore Agrippa d'Aubigné, had been converted to Catholicism and was a devout member of the Church. She did not bear as much of the responsibility for Louis XIV's religious policies as

James II, after his flight from England, meets Louis XIV.

success—to dominate Europe

her contemporaries supposed, but she could not conceal her satisfaction when those policies induced the Protestants to recant. She was a pious woman and felt it her duty to convert those who had strayed.

Although not a deeply religious man, Louis was scrupulous in his observances: he heard Mass nearly every day of his life. As a Christian king and head of the Catholic Church in France, he believed that one of his principal duties was to induce all his people to accept Catholicism and to carry out the promise that had been contained in the coronation oath since the

Madame de Maintenon: blamed for the massacres of Protestants that took place after she became Louis XIV's second wife.

time of Henry IV: "seriously to endeavor to extirpate all heretics, so branded by the Church, out of my land."

To achieve that ambition, a campaign was mounted against

the country's million Protestant Huguenots. Missionaries were sent into Normandy, Languedoc and Poitou—areas where the Huguenots were particularly numerous—and proclamations were issued excluding Huguenots from holding public office.

Violence was proscribed, but orders for the billeting of troops in the houses of Protestants inevitably resulted in bloodshed. The poor could not afford to feed and lodge the soldiers; the rich could not bear rough troops ruining their homes. Reports reached Paris of dragoons driving Protestants to Mass, forcing them to listen to the missionaries and sprinkling them with Holy Water.

These methods were strikingly successful: the populations of some towns, following the example of the leading Protestant families in the districts, were converted to Catholicism en masse. Other towns lost nearly all their Protestants by conversion or emigration. By the end of 1685 there were only a quarter of a million Protestants in France. They remained obdurate in their faith, clinging stubbornly to their church councils and schools. They relied on the protection of the 1598 Edict of Nantes, which guaranteed their religious freedom and granted them a recognized position.

Revocation of the Edict of Nantes

Louis determined to eliminate the remaining Protestants and fulfill his pledge of "uniting to the Church those who had strayed from her" and "wiping out all memory of the

A Protestant prayer meeting being broken up by soldiers of the Duc de Guise, after the Revocation of the Edict of Nantes.

troubles, confusion and evil caused in our Kingdom by the progress of that false Religion." On October 18, 1685, he signed the Revocation of the Edict of Nantes: Protestant churches were to be demolished, Protestant schools closed, and children born into Protestant families to be baptized Catholics.

The Revocation was welcomed throughout France by the majority of Catholics since it meant the end of religious wars. The hated Huguenots, so hardworking, prosperous and intolerant of laxity, would have to go. Madame de Sévigné declared that a king had never done and never would do anything more beautiful, and Jacques-Bénigne Bossuet, the Court preacher who had converted the Huguenot Marshal Turenne, compared Louis to Constantine, Theodocius and Charlemagne.

Greeted with such pleasure in France, the Revocation was condemned throughout the Protestant world as an act of unpardonable cruelty. It was also one of the greatest political blunders of Louis XIV's reign. Over 200,000 Huguenots—including many of France's most valuable citizens, talented scientists, financiers and businessmen—chose to emigrate rather than renounce their faith. Settling in England, Holland and Denmark, they established industries in direct competition with those of France, and represented a permanent reminder of the Catholic King's iniquity.

Thirteen years after the Revocation, Louis XIV, who had done so much for France, celebrated his sixtieth birthday. In that year, in Moscow, another, younger ruler promised to do as much for Russia.

William and Mary, whose joint rule ensured the Protestant succession.

A Window on the West

The Grand Embassy that set out from Moscow in 1695 was officially led by François Lefort, tutor to Russia's young Tsar, Peter I. Lefort's entourage included a twenty-three-year-old soldier of imperial mien who called himself Bombardier Peter Mikhailov. Mikhailov—as every member of the Embassy and every crowned head in Europe knew—was Tsar Peter himself. Traveling "incognito" through Western Europe, the young ruler obtained interviews with the Emperor of Austria, the kings of Poland and England, and numerous German princes. As the Embassy made its slow circuit of Europe's capitals, Peter studied Western industries at first hand—and by the time he returned to Moscow he had mastered fourteen special technical skills. His extensive knowledge of European technological advances enabled Peter to Westernize his nation and his army in less than a decade—and helped him achieve the age-old Russian dream of "a window on Europe."

At a time when London, Paris, Rome and Vienna were already flourishing capitals, Moscow was little more than a small village, lost in the forested wilderness of northern Russia. The city is first mentioned in official chronicles in 1147; a century later it became the fief of Prince Daniel, younger son of the famous Alexander Nevski. Under his descendants the small princedom was transformed—through treaties, marriages and territorial sales—into a powerful state whose rulers, the grand dukes, succeeded in shaking off the yoke of the Mongols. Assuming the title of tsar, the Muscovy princes organized a centralized government which eventually administered a vast area that included part of Siberia.

The period of troubles that began with the extinction of the house of Rurik in 1598 and ended with the election of the new dynasty of the Romanovs only temporarily interrupted the evolution of a young and already promising nation. But during the period of Asiatic domination (1223-1380) there had been little contact between Russia and the civilization of the West, and during the troubles that occurred early in the seventeenth century, Muscovy was deprived of all access to the sea. It remained an underdeveloped, feudal country, populated by some 10 million pious but ignorant peasants and dominated by an autocratic monarch who considered himself an heir to the Byzantine emperors. These tsars found only feeble supporters in a fanatical clergy and in a class of indolent noblemen, the boyars. The West remained as much a closed book to them as it did to their subjects. Nevertheless, national defense and urgent commercial considerations dictated a closer connection with the feared and despised West. The idea of an outlet to the sea began to haunt the best minds of a nation that, until then, had kept its eyes fixed on the steppes. Peter the Great, the tsar-reformer, was the man who realized that dream.

Born in Moscow in 1672, Peter led a stormy childhood amid dynastic quarrels, clan rivalries and popular uprisings. His father, Tsar Alexis, pious

and easygoing, had two unpromising sons by an earlier marriage: the sickly Fëdor and the partially blind and feebleminded Ivan. When Alexis died in 1676, Fëdor inherited the throne. His reign lasted only six years, and upon his death the incompetent Ivan and ten-year-old Peter were proclaimed joint sovereigns of all the Russias under the regency of their half sister Sophia, an intelligent and ambitious virago of fifty. Although she was frequently compared to Elizabeth I of England—and although she consciously modeled herself on the Empress Pulcheria of Byzantium—Sophia was unable to maintain order in her own country. Relegated to the background, the adolescent Peter witnessed scenes of bloodshed that gave him a horror for the atmosphere of the Kremlin and for the traditional habits of the old Muscovy.

The young prince was brought up by his mother, Natalia Naryshkin, in a country setting on the outskirts of Moscow. There he supplemented an adequate education through contacts with the humble foreign artisans who lived in the nearby German quarter. Peter, who had a passion for soldiering (a list of his early toys includes pistols, carbines, bows and arrows, drums and cannon), organized his companions—gentlemen's sons, stableboys and street ragamuffins—drilled them and learned with them how to handle arms. Other boys joined the ranks, and the games grew more ambitious. Using boats, they mounted a full-scale assault on a small fortress that Peter had had built on a little island not far from his home. At the end of a few years he had two well-trained battalions of several hundred men each. With this nucleus of what was to become a famous army, he executed a coup d'etat in 1689 to free himself from the hampering tutelage of Princess Sophia, put an end to her dangerous intrigues and take over actual power.

At this time two remarkable men became his tutors in the military profession and in the art of Western living: an old mercenary, Patrick Gordon,

The Empress Natalia Kirillovna, mother of Peter the Great.

Opposite Emperor Peter the Great as a shipbuilder at Deptford during his stay in England. His interest in the sea led him to attack the Turkish port of Azov, so that Russia would have an outlet to the sea.

The "Grand Embassy" visits Europe

Peter the Great as a child with his elder half-brothers, Fedor and Ivan, patriarch Adrian and a Metropolitan.

scion of an illustrious Scottish family, and young François Lefort, another soldier of fortune and a native of Geneva. Under the influence of these two friends Peter revived the old dream of giving Russia access to the sea. In 1695 he flung himself into a war against Turkey and captured Azov at the mouth of the Don. But even in the moment of victory he realized that his land and naval forces were inadequate to gain him mastery of the Black Sea. He decided to send a "Grand Embassy" to various Western countries, not only to secure the help necessary to continue the war or to conclude an advantageous peace, but also to build up a corps of specialists by initiating young representatives of his nobility into European science.

To everybody's astonishment Peter himself joined the embassy, traveling incognito. For eighteen months the Tsar of All the Russias traveled with his apprentices through the Baltic countries, the German states, Holland and England, vainly attempting to escape notice under the borrowed name of "Bombardier Peter Mikhailov." Officially, the embassy was led by François Lefort, seconded by two Russian dignitaries. But all eyes were naturally turned to the young sovereign, taller by a head than any of his companions, who distributed lavish gifts and was received at every court.

At Königsberg he met the Prince-Elector of Brandenburg; at Koppenbrugge, the princesses of Hanover. In Holland he had his first interview with William of Orange, King of England, whom he was to meet again in London. In Vienna he was on intimate terms with Emperor Leopold of Austria. And on his way back to Russia, at Rawa Ruska, he made friends with Augustus of Saxony, who had just been elected King of Poland.

Diplomatically, the results of Peter's Grand Embassy were rather slight, since none of the European cabinets was ready to support the Russian plans for a crusade against the Turks. But the royal traveler had other interests. His goals included developing his naval building program, organizing a powerful artillery, inviting selected specialists—from among the captains, seamen and engineers he met—to Russia, and building up a corps of his countrymen instructed in the most recent scientific and technological methods. He wanted to superintend the apprenticeship of the young noblemen that he had brought with him, and he cherished the ambition of serving as their model. His biographers never fail to point out that he ended by mastering fourteen skills, not counting that of statesman: at various times he functioned as engineer, cannoneer, carpenter, boatman, armorer, drummer, blacksmith, joiner and tooth-puller.

Peter even spent a week with his old friend Gerrit Kist (who had been a blacksmith in Moscow) in the little Dutch village of Zaandam, working in Master Rogge's yard under the name of Master Peter, exploring the canals and visiting the local spinning mills, sawyards and oil works.

In Amsterdam, where he was to spend more than four months, the Tsar concentrated on increasing his knowledge of shipbuilding. Although he slighted neither the museums nor the laboratories nor the dissecting rooms, he spent the greater part of his time in the East India Company shipyards. But it was in England, in the yards of Deptford and the arsenals of Woolwich, that he completed his apprenticeship and became an accomplished master of the art of shipbuilding. "If I had not come here," he was to say later, "I should never have been more than a plain carpenter." He also perfected the technique of navigation, spent hours rowing and sailing, attended

The *streltsy* fighting Peter's troops, who are led by Patrick Gordon. The *streltsy* were regarded by Peter as his chief enemy as they supported the Regent, Princess Sophia.

A boyar or Russian noble.

Left An Easter procession outside of the Kremlin in Moscow.

Below Cutting the boyars' beards: Peter's reforms affected the lives of all his subjects, but the beard cutting was of symbolic importance.

the maneuvers at Spithead and revived the courage of British sailors during a storm by asking them: "Have you ever heard of a tsar being drowned?" Later, remembering this period in his life, he often said to his courtiers, "The life of an English admiral is infinitely happier than that of a ruler of Russia."

When he was not on the water, Peter inspected the collection of weapons at the Tower of London; visited the Mint and the Greenwich Royal Observatory; went to a masked ball, the theater, a bear fight and a cock fight; paid court to an actress; and incidentally wrecked the elegant house that he and his party were living in. He even found a moment to watch, through an attic window, the opening of Parliament (thus giving a wit the chance to remark: "Today I saw something unique in the world—one sovereign on the throne and another on the roof").

A few months later, as Peter was finishing his conversations in Vienna, he was suddenly obliged to return to Moscow because of an uprising of the *streltsy*, the undisciplined, turbulent and reactionary local militia guards. The *streltsy* were survivors of the old Muscovite regime. Armed with muskets and sabers, unadapted to modern warfare, they occupied separate quarters near the capital and in frontier towns. They had been partisans of Princess Sophia, had participated in all the recent upheavals and were prepared to fight to the last for the maintenance of the old order of society, which they felt was being menaced by an "ungodly tsar" who had gone abroad for unknown reasons. Determined to reestablish Sophia on the throne and to exterminate the nobles and the boyars, they had marched on Moscow—and nothing but the courageous intervention of General Gordon had prevented the success of their plan. With remarkable speed he had dispersed isolated detachments of the *streltsy* before they had had time to concentrate, had encircled their main forces and had

Peter declares war on Sweden

Eudoxia, wife of Peter the Great. The Czar did not get on with his wife who was the daughter of a Court official.

Above right Bust of Peter by Rastrelli.

Below right A plan of a battle between Denmark and Sweden: Peter's keenness to have an outlet on the Baltic led him into continuous wars with Sweden, in which the Danes were usually his allies.

One of the *streltsy* soldiers.

Moscow on August 25, 1698, there was nothing left for him to do but to act as judge.

Peter returned to his country the possessor of intellectual and technical equipment such as no Russian before him had commanded. He knew that his nation was at the crossroads, and that it would be unable to maintain its role in the world without the radical reforms that he was prepared to accomplish. The *streltsy* were barring his way and he considered it his duty to finish with them once and for all. He subjected them to terrible reprisals, participating personally in the interrogations that took place in torture chambers. Three hundred and forty-one rebels were condemned to death, brought in carts to Red Square and hanged from the crenelated walls of the Kremlin, where their emaciated skeletons remained exposed to the horror of passersby.

More executions followed during the ensuing weeks; the number of victims finally reached 799. The sixteen *streltsy* regiments were disarmed and disbanded; the families of the condemned men were turned out of their homes. Princess Sophia, considered responsible for the whole upheaval, was deprived of her rank and obliged to take the veil.

At last Tsar Peter was free: he had broken with the past and was now prepared to lead his country into a gigantic military and reforming enterprise. The horrors of the executions were soon overshadowed by the glory of his victories and of his reforms.

On August 8, 1700, Peter made his historic decision to declare war on Sweden, in order to open a road from Russia to the West by the conquest of the Baltic littoral. He had secured the collaboration of Poland and Denmark, but his alliance with these two rivals of Sweden was to prove ineffectual. With nothing to rely on but his own forces, Peter was defeated at Narva by the valiant Swedish King, Charles XII. Refusing to be discouraged by this defeat, Peter raised and equipped new armies; he put immense effort into creating a good artillery; he worked with his own hands on the construction of the frigates that were to give him mastery of the

Baltic. Then his disciplined and well-trained regiments seized the mouth of the Neva and entrenched themselves along the coveted littoral. On June 27, 1709, in a battle at Poltava, he put his great adversary, Charles XII, to flight.

To achieve this brilliant success, Peter had been obliged to subject the entire structure of his country to a basic transformation. In a certain sense Russia emerged completely "Europeanized" and "Westernized." Even before venturing into war, Peter had undertaken to change the outward aspects of his fellow countrymen or, more precisely, of his own entourage. During his journeys in Western Europe he had observed how ridiculous the long medieval gowns and long beards of the Muscovites looked to the outside world. The day after his return from abroad, Peter received the boyars who came to greet him with a large pair of scissors in his hand—and chopped off the beards of the most eminent among them. At a banquet later in the same week, the Tsar's jester (an ancestor of the novelist Turgenev) circled the table and cut off the beards of all the

guests who had not yet adopted the new fashion. Three days later nearly all beards had disappeared from the court. Within a few months Peter was also wielding the scissors on the exaggeratedly long sleeves of his attendants. "With these full sleeves," he said, "accidents are always happening: sometimes they get dipped in the soup, sometimes they break windows."

Resistance, of course, was greater in the case of more serious reforms, but Peter nonetheless had his way. He established conscription as a means of recruiting a permanent and regular army with an adequate number of specialists, and he did the same for the fleet. He subjected a recalcitrant Church to his authority by replacing the all-powerful patriarch by an ecclesiastical body, the Holy Synod, which was given strictly limited functions. He replaced the hereditary aristocracy by a "nobility of service" open to all deserving officers and functionaries. And to put an end once and for all to the old customs and habits, he left Moscow and the Kremlin and moved his residence to a swampy, deserted region at the mouth of the Neva, newly conquered from Sweden. There he built his new capital, St. Petersburg (renamed Petrograd in World War I and Leningrad by the Communists in 1924)—"a window on Europe," as he put it.

Permanent connection with the West—the final goal of all his efforts—was not easily established. For long years the cabinets of Europe turned a cold shoulder to the upstart Tsar who took no interest in the great Spanish problem then in the limelight, and who persisted in fighting the "invincible" King of Sweden in what was considered a perfectly "useless" war. Russia's prestige was very low at Versailles, Vienna and The Hague. It was only after the victory of Poltava that all Europe turned its eyes to the East.

Following Poltava, the French cabinet expressed interest in a rapprochement with Russia and in acting as mediator between Russia and Sweden. Peter set off for Paris immediately and soon entered into a friendship with the French regent. His second appearance in the countries of the West was as

pregnant with consequences as the first had been. By directing his ministers to sign the Amsterdam Agreement with France and Prussia in 1717, Peter inaugurated a system of interchangeable alliances that was to be employed by his successors on a great scale. By submitting to the admiration of the Parisian populace, by showing a charming affection for the boy king, Louis XV, and by visiting Madame de Maintenon, Louis XIV's durable mistress, Peter laid the foundation for his fame throughout the world.

In Russia that fame was marred by Peter's treatment of his son and heir, the Tsarevich Alexis. The two men could hardly have been more different: while Peter was creating a new Russia, Alexis preferred the old Russia, with its indolent quietism and its horror of innovation. Incapable of leading a revolt himself, he became—quite without premeditation—a symbol around whom all the malcontents in Russia rallied. The contest between the two came to a climax in 1718 when Peter imprisoned Alexis and appointed a supreme court that condemned him to death. It was one of Peter's few—but lasting—blunders.

As the years wore on, he had many victories. The surrender of the Swedish fleet after the naval battle of Hangö in 1714, the military occupation of Finland, and two raids into Skane in southern Sweden led to the signing—on August 30, 1721—of the Treaty of Nystad. That document ceded Russia all of Estonia, Livonia, Ingria and Karelia, and part of Finland, including the fortress of Vyborg.

Peter's triumph was complete. He had conquered the Baltic littoral, his coveted objective. He had further succeeded in establishing a sort of veiled protectorate over Poland and in setting up a series of duchies along the western Baltic. On October 22, 1721, three years before his death, he was proclaimed "Emperor of All the Russias," and the senate bestowed upon him the title of "the Great."

Like a warship launched from the ways, Russia had made her entrance into Europe to the clang of hammers and the thunder of guns.

CONSTANTINE DE GRUNWALD

Peter the Great Square and the Senate in St. Petersburg. Peter built St. Petersburg as a new capital for his kingdom, perhaps because of its proximity to the sea.

Above left The Battle of Poltava, 1709, at which Russia won a decisive victory over the Swedes. This victory secured for Peter Livonia and Estonia as well as a Baltic foothold.

Sweden and Russia—giants of the North

Russia's entry into European affairs coincided with the downfall of Sweden. During the reign of Gustavus Adolphus (1592–1632), Sweden had become a first-class power. With the help of French financing, Sweden had emerged from the Thirty Years' War with an outstanding military reputation, a seat in the German Diet and undisputed control of the Baltic. As a champion of Protestantism, Gustavus Adolphus had taken his army south in the Thirty Years' War. His presence had prevented the Austrian Emperor from acquiring any outlet to the Baltic and had thereby eliminated a potentially dangerous rival sea power.

Sweden retained her commanding position in northern Europe during the reign of Queen Christina, Gustavus Adolphus' strange and gifted daughter, who came to the throne when she was eighteen. But the wayward, extravagant and self-centered Christina soon wearied of government. Aware of the unrest that her unusual personal behavior was causing in Sweden, she abdicated in 1654 in favor of her cousin, Charles Gustavus, who became King Charles X.

Within a year of his coronation,

The entry of Christina of Sweden into Rome after her conversion to Catholicism.

Charles persuaded the *Riksdag* that a campaign against Poland was to Sweden's advantage. Leading an army of 50,000 men into Poland in July, 1655, he occupied Warsaw, forced the Polish King John Casimir to seek refuge in Silesia, and captured Cracow. The brutality of Charles' troops—most of whom were mercenaries—the arrogance of his rapacious officers and his own ill-concealed contempt for national and religious feelings aroused the Polish people. Charles lost Warsaw and more than half his troops in a protracted campaign against large bands of guerrillas and a reorganized Polish army led by John Casimir. Only by buying the help of the Elector Frederick William of Brandenburg was his combined Prussian-Swedish army able to reoccupy Warsaw and defeat the forces of the Polish King. The Poles refused his peace terms, and war was resumed. In June, 1657, the Danes gave Charles an excuse to extricate himself from his exhausting and profitless war by declaring war on Sweden.

Charles' early military successes against Denmark were astonishing: a powerful thrust carried him across Jutland to Fredericksodde, and across the frozen expanse of the Great and Little Belts to Zeeland. Although the treaties of Taastrup and Roskilde in 1658 ceded almost half of Denmark to Sweden, Charles was still greedy for more territory and greater military renown. He resumed the war, but met with little success due to the intervention of Holland, France and England—who feared the obliteration of Denmark by an increasingly powerful Sweden. Upon the King's premature death in 1660, the Council of Regency signed two peace treaties. By the terms of the Peace of Oliva, Sweden's possession of Livonia was confirmed but the Elector of Brandenburg acquired the Duchy of Prussia; by the Peace of Copenhagen, Sweden gained the three Scanian provinces from Denmark in return for giving up the island of Bornholm.

Charles XI

During the years of Charles XI's minority, Sweden's strength rapidly declined, war with Denmark broke out again and the Swedish army was defeated by Brandenburg at Fehrbellin in 1675.

When the young King came of age in 1672, he set out to revive Sweden's power. Boorish and ill-educated—but determined and brave—Charles followed the advice of his shrewd minister Johan Gyllenstjerna. He reorganized the national armaments and his demoralized army, recovered the alienated crown lands, deprived the corrupt *Riksdag* of its control over finance and administration, and converted the government of Sweden into a semi-absolute monarchy. The treaties of Nijmwegen and St. Germain in 1679 ended the wars and confirmed Sweden's possession of Finland, Ingria, Estonia, Livonia, numerous islands in the Baltic and large parts of present-day Denmark, Germany and Poland. Those vast territories were poor and sparsely populated by a variety of races with their own languages and customs. More than three-quarters of Sweden's 3 million people were peasants, most roads were no more than tracks, and few cities were worthy of the name—yet Charles XI made the army a powerful, well-equipped and well-trained one once more.

Charles XII

When Charles XI died in 1697, his fourteen-year-old son, a clever, precocious and austere boy, succeeded him as Charles XII. The *Riksdag*, jealous of the power of the regents, offered him full sovereignty the following year. Charles accepted, and proceeded to attack a coalition that had been formed by Denmark, Poland and Russia to dismember the empire his father and grandfather had built. Charles first advanced on Denmark—whose army had invaded Holstein—landing his troops in Zeeland, a

Gustavus Adolphus, the Protestant King of Sweden.

—battle for supremacy

Swedish Empire under Charles XII

- → Charles XII's campaigns 1700-18
- ● Territory gained before 1660 and still held in 1721
- ○ Territory lost 1719-21

had time to reorganize his armies and reoccupy the Baltic provinces.

After a battle on the Warbis River, the Swedes forced Peter's army to retreat. In the appallingly cold winter of 1708—the most bitter Russian winter in a hundred years—the Swedes pursued their retreating foe across a burned and desolate countryside. By the time they caught up with the Russians on the Vorskla River, the Swedish force had been reduced to 20,000 men. At the Battle of Poltava on June 27, 1709, the vastly superior Russian army overwhelmed the Swedes. Charles, who had been wounded on June 7 and was too feverish to lead the battle himself, rode south to seek refuge in Turkey with a small force of cavalry, leaving behind an all but annihilated army.

Charles stayed in Turkey for four years and persuaded the Sultan to declare war on Russia three times, with inconclusive results. In 1715, after an absence of fourteen years, Charles returned to Sweden. Aided by his powerful minister, Baron Görtz—who shared his belief that Sweden was still a great power—Charles raised another army and attacked Norway, hoping to capture enough territory to give him a strong hand in negotiating with his enemies. It was his last campaign: on December 11, 1718, while laying siege to the fortress of Fredriksten, Charles was shot.

In reality, the fate of Sweden and the outcome of the Great Northern War had been decided nine years earlier, at Poltava. By the terms of the Treaty of Nystadt in 1721,

Sweden lost her empire, Denmark moved into Holstein and Augustus II regained the Polish throne. Russia replaced Sweden as the controlling power in the Baltic.

Charles XII, who became King of Sweden at fourteen. His military ambitions proved financially ruinous.

While Charles XII was campaigning in Russia, Charles II of Spain died and bequeathed his possessions to Louis XIV's grandson, Philip—thus plunging Europe into the War of the Spanish Succession. The victories of the Duke of Marlborough, commanding the English armies, and Prince Eugene of Savoy, commanding the Austrian, were followed by the Peace of Utrecht.

few miles north of Copenhagen, in August, 1700. Two weeks later, by the terms of the Peace of Travendal, Charles gained a large indemnity and a guarantee that Denmark would make no further hostile moves against Sweden.

Charles then turned his attention to Russia. Against the advice of his generals, he took his army on a week's march through Ingria to attack the Russian fortified camp at Narva. On November 20, 1700, in a heavy snowstorm, his troops overwhelmed a Russian army four times their size in one of the most decisive victories of modern times. Charles captured eighteen generals and 145 cannon. His losses were light—nine hundred men—while Russian casualties were more than nine thousand.

Charles could have marched on to St. Petersburg, but fearful of the enemies who lay undefeated behind him, he turned back to attack Poland. Charles was determined to depose Augustus the Strong of Saxony, who had recently secured his election as Augustus II of Poland, and to replace him with his own candidate, Stanislas Leszczynski. He entered Warsaw in May of 1702, and on July 2 defeated a large army of Poles and Saxons at Klissow. Three weeks later he captured Krakow. In 1703 Sweden won another victory at Pultusk and seized the fortress of Thorn. Finally, in July, 1704, soon after the King's

twenty-second birthday, Stanislas Leszczynski was elected King of Poland in Augustus II's place.

Supremely confident, impulsive and unstable, Charles seemed addicted to the excitement of war. His schemes became ever more ambitious and increasingly ruinous to the finances of his country. In August, 1707, he again attacked Russia, marching on Moscow at the head of an army of 44,000 men. Unfortunately for Charles, while he had been "immersed in the Polish bog," Peter the Great had

The Battle of Poltava, 1709, at which Charles' army was destroyed by the Russians.

Twilight of the Sun King

Louis XIV's claim to the Spanish Netherlands was a tenuous one at best—and all Europe was incensed when the French monarch's troops occupied the Low Countries in 1667. Forty-six years, two inconclusive wars and one inconsequential treaty later, the territorial ambitions of the Sun King were finally curbed and peace was restored to Europe. The treaties signed at Utrecht in 1713 and at Rastatt a year later established a new balance of power among the nations of Western Europe—one that was to last for nearly a century. The militarily humbled French Empire was shorn of several of its overseas possessions; Holland, already weakened, was reduced to second-class status; and Russia, Prussia and England emerged as the dominant European powers. More important, the defeat and subsequent death of Louis XIV ended the Age of Absolutism in Continental politics and inaugurated an epoch of enlightened despotism.

Philip V of Spain. After the Treaty of Utrecht he renounced his claim to the French throne.

Opposite Marlborough and his staff at the battle of Blenheim. This battle ended sixty years of French invincibility—a fact formally acknowledged nine years later by the Treaty of Utrecht.

The treaties concluded at Utrecht in 1713 and at Rastatt in 1714 finally ended the long years of European wars that had resulted from Louis XIV's efforts to extend French hegemony. They also established a new European balance of power that was to survive until the French Revolution.

From the moment Louis XIV took control of the French government in 1661, he was intent on providing France with the best army in Europe—and then using that army, in conjunction with the skilled French diplomatic corps, to make France the most powerful nation on the Continent. Until 1688 it seemed that he would succeed. In 1668 Louis marched into the Spanish Netherlands, using as a pretext Spain's failure to pay the dowry promised him when he married Marie Thérèse, daughter of Philip IV. When the Dutch Republic formed a defensive alliance with England and Sweden, Louis made plans to punish the insolent little nation and at the same time destroy the Dutch as trade rivals. In 1672 he invaded the Republic, thus beginning the first of his great wars. The Dutch managed to keep the French army from advancing on the province of Holland by opening the dikes and inundating the land, and by 1678 Spain, England and the Holy Roman Emperor, Leopold I, had joined the Dutch against France. The war was a stalemate.

The anti-French coalition only temporarily checked the French drive toward supremacy in Europe, however. During the next ten years Louis turned from war to diplomacy and nearly succeeded in making himself master of Europe. He annexed several cities, including Strasbourg, on flimsy legal grounds, and fear of France once more led to the formation of a defensive alliance. Known as the League of Augsburg, that alliance centered around Leopold I and ultimately included most of the German states, Sweden, England, Spain, the Dutch Netherlands and Savoy. From 1688 to 1697 the League—also known as the Grand Alliance—waged a dreary, indecisive, exhausting war with France.

The war ended with the treaty of Ryswick in 1697, but nothing was really settled.

The threat of French hegemony had not been the only irritant to European stability before 1697. Maritime rivalry between France and Spain on the one hand and England and Holland on the other, and ideological differences between the Catholic and the Protestant countries had also been sources of conflict. Now a further element was added: the question of who would succeed to the Spanish throne. Louis had claimed that throne on behalf of his grandson Philip of Anjou; Leopold I had claimed it for his grandson Charles.

Louis, exhausted by the War of the League of Augsburg, was quite ready to renounce in part his claims to the Spanish throne, and to put an end to hostilities by coming to terms with the maritime powers. In 1700, however, Charles II of Spain died, bequeathing to Philip of Anjou his great inheritance. Louis accepted on behalf of his grandson, and from that moment onward war was virtually inevitable.

The War of the Spanish Succession was to last ten weary years. Right from the start, the participating powers spent as much time in negotiations as in fighting. The coalition against France was led by a "triumvirate" consisting of England's Duke of Marlborough, Prince Eugene of Savoy and Antonius Heinsius of the Dutch Republic. It was in the interests of all three of them to prolong the war until France was finally forced to surrender. In 1710, however, Marlborough fell into disgrace and the Tories, who took over the English government from the Whigs, were in favor of making a reasonable peace with France. A year later Emperor Joseph I died, leaving his throne to his brother Charles VI, who was also the Austrian pretender to the Spanish throne. England, which felt just as threatened by an alliance between Austria and Spain as by one between France and Spain, withdrew from the war and signed a preliminary treaty with France on October 8, 1711.

The Treaty of Utrecht was finally brought to a

Charles VI capitulates at Rastatt

Spanish America. She was allowed to send one "authorized ship" annually to trade in Spanish waters, and she secured a monopoly of the slave trade for the next thirty years.

Holland, on the other hand, derived very little benefit from her efforts, apart from the fact that France renounced all claims to the Low Countries, which came under Austrian rule. Spain had to give up all her European possessions outside the Iberian Peninsula to Austria and to the Duke of Savoy, who had been proclaimed King of Sicily.

Surprisingly, the English reacted unfavorably to the Treaty of Utrecht. The opposition was led by the Whigs, who were critical of the Treaty for several reasons. First, they were bitter because they had lost power scarcely twenty years after the Glorious Revolution of 1688 (which had led to the deposition of the Catholic monarch James II and the accession of William and Mary to the English throne). The Whigs of course had brought about the Revolution and, not surprisingly, they had hoped to reap the benefits from it. They therefore opposed the peace treaties, at least in part, simply because they had been drawn up by their opponents, the Tories. More fundamentally, they felt that the whole spirit of the Glorious Revolution had been betrayed by a peace treaty that had preserved the French monarchy practically intact and that had not interfered with the Spanish overseas possessions. Finally, they pointed out the striking contrast between the ever-growing popularity and influence of English ideas on the Continent and the Tory leaders' meek attitude toward two Catholic monarchs who, for all intents and purposes, had been defeated.

It was quite another story on the Continent, especially in France. Although the failing Louis XIV persisted in his rigid absolutism, French thought and writing was becoming more and more permeated with the subtle influence of English science and rationalism. From the year 1715 on, the regent,

Charles XII of Sweden, whose eventual defeat heralded the arrival of a new power in Europe—Russia.

Right Prussia, led by Frederick William I, built up the finest army in Europe, thus laying the foundations of the German military tradition.

successful conclusion after Philip of Anjou—now Philip V of Spain—had renounced all rights to the French throne on July 8, 1712. Even then Charles VI was reluctant to give up his rights to the Spanish throne and delayed signing the peace treaty until the following year at Rastatt.

Those treaties marked the end of French expansion in Europe; they also represented a great victory for England. Louis XIV was forced to recognize the Protestant succession in England and to expel the Stuart pretender, the son of James II, from French soil. Philip V's renunciation of all rights to the throne of France and the French princes' renunciation of the Spanish succession were declared to be inviolable law. Moreover, Louis XIV ceded to England Hudson Bay and Strait, Acadia, Newfoundland and the island of Saint Christopher in the Lesser Antilles. The port of Dunkerque was to be filled up and its fortifications demolished. Britain received Gibraltar and Minorca from Spain and, far more important, she was granted certain exclusive trading rights with

Philippe of Orleans, and his minister Cardinal Dubois adopted a pro-English policy, encouraging more cordial relations between the two countries. (Later on, the Whig Minister, Sir Robert Walpole, was to support that entente.) During that period, the intellectual links between the two countries grew much closer. Montesquieu and Voltaire, in particular, were profoundly influenced by English life and literature. The England of John Locke, George Berkeley, Daniel Defoe and Jonathan Swift set the trend for the age of the *philosophes*.

In short, England now represented the country of freedom, the land where the popular press and partisan pamphlets played a decisive role in the political arena. People on the Continent knew all about the political pamphlets written by Swift and Defoe in the course of the fiery polemic that had developed as a result of the Utrecht peace talks. England seemed to be the only country where public opinion was sometimes a decisive factor in influencing governmental decisions. Her economic prosperity seemed to be a fitting recompense for her liberal and enlightened government.

Clearly, that contemporary concept of England was based partly on illusions. The corruption so vividly denounced by Hogarth was completely ignored, while enormous interest was shown in the progress of industry and trade, in the amazing discoveries of Isaac Newton, in the promotion of new ideas by the National Academy of Sciences (the Royal Society), and in the predominant role played by the London Stock Exchange. The Treaty of Utrecht brought England a lasting prestige on the Continent, both with her former enemies and with her former allies. The eighteenth century was dominated by England in the way that the preceding century had been dominated by France and the sixteenth century by Spain.

The Treaty of Utrecht reshuffled the European powers into a new pattern of relationships that was to remain in force for nearly a hundred years. Further, the consequences of the adventurous policy of Charles XII of Sweden in northern Europe, and the victories of Prince Eugene over the Ottomans affected the European balance of power just as much as the Treaty of Utrecht. With the final defeat of Charles XII a new major power appeared on the eastern horizon: Russia, whose Tsar Peter revealed his intention of taking an active part in European affairs from that time on.

Russia's emergence as a major power came at the time of the decline of two other formerly powerful states: Poland, which had been weakened as a result of internal anarchy, and Sweden, which had been reduced by the actions of Charles XII to the status of a second-class nation. The Ottoman Empire was

Left Prince Eugene of Savoy who, together with Marlborough and Heinsius, formed the "triumvirate" against France.

Below left George I, first of the Hanoverians, came to the English throne the year after the Treaty of Utrecht. During his reign the Monarchy took the form it retains today.

Claude, Duke of Villars. The greatest French general of the eighteenth century, who defeated Eugene of Savoy at Denain.

Prussia—Germany's emerging giant

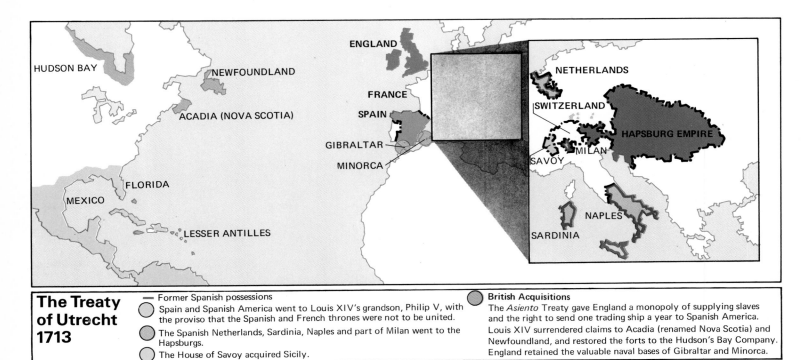

another great power that was in a state of decline during that period. Although it still ruled over vast territories, it no longer constituted a serious menace to the Austrian states. Prince Eugene's Austria, on the other hand, had been victorious against both Louis XIV and the Ottoman Sultan and was far more solidly established on the banks of the Danube than it had ever been before.

In Germany, the new kingdom of Prussia was emerging as the heir to the former Swedish territories. The nebulous concept of a loosely knit group of German states, deliberately fostered by the treaties of Westphalia, was in the process of becoming clarified and condensed, while the German people, having recovered from the disasters and ruin of the Thirty Years' War, were becoming aware of their identity. At the time, Prussia was still only one of several powerful states within Germany. Saxony and Bavaria were equally powerful German states, but the former was hindered rather than strengthened by the enormous dead weight of Poland, while the latter was growing progressively weaker, without any apparent gains, as a result of its abortive, imperialist ambitions. Prussia, on the other hand, had a history of strong rulers who had developed the Prussian army into the best in the world. That army was the base on which Prussia rose to great power during the reign of Frederick William I (1713-40).

In Italy, the north and central regions were dominated by Austria, while the Republic of Venice was falling into a fatal state of decline. Neither the Papal States nor the Kingdom of Naples were in a position to play a decisive role in the affairs of the country. The newly created Kingdom of Sardinia, on the other hand, had its eyes fixed more and more determinedly on the fertile plains of the river Po in the north. At the same time, it was playing off the

Bourbons of France against the Hapsburgs of Austria —a diplomatic game that had proved most successful up to that time.

Spain, now that her European possessions had been taken away from her, had turned her attention to internal reforms, as well as to the development of her vast overseas empire. Geographically almost as isolated as England from the European continent, and in possession of a powerful fleet of ships, there was nothing to prevent Spain from becoming a great maritime power. Unfortunately, a nostalgia for her former Italian possessions, combined with the ambitions of Elizabeth Farnese, the second wife of Philip V, diverted Spain from her main course into a fruitless attempt to bring about a revision of the Treaties of Utrecht and Rastatt. Elizabeth's ambitious scheme,

which was supported by both Charles XII and the Stuart pretender, was to prove disastrous for all.

France was equally split by memories of past glories and concern for the future. She soon recovered from the exhaustion of the long wars, but a violent division of opinion still existed: on the one side were those people who held the traditional anti-Austrian views, dating back to the time of Francis I and Richelieu, and who were now reinforced by supporters of the new enlightened thought; on the other side, the Ultramontane Catholics were hoping for a reconciliation between the Catholic Bourbons and Hapsburgs. The policy of the latter group was to be triumphant with the Family Compact, a series of alliances between the French and Spanish branches of the Bourbons. The former attitude involved

France in the War of the Austrian Succession and reappeared during the French Revolution in the policy of the Girondists, who in 1792 succeeded in having war declared on Austria. Everyone in France was agreed, however, that England was their greatest rival.

While the Continent was busy solving its immediate problems, England had quietly arranged the disputed maritime and colonial affairs to her own advantage. For although the Treaty of Utrecht had placed her in a relatively favorable position in general, it had failed in these areas to give England the decisive victory that the Whigs had hoped for. On the surface, England seemed to be even more divided on the right policy to adopt than the Continental powers were, but that dissension was more

The announcement of the Treaty of Utrecht in the streets of The Hague ten days after it was signed.

Left top The allies meeting during the treaty negotiations to discuss peace terms.

Left above The exchange and signing of the treaty.

An engraving of the city of Utrecht produced to celebrate the signing of the Treaty on May 12, 1713.

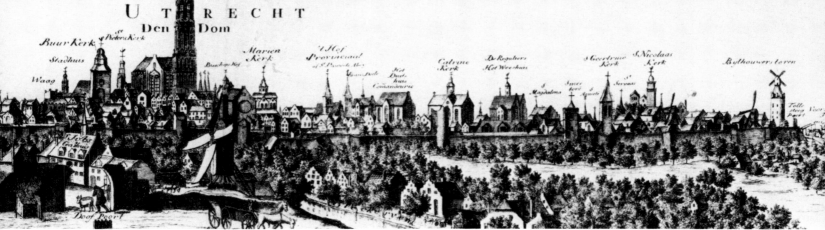

4/97

John Churchill, Duke of Marlborough

apparent than real. The English knew very well that the future of their country lay on the high seas rather than on the European Continent. After the middle of the century they took no further interest in European affairs, except when it was a question of weakening French naval power.

The confrontation of two opposing political views all over Europe was more striking after the Treaty of Utrecht than perhaps at any other time in modern history. On the one side were the traditionalists, who stubbornly persisted in views that very often dated back to the wars of religion. On the other side were the supporters of a new, enlightened policy whose only concern was the reality of the present. Public opinion, when it existed, was equally divided between these two currents of thought.

Cabinet decisions in the eighteenth century, although they did not neglect material interests or ancient traditions, paid little attention to the aspirations of the common people. During the War of the Spanish Succession, the Catalans had demonstrated heroic loyalty toward the Austrian pretender, mainly because they hated the centralist policy of the Castilian government. The people of the German Tyrol showed a similar loyalty toward the Hapsburgs when they were invaded by the Bavarians. Such actions were ignored during the peace talks, however. At that time, the people were still treated like herds of cattle, to be exchanged at the will and convenience of princes and kings, who did not consider the peoples' own wishes on the matter. For example, Sicily was given to the Duke of Savoy, only to be taken away from him a few years later, in exchange for Sardinia; Lorraine was given by Louis xv to his father-in-law, Stanislaus i, ex-king of Poland, as compensation for the loss of the Polish throne. There were numerous similar examples.

John Churchill, first Duke of Marlborough, whose victories over the French at Blenheim, Ramillies, Oudinarde and Malplacquet convinced Louis of his inability to join the thrones of France and Spain.

Right Blenheim Palace, designed by **Vanbrugh**, was given to Marlborough by a grateful nation after his victory.

A new generation of philosophers

It is worth noting, however, that one of the colleagues of the French representative at the Utrecht peace talks, Cardinal de Polignac, was the same Abbé de Saint-Pierre who published, in the very year that the Treaty was signed, his *Projet du Paix Perpétuelle*. That project was considered for many years to be nothing more than a pleasant utopian dream, a revival of the ideas expressed in the *Mémoires* of Sully. Yet by writing his book, as well as by founding, some years later, the *Club de l'Entresol*, the Cardinal was ushering in the new generation of economists and philosophers who believed that the best antidote to war was the general prosperity of the country. Their influence spread far beyond the frontiers of France and England, the most advanced countries of the day. Saint-Pierre drafted a program for "enlightened despotism" which, although it was not directly concerned with the wishes of the people, at least showed an interest in their well-being, since it encouraged the creation of greater prosperity.

Thus the Treaty of Utrecht not only put an end to a series of wars that had proved disastrous to all concerned, it also marked the opening of new perspectives that were totally alien to the spirit of domination reflected in the absolutism of Louis XIV.

JACQUES MADAULE

Above left Louis XIV, whose ambition of uniting the thrones of Spain and France was finally frustrated by the Treaty of Utrecht.

Above Louis XV taking his seat in *Parlement* for the first time, from a contemporary engraving.

Queen Anne with Knights of the Garter. Under Queen Anne's rule, and particularly as a result of the Treaty of Utrecht, Britain's colonial territories increased.

Europe is conquered by French culture where

Corneille, whose independence was crushed by his subservience to Cardinal Richelieu.

The almost continuous wars that were fought in Europe throughout the seventeenth century did not prevent its being an age of unparalleled advancement in the development of art and in the improvement of standards of living. And although most of the countries of Europe had, at one time or another, been ranged in conflict against France, French culture had not suffered in the esteem of the civilized world.

The genius of the French dramatists of the seventeenth century was indeed undeniable. Pierre Corneille, whose early comedy *Mélite* was enthusiastically received in Paris in 1629, produced a succession of plays that included *Le Cid*, a masterly piece that marks the beginning of the greatest period in French drama, and *Le Menteur*, a comedy of remarkable originality.

For a time Corneille was one of Richelieu's "five poets" and was obliged to produce plays on themes presented to him by the Cardinal. Corneille, awkward and independent, was quite unsuited to such profitable but restricting work, and soon offended Richelieu by declining to follow his master's schemes. Jean de Rotrou, the only one of the five poets worthy of comparison with Corneille, died of the plague at the age of forty—but by then he had produced an extraordinary number of plays, of which four (*Le Véritable Saint Genest, Don Bertrand de Cabrère, Venceslas* and *Cosroès*) are acknowledged masterpieces.

While *Cosroès* was being performed in Paris, a popular theatrical company was touring the provinces. One of its number was Jean Baptiste Poquelin, whose stage

name was Molière. Molière had already proved his gifts as a comic writer, but it was not until his *Précieuses Ridicules* was published in 1659 that he achieved his first real success. Kindly, overworked, anxious and painstaking, Molière was an authentic genius. A most fertile and inventive comic dramatist, he was an inspiration to successive generations of writers for the theater, none of whom were able to match his mastery as a creator of artificial comedy and of scintillating dialogue. Although suffering from serious lung disease, Molière insisted upon taking the part of the *malade imaginaire* in the seventh presentation of his play by the same name.

Jean Racine, whose earliest play, *La Thébaïde ou Les Frères ennemis*, was acted by Molière's company at the Palais-Royal in 1664, was as supreme a tragic poet as Molière was a comic dramatist. Racine retired from dramatic work at an early age, writing nothing for the stage after 1677 apart from two religious pieces for Madame de Maintenon's schoolgirls at Saint-Cyr. His best work was written between 1667—when *Andromaque* appeared—and 1677—when *Phèdre* was first presented.

While Racine was writing in France, the English theater—closed during the Commonwealth—reopened in London. It was no longer a national theater, as it had been in Shakespeare's time; indeed, until the civil war the most notable

Molière, France's leading comic dramatist, as *Le Bourgeois Gentilhomme*.

productions of the English stage were court masques—stylized, allegorical and spectacular pageants on which Ben Jonson and Inigo Jones lavished their respective talents as poet and scenic designer.

Apart from Thomas Shadwell, who was far more prolific as a comic writer than as a playwright; Thomas Otway, whose greatest work, *Venice Preserved, or a Plot Discovered*, appeared in 1682; and John Dryden—English writers for the theater in the Restoration period were more successful in comedy than in tragedy.

Racine, who despite his education among the theater-hating Jansenists, became France's greatest tragic playwright with a reputation exceeding that of his older contemporary Corneille.

Rise of the Opera

Earlier, in Italy, the first genuine operas had been performed. Jacopo Peri and Giulio Caccini had paved the way with *Dafne* and *Euridice*. Claudio Monteverdi, who spent the last thirty years of his life as director of music at St. Mark's in Venice, applied and extended the ideas of the *Nuove Musiche* (new music): his *Orfeo*, first performed at Mantua in 1607, marks an important advance, and his *Il Ritorno d'Ulisse* and *L'Incoronazione di Poppea* are further developments of the genre. Henry Purcell, who was clearly influenced by the new Italian masters, further developed the operatic form with his *Dido and Aeneas*, written in 1689.

The first opera house was opened in Venice in 1637, and others followed: the London opera opened in 1656, the Paris opera in 1669, Rome in 1671 and Hamburg in 1678. As the performances improved, so did the skill of the instrument makers. At Cremona in

northern Italy, the Amati, Guarneri and Stradavari families began making string instruments, particularly violins, of unprecedented quality.

Art on the Continent

Painters as well as musicians drew their inspiration from Italy. Dutch art in particular developed under powerful Italian influences (although with its own distinction and beauty and its own concern for detail). Not only Frans Hals and Rembrandt van Rijn, but Terborch, Pieter de Hooch, Jan Vermeer, Karel Fabritius, Jakob van Ruysdael, Aelbert Cuyp and Meindert Hobbema all belong to this astonishingly fruitful period. So do Rubens, Jordaens and Van Dyck.

Spain's artistic genius, El Greco, died in 1614, but Francisco de Herrera, Francisco Pacheco, Velasquez and Murillo continued to produce canvases until mid-century. In France, the highly individual work of the Le Nain brothers, Antoine and Louis, was as prized as the delightful work of Nicolas Poussin, Gaspard Poussin and Claude Lorrain—all of whom were French landscape painters working in Rome.

Art in England

The persecution of Protestants in the Spanish Netherlands—and the patronage accorded them at the English Court—brought many Dutch and Flemish painters to England. Daniel Mytens served as Sergeant-Painter to James I, and Cornelius Johnson held the same post under Charles I. Van Dyck and Rubens also found a valued and astute patron in Charles—and Van Dyck's English pupil, William Dobson, succeeded him as Sergeant-Painter to the King. During the Commonwealth, the only painters of note were Samuel Cooper and Peter van der Faes (better known as Peter Lely), who had come to London to follow the example of Van Dyck. After the Restoration, Lely's success at court was emulated by Godfrey Kneller, whose portraits hung on the walls of almost every great house in the country.

The most fashionable of these houses were built in the Palladian style that Inigo Jones introduced to England after a lengthy tour of

French arms had failed

Congreve (*left*) whose comedies shocked and delighted Restoration England; and John Dryden, one of England's few successful tragic writers of his time.

Italy. (The work of the great Italian architect, Andrea Palladio, filled Jones with admiration, provoked him to open imitation, and inspired a tradition that was carried on in England by Roger Pratt.) After the Great Fire of 1666, Christopher Wren—who had already been responsible for fine work at Oxford and Cambridge— undertook to rebuild many of the City's churches and St. Paul's Cathedral.

If St. Paul's is England's great monument to the genius of the age, Versailles and the Paris of Louis XIV are monuments to the genius of the French. Jules Hardouin Mansard designed the Grand Trianon and other buildings at Versailles, the château of Marly, the Places des Victoires and the Place Vendôme. The gardens of Versailles were laid out by André Lenôtre, father of French landscape gardening.

Law's system

For all the elegance of the more fashionable parts of Paris, France at the end of the War of the Spanish Succession was on the verge of financial ruin. The country had rich resources, but its government was without credit and it could raise loans only at enormous cost. The government's financial position was such that a declaration of national bankruptcy was seriously considered.

Among the French Regent's distraught advisers was a Scotsman, John Law, who appeared entirely confident that if a proper fiscal system were adopted, the crisis could be resolved. Law, the adventurous, attractive and keenly intelligent son of an Edinburgh goldsmith, had led a dissolute youth in London and had fled to Holland in 1694 after killing a man in a duel.

Since that time he had traveled widely, studied the operations of the banks of Europe, lived by gambling and speculation, and endeavored to persuade various governments to adopt his schemes. His contention was that finance was a science, resting on fundamental principles and able to support a coherent policy. He assured the Regent that France's troubles were entirely due to past financial mismanagement, that trade depended upon money, and that the solution lay in creating a supply of money to meet its present scarcity—a supply that would never be hoarded and could never become scarce. What Law meant was that paper— or, in other words, the credit of the State—must henceforth be used for money.

Impressed by Law's confidence and ingenuity, the Regent allowed him to found a private bank with the right to issue notes. The bank was immediately successful; its notes combined the advantages of fixity of value with convenience. A decree, issued on April 10, 1717, ordered tax collectors to receive them as payment and to exchange them for coins.

Having successfully established his bank, Law was permitted to set up a commercial company, the *Compagnie de la Louisiane ou d'Occident*, for the purpose of colonizing and commercially exploiting that North American region. In December, 1718, Law's bank became *La Banque royale*. Its notes were guaranteed in the King's name and made legal tender throughout the kingdom. Branches were opened in five principal French towns. Law's company rapidly amalgamated with other companies, and under its new name, *La Compagnie des Indes*, it developed a virtual monopoly of French foreign trade. To exploit its opportunities, capital was needed—and 50,000 shares

of company stock were therefore issued at 500 *livres* each. The price of those shares rose rapidly, another issue of 50,000 shares was made, and two annual dividends of 6 per cent were promised. Speculation in the company's shares naturally increased.

Law now proposed to take over the national debt and to manage it on terms advantageous to both the government and the *Compagnie des Indes*. The Company agreed to lend the bankrupt French government 15 million *livres* at 3 per cent interest, and financial transactions involving huge sums of money followed. Immense fortunes were made as the price of the five-hundred-*livres* shares rose to 12,000 and then to 20,000 *livres*. For months the rage of speculation continued. Provincial families sold all they had and came to Paris to play the market. John Law became, in Lady Mary Wortley Montagu's words, "absolute in Paris."

In March, 1720, the title Superintendent of Finance was revived, and promptly bestowed upon the Scotsman. By that time, Law's System was already in decay. It was clear that the prosperity was artificial and that the Company could not conceivably pay the dividends expected. Men began to sell shares to invest in property and coin, the price of the shares fell and the worth of paper money depreciated. By declaring dividends as high as 40 per cent, the Scot endeavored to stimulate the circulation of the Bank's notes, but in May it was decreed that their value should be reduced by half. Confusion became panic: the police dispersed speculators in the Paris streets as the Bank, the Company and the System collapsed in ruins.

John Law's initial success in manipulating credit encouraged the launching of a similar scheme in London, one that was soon to collapse as dramatically and devastatingly as had the *Compagnie des Indes*.

John Law, France's Superintendent of Finances, who caused a financial crisis similar to England's South Sea Bubble.

DOMINE

IN TE

SPERAVI

Sarga Finissima de Inglaterra
de la Nueva Fabrica
Nᵒ Con Yards

RIO DE   LONDRES

The South Sea Bubble

In January of 1720, a newly formed English trading corporation known as the South Sea Company issued stock worth £31,000,000—enough to cover England's enormous war debt, which the Company absorbed. Shares of Company stock sold at first for £128 each; by July of the same year the Company's enterprising directors had pushed the value of those shares to £1,000. Generous bribes to high government officials, coupled with equally generous loans to investors (loans that enabled those investors to reinvest their original cash outlays in subsequent issues of Company stock) fed a dangerous inflationary spiral—and led to the Company's inevitable collapse. The bursting of the "South Sea bubble" toppled the government, bankrupted countless small investors and eventually altered England's financial structure.

At nine o'clock on the evening of September 17, 1720, sixteen of the most important men in England met at the General Post Office in London. Their chairman was James Craggs, England's Postmaster General and a senior member of the government that was led by Stanhope and Sunderland. Craggs was joined by five other ministers: his son James, Secretary of State; William Aislabie, the Chancellor of the Exchequer; the Duke of Kent, who was Lord Privy Seal; and two politicians who had recently joined the ministry (following the settlement of a rift in the Whig party), Robert Walpole and Charles Townshend. The other men present were leading members of the governing bodies of the Bank of England and of the South Sea Company.

The meeting lasted six hours. Its purpose was to consider a way to stave off the impending collapse of the market in South Sea stock. From a modest 128 pounds per share—the asking price at the beginning of the year—that stock had soared to nearly 1,000 pounds per share by July of 1720. On September 1 it had sunk to 775, and on the day of the meeting it was being quoted in Exchange Alley at 520. (By the end of the year it would be back to 155.)

Much the same thing was happening that same autumn in Paris, where the elaborate financial "system" constructed by John Law had expanded to encompass the whole of the French national economy, including its currency. Indeed, the growth of the "South Sea Bubble"—as that stock's inflationary spiral was dubbed—was not an isolated incident in British economic history but rather was part of a wave of speculation that swept over Western Europe in the second decade of the eighteenth century. Its influence was felt in Portugal and Switzerland, Hamburg, Vienna and Amsterdam. Much of the dealing, in fact, was international and competitive: the canton of Berne invested in South Sea stock, and Law, speculating on a fall in price, tried to mount a "bear" operation against it by dumping thousands of shares on the market.

The South Sea Company had been founded in 1711 by Harley's Tory government, which had swept into power by promising to wind up the wars waged by Marlborough and, if possible, to dispose of the legacy of debt that had resulted from them. (The discovery that wars could be fought on credit had enabled Marlborough to finance his victorious campaigns at Blenheim and Malplaquet. It had also left the country deeply in debt.) Harley's scheme was a relatively simple one: he created an impressive-looking trading company with power to issue stock, and then invited the holders of certain government debts to exchange them for stock. In return the company received an annual payment from the Exchequer that was more or less equivalent to the interest on the debt that the company had taken over. Although the company was said to have commercial prospects, the scheme was not much more than a camouflaging of the war debt to make it more acceptable to the squires who formed an important part of Harley's majority in Parliament.

It may well have been John Law's stupendous success in manipulating French credit that encouraged the South Sea Company to launch the scheme that culminated in the extraordinary South Sea Bubble of 1720. The leading member of the group of financiers that controlled the Company was John Blunt, a blustering Baptist who had long been jealous of the financial privileges of the Bank of England. The Bank of England was traditionally Whig, and there was more than a hint of Tory reprisal in Harley's decision—based on Blunt's counsel—to create the rival South Sea Company. In any case, the mainspring of the promotion was the ambition of Blunt and his associates.

Early in 1720 the South Sea Company obtained an act of Parliament under which virtually the whole of the outstanding national debt of 31 million pounds could, at the option of the holders, be converted into South Sea stock. In theory, that act authorized the company to create one hundred pounds' worth of stock for every one hundred pounds' worth of debt that it took over. In practice, the rate

Sir Robert Walpole who gained power in England's House of Commons as a direct result of the South Sea Bubble scandal, and during his period in power created the British premiership.

Opposite The trade label of the South Sea Company.

A gift of seven million pounds

John Law, the Scot whose financial innovations in France led to speculation similar to that in the South Sea Company.

at which debt was exchanged for stock was left to the Company—and it was no secret, from the very beginning of the scheme, that the stock would be issued at a premium. That action would create a stock surplus (because the Company would be able to issue more shares than it needed for the exchange operation) and that surplus—said the promoters—could then be sold for the Company's benefit. The stock's promoters therefore urged debt-holders to exchange their government bonds at a rate that clearly favored the Company. They argued that such a move would actually increase the debt-holders' profits because the Company in which they had become shareholders would have more surplus stock to sell. So great was the confidence of the promoters that they undertook to make the national Exchequer an outright gift of 7 million pounds out of proceeds from the sale of surplus stock. This huge public bribe was necessary to outbid the Bank of England, for the Bank's directors, seeing their privileged position threatened, had also made proposals for taking over the national debt and converting it into Bank stock. Parliament, in fact, held a kind of auction between the two great financial institutions to decide which of them should wield the great, new and ill-understood engine of credit.

In those days the stock exchange, which revolved around Garraway's Coffee House and the little maze of lanes in which it stood, was a smallish affair and largely unregulated. There were already licensed brokers in existence, but the stocks that they quoted were limited—until the South Sea Year—to government issues and to the stocks of the East India Company, the South Sea Company, and the Bank of England and a few issues bearing the names of companies that had survived the great turn-of-the-century enthusiasm for joint stock promotion. Such companies had originally operated under charters entitling them to carry on a specified enterprise, but by 1720 almost all of them had been converted into "shells"—companies that had ceased the activity for which they had been incorporated—by financial syndicates.

The triumph of the South Sea Company in the spring of 1720 had not gone unopposed in Parliament. It had been fought by a determined group of supporters of the Bank of England—notably Robert Walpole—and its path had been eased by large bribes to certain ministers and parliamentarians. Those bribes characteristically took the form of stock in the South Sea Company, nominally transferred to the legislators at market prices and actually delivered free on demand. The value of the bribes was thus, ironically, proportionate to the success of the scheme. Among those probably bribed in this fashion by Blunt and the South Sea Company's cashier, Robert Knight, were Aislabie, the Chancellor of the Exchequer; Charles Stanhope, the Secretary to the Treasury; the two Craggs; and the Earl of Sunderland who, with James Stanhope, was the government's leading minister. Through Aislabie, King George I, who was titular governor of the Company, also benefited—and so did his two mistresses, the Duchess of Kendal and the Countess of Darlington.

At first matters went well enough. The actual conversion began in May at the rate of 375 pounds' worth of debt to secure only 100 pounds' worth of stock, and large quantities of stock were then marketed at vastly inflated prices. (By August, the going rate for a block of stock purchased at 100 pounds in May had risen to the sum of 1000 pounds.) To promote additional speculation the Company interspersed its issues of stock with loans to purchasers of stock, thus constructing a kind of financial pump by which the same limited supply of cash was used over and over again to force the price of stock to ever greater heights.

The South Sea directors had never expected a boom on this scale, and they did their best to damp down competition. They even obtained an act

An emblematical print of the South Sea Bubble. In the fever of speculation which gripped the city of London the price of stock in the South Sea Company and other companies rose to unrealistic levels.

against unauthorized joint stock companies. (That piece of legislation, the so-called "Bubble Act," remained on the statute book until 1825 and severely restricted joint stock enterprise throughout the eighteenth century.) Their efforts were to no avail, however, and by September of 1720 it was evident to the entire English financial community that the South Sea Bubble was about to burst. Many factors contributed to the crash: the collapse of Law's financial system in France, the panic induced by the arrival of a fresh epidemic of plague, and the sudden realization that even a guaranteed dividend of fifty

per cent—which the Company's desperate directors promised their stockholders in August—gave the stockholder who had bought at one thousand only five per cent on his money. But the chief reason for the slump was that a mountain of short-term credit had been extended during the preceding months of intense speculation—and that credit could not be supported by those who had incurred it.

This was the problem that Craggs and the group at the Post Office confronted on the evening of September 17, 1720. They were unable to solve it, and by the end of the year trade was virtually at a standstill and there was widespread unemployment. A parliamentary inquiry was set in motion and it soon began to dredge up the murky story of the passage of the South Sea Act. Blunt became a willing witness against his fellow directors but not before his colleague Knight—of whom the Committee "found it proper to observe that it has appeared to them, throughout their examination, that Mr. Knight, the cashier of the South Sea Company, was principally concerned in their most secret transactions"—was able to abscond to the Netherlands.

During the spring of 1721 the ministry evaporated in a cloud of death and disgrace: Postmaster General Craggs committed suicide; his son, the Secretary of State, died of smallpox: Stanhope, the Prime Minister, burst a blood vessel while defending his government in the House of Lords; and Aislabie, the Chancellor, was expelled from the House of Commons.

The country was in an uproar. "They are *Rogues of Prey*, they are *Stock Jobbers*, they are a *conspiracy of Stock Jobbers*, a name which carries along with it such a detestable deadly image, that it exceeds all humane

Change Alley where dealing in stocks and shares took place.

BUBBLE CARD.

A satirical "bubble card" showing "headlong fools" plunging into frenzied investment and eventually into the water.

The House of Commons in George I's reign, by Tillemans; a number of members of the House were involved in the South Sea Company.

Sir James Craggs, Postmaster General, who kept the House informed of developments during the crisis.

invention to aggravate it," screeched one anonymous publicist, the author of *Cato's Letters*. Soothing that tempest, which had destroyed the government and shaken the Hanoverian settlement itself, was Robert Walpole's supreme achievement. Walpole, who succeeded to the perilous office of First Lord of the Treasury upon the resignation of Sunderland in April, 1721, confronted, opposed and finally defeated the "party of revenge" during the next three months.

The Age of Walpole—and of the Pelhams after him—is one of the longest periods of political and economic stability in British history, an era that witnessed the establishing of certain traditions that have survived to this day. The consolidation of power in the House of Commons, the heritage of mistrust of overt collaboration between government and business, and the concept of the importance of a basic continuity in affairs of state—all date from the long period of calm that succeeded the shock of the South Sea Year. So too does the enduring domination of the country's finances by the Bank of England. Sir Gilbert Heathcote, speaking for the Bank at the Post Office meeting, made it a condition of the Bank's collaboration that in the future the South Sea Company's account should be kept by the Bank of England and by no one else. The Bank and the Treasury justified the confidence they demanded. British public finance, from Walpole's time, became the best managed and the soundest in Europe, and its techniques steadily improved. The fact is of incalculable importance for the history of the next 250 years.

Walpole achieved domestic stability not through the offices of the Bank of England but by falling back on the landowners, and their interests and prejudices were to remain uppermost in the minds of British politicians for the next hundred years. It is true that British commerce continued to grow, that London supplanted Amsterdam as the financial capital of Europe, that business families made marriages with the landed gentry and that the importance of trade to the country was everywhere lauded, but business in England never achieved equality of respect with landed wealth. A landed estate remained the ideal security for an Englishman. The former great commercial powers—Florence, Venice, Amsterdam—had been dominated by merchant princes; England lacked them, even in the period of her greatest commercial power.

England's social structure hardened during this period. The absurd inequities of the unreformed House of Commons—to which members were returned on the decision of a single magnate or a tiny caucus of electors—were perpetuated by a series of eighteenth-century decisions concerning the right to vote and the respect paid to landed property. The "Venetian oligarchy" denounced by Disraeli, the system of patronage by which progress in life depended primarily on influence, and the deep conservatism that allowed almost no change in social or constitutional law between 1720 and 1780—all these are marks of this remarkable era of stability. Its saving grace was that it was a diffused not a centralized stability. The rights of individuals and, above all, the rights of corporate bodies—be they local authorities, colleges, charities, or guilds—are the stuff and tissue of eighteenth-century English society.

To some extent the period following the South Sea Year can be called stagnant as well as stable. It contrasts vividly with the preceding thirty years, during which the enduring outline of the British constitutional settlement had been established. The conquest of Ireland, the union with Scotland, the Hanoverian succession, the supremacy of Parliament and the shape of ministerial government were all achieved in the generation following the Revolution of 1688. It was a period of greatness and promise, not only in politics but in economics, science, and letters. It was an age of new vitality that accompanied Britain's emergence as a great European power. The tendency, unquestionably, was toward political stability, but in another sense the chaotic South Sea Year was a culmination of effervescence.

The succeeding years fell short of the promise of the first twenty of the century. Except in the field of agriculture, technology was slow to find application, despite the earlier progress of scientific theory. For reasons which have never been satisfactorily explained, even the rate of growth of the population decelerated until about 1740, when it resumed a sharper upward trend. It is not unreasonable to attribute some of this slowing down of progress to the recollection of the almost insane burst of optimism which had ended in the disaster of 1720.

That disaster can perhaps best be explained as the impact of new, barely understood financial techniques upon an economy that was still predominantly agricultural. It was in part the penalty that

A system in need of reform

The Brabant Screen, a satirical print of 1721: on the right behind the screen three directors of the company are hiding, on the left the South Sea Company Treasurer, Knight, receives a letter from a royal favorite, authorizing him to flee to the Low Countries. The pictures on the screen attack the morality of the directors and the Treasurer. It was thought at the time that royal patronage was used to hush up the crisis, as members of the royal family were involved in the Company and its ruin.

Old Custom House Quay in London during the 1720s: the immense expansion of trade that accompanied the growth of Britain's foreign empire was one of the factors that caused the South Sea Bubble.

England paid for becoming the first nation-state to assume the commercial leadership of Europe. The later period of comparative stagnation—the age of Walpole and the Pelhams—can be seen as one in which the new nation-state, still led by its landed gentry, gradually assimilated its new role in Europe and the world.

The contrast between the aftermaths of the speculation in London and Paris is not insignificant. In Paris, an effort was made to wipe away the memory of Law and his system, and huge piles of paper—representing the era of credit—were publicly burned. Law's real success—for he had succeeded, during his five years of power, in revitalizing the French economy as well as inflating the currency—was lost in an almost religious revulsion for high finance that swept the country. France settled down to a long period of backward-looking despotism that was relieved only by her native sons' essentially critical intellectual brilliance. In England, where many had been ruined (and more cheated of wholly imaginary gains) and an extensive reconstruction of the South Sea Company had been necessary, there was no bankruptcy. In the end, the Company's obligations to its shareholders were honored and South Sea annuities remained a feature of the British national debt until Gladstone abolished them upon becoming Chancellor in 1854. The period of stagnation that followed the slump was an age of digestion rather than decay. The commercial and constitutional vitality of the early years of the century was checked, but not destroyed.   JOHN CARSWELL

Throughout Europe philosophers plead for

Europe after Louis XIV

When the South Sea Bubble burst, Louis XIV had been dead for five years and his nephew, Philip, Duke of Orleans, was ruling as Regent for Louis' five-year-old great-grandson. In defiance of the Treaty of Utrecht, Philip V of Spain—first of the Bourbon kings and Louis XIV's grandson—had also claimed the regency, but with the help of England and Holland, which had sworn to guarantee the Utrecht treaty, the Duke had thwarted Philip's designs. Undaunted, Philip invaded Sardinia and Sicily in 1717 at the insistence of his wife, Elizabeth Farnese, who wanted a secure inheritance for her sons. His provocative act led to the Quadruple Alliance of Austria, England, France and Holland—and when a French army crossed the Pyrenees and an English fleet under Admiral George Byng destroyed the Spanish fleet off Messina, Philip was forced to make peace and to renounce his claims to the former Spanish possessions in Italy.

Philip's ambitions were further thwarted when Louis XV—who came of age in 1723—rejected the hand of his Spanish cousin, the Infanta, and married Maria Lezczynska, daughter of the former King of Poland. Delegating responsibility for most of the country's affairs to Cardinal André Hercule de Fleury, Louis devoted himself to hunting and to a succession of mistresses, of whom Madame de Pompadour, the dominant figure at Versailles for almost twenty years, was by far the most remarkable.

The year before Louis XV ascended to his great-grandfather's throne, Queen Anne, daughter of James II and the last of the Stuart monarchs, died. Not one of her numerous children had survived, and the crown passed to James I's great-grandson, the Elector of Hanover, who was crowned King George I of Great Britain and Ireland according to the Act of Settlement of 1701. During the reign of George I, the policy of the British government was dominated by the necessity of maintaining the Elector's family on the throne. As a result, the Whig oligarchy became entrenched in power and those Tory squires who might otherwise have supported a restoration of the

Voltaire, the embodiment of the Enlightenment.

Stuarts were kept occupied in local affairs.

The government's success in maintaining domestic tranquility and in restoring confidence after the South Sea panic owed much to Sir Robert Walpole. As leader of the administration from 1721 to 1742, Walpole established the system by which England has since been governed, a system that made the Cabinet collectively responsible for the government's policy and established the supremacy of the First Lord of the Treasury as Prime Minister in both Cabinet and the House of Commons. The Cabinet—a group of ministers who were all members of Parliament, dependent upon the favor of Parliament and collectively answerable to Parliament for their actions—had not been envisaged in the Revolution Settlement of 1689. Nor had the office of Prime Minister. But under Walpole both Cabinet and Prime Minister evolved and developed in answer to the country's needs. There was no written constitution; nor, apparently, was there a need for one.

Voltaire and Montesquieu

Walpole's system of government aroused deep admiration among foreign observers of the time. Voltaire, who came to be recognized as the very embodiment of the eighteenth-century Enlighten-

ment, arrived in England during Walpole's premiership in 1726 and was profoundly impressed by what he saw. Voltaire was thirty-one at the time, and he had already achieved notoriety in France as a poet and dramatist—and as a satirist who had been banished from court and eventually imprisoned for lampooning the Regent. He had been forced to seek refuge in England after rashly challenging the Chevalier de Rohan-Chabot to a duel, and he arrived bitterly indignant at the tyranny and injustice he had left behind him in France.

The French government that Voltaire railed against had failed to impose an equitable system of taxation—and in an effort to win the support of various sections of the community, exemptions had been granted to whole classes of the

Montesquieu: full of praise for England's liberal political system.

people. Not only the nobles and the clergy, but a large proportion of the middle classes had been exempted from the *taille*, or property tax, and entire provinces had been granted other forms of relief. Even worse, the French government appeared totally incapable of reforming that system.

Upon Louis XIV's death, the *Parlement* of Paris was restored to its former authority, but its members (and those of the twelve Provincial *Parlements*) were blind to the need for reform and totally opposed to any proposal that might lead to it. A more representative legislative assembly, elected by the people and responsible to them, was so out of keeping with French tradition that the idea was never even proposed with any sort of conviction. And even those writers who had found cause to criticize the autocracy during the later

Sir Robert Walpole talking to the Speaker in the English House of Commons.

freedom in politics and religion

years of the King's reign suggested a return to ancient methods of government rather than a progression to new ones.

To Voltaire, the Englishman's freedom seemed so refreshing as to be an inspiration. In England the press was free, there was a measure of religious toleration inconceivable in France, and there was parliamentary government. Torture, arbitrary imprisonment and arbitrary taxes were evils of the past. The Frenchman's *Lettres sur les Anglais*, a work that increased the disfavor in which Voltaire was held at the French court, provided his countrymen with a glimpse of a society that was much more fortunate than their own.

Charles de Secondat, Baron de la Brède et de Montesquieu, whose *Lettres persanes* was a biting satire of French society, arrived in England in 1729 to study political and social institutions. His verdict was every bit as favorable as Voltaire's had been. "It was the freest country in the world," he decided. "I make exception of no republic. And I call it free because the sovereign, whose authority is controlled and limited, is unable to inflict any imaginable harm on anyone."

Locke on liberty

Both Montesquieu and Voltaire studied the writings of John Locke, the founder of philosophical liberalism. Locke's ideas had deeply influenced the course of the English revolution and his works had provided the eighteenth century with its most worthwhile and durable analysis of the intellectual revolution of the seventeenth. His *Letters on Toleration* defended religious liberty; his *Treatises on Government* upheld political liberty; and his *Essay Concerning Human Understanding* insisted upon intellectual liberty.

For all the enthusiasm that the English constitution aroused in foreign observers, however, it had far more serious defects than they were willing to recognize. For one thing, religious toleration was severely limited: nonconformist dissenters were excluded from both Parliament and the universities of Oxford and Cambridge, and until 1779 Roman Catholics were forbidden to practice their religion in public. For another, the government of England was still an aristocracy, and that aristocracy

The Battle of Culloden at which "the Butcher" Duke of Cumberland, with his redcoats shattered the hopes of the Jacobites.

controlled Parliament. Many of the members held their seats through family influences and bribery, and under their rule social injustices continued unchecked. Moreover, although it was often mitigated in practice, the penal code was ferocious. There was

The entrance to Newgate Prison, London. Despite England's reputation for liberty, more crimes were punishable by death than in any other European country.

scarcely another country in Europe where so many crimes were punishable by death—and the number of capital statutes was increasing. Thirty-three new capital offenses were created in the reign of George II alone—or roughly one for every year of the monarch's reign.

Yet despite the miseries of the unheeded and largely unseen poor, England was a happy country. The Industrial Revolution had not yet brought the tragic problems of the dark, satanic mills to the north, there were few slums in the small towns, and farmers prospered. In the provinces, the power of the Tory squire to govern the life of his tenants and dependents went unquestioned. All in all, life in early Georgian England was stable, placid and self-satisfied. In 1715 and again in 1745, the Jacobites, supporters of the exiled Stuart kings, attempted to overthrow the House of Hanover, but they failed to arouse the English people, who refused to imperil the safe, Protestant monarchy by rallying to the cause of a romantic pretender. At Culloden, on April 16, 1746, Jacobite hopes were dispelled forever by the army of William Augustus,

Duke of Cumberland, the second son of George II. By 1765, Horace Walpole could write that Jacobitism was extinct.

By the middle of the eighteenth century, English optimism was shared by the political writers of France. For all their burning anticlericalism and lost faith in the doctrines of the Church, French intellectuals had not lost their faith in the dignity of man. Man was innately good—and good legislators could make him infinitely better. He could also be made better, and his environment improved, by increasing his knowledge—and it was with a view to increasing man's knowledge that Denis Diderot set about the task of compiling his great *Encyclopédie* in 1741. "The aim of an encyclopedia," as he put it, "is to assemble the knowledge scattered over the face of the earth; to explain its general plan to the men with whom we live, and to transmit it to those who will come after us, so that the labors of past centuries may not be useless to future times; so that our descendants, by becoming better informed, may in consequence be happier and more virtuous . . ."

An Encyclopedia for the Enlightenment

The task assigned to Denis Diderot in 1742 by a consortium of leading Parisian publishers was a relatively simple one : to translate Quaker Ephraim Chambers' single-volume Cyclopedia *into French. Diderot's immediate, ambitious revision of his employers' assignment led to the publication of a thirty-five volume* Encyclopedie *that both summarized and exemplified the Age of Enlightenment. The process took twenty-five years and was conducted semiclandestinely, without the approval of government censors. The series, which was suppressed by the State Council and expressly condemned by the Church, numbered among its contributors the greatest names of the Age of Reason : Rousseau and Voltaire, Quesnay and D'Alembert. The encyclopedia's influence on the courts, councils, and cognoscente of Europe was profound. In France itself, Diderot's work was quoted at court to settle arguments—and was quoted elsewhere, by opponents of the King, to stir a revolution.*

Many of Diderot's friends wrote articles for his encyclopedia: Rousseau for example wrote on music.

Opposite Diderot, who developed the original idea of a translation of Chamber's *Cyclopedia* into French. .

Soon after the publication of Diderot's *Encyclopédie*, a book of pirated selections was advertised as containing "the most interesting, the most pleasant, the most piquant, the most philosophical articles of the Great Dictionary," intended to attract all kinds of readers, "and in particular men of the world." The advertisement indicates something about the reading public of the *Encyclopédie*. Men of the world, including the crowned heads of many countries, did indeed have the volumes in their libraries. The Sultan in Constantinople instructed his engineers to make use of the illustrative plates to improve his gun foundry, and learned people all over Europe used the articles to better their knowledge and to write refutations. Army officers, lawyers, economists and clergymen are found on the various lists of subscribers. No other book has had such a dramatic impact on so widespread and influential an audience.

The great French *Encyclopédie* of Denis Diderot and Jean Le Rond d'Alembert is a landmark in the story of the human mind. It is a whole library, and its long list of contributors includes the most famous names of the age. The entire French literature of the eighteenth century is represented in these volumes—not only belles lettres, but also writings on philosophy, natural history, economics, politics and many other subjects. What is still more important, all the contributors were united in the task of creating a new and revolutionary way of thinking, in contrast to the still dominant traditions of the Church in politics and nearly all ways of life. New light was to be shed, and the term "Enlightenment" became the watchword for the whole epoch. The *Encyclopédie* was not the sole instrument of that great movement, but it was by far the most powerful and decisive vehicle.

The war on tradition had begun in the seventeenth century, when scientists and philosophers began attacking what for centuries had been the traditional patterns of European civilization: a divine monarchy; a privileged Church and hereditary aristocracy; a formally maintained, stratified social hierarchy; a legal system that favored the group rather than the individual; and decentralized state government that accounted for considerable local variety and regional autonomy. Both religion and the social order had been accepted on faith, unchallenged.

In addition, the seventeenth century saw new scientific discoveries—particularly Isaac Newton's investigations of motion—bring about startling changes in thought. Newton's investigations and the thinking of Descartes, Francis Bacon and John Locke helped develop a belief in natural law and a universal order. Most important, they developed the confidence that human reason, using the scientific method, could discover truth. Skepticism replaced blind faith, all the old orthodoxies were questioned, and the belief in change and progress replaced the commitment to stability. Nature, the new rationalists believed, was mechanical, ordered and subject to unvarying laws; man, through the use of reason, could discover these laws. Progress and perfection were possible on earth.

By the eighteenth century the Enlightenment—or the Age of Reason, as it has been called—was in full swing. The new ideas had by then become widely disseminated, popularized by the *philosophes*, who addressed themselves to the general public. Those *philosophes* were the men who contributed to the book that became the bible of the Enlightenment, Diderot's *Encyclopédie*. That great work epitomized the rationalism and skepticism of the age, recording scientific achievements, the advance of industrial technology and the reorientation of thoughts. Its

Button making, a typical illustration from the *Encyclopédie* which dealt with practical matters as well as ideas. The first volume of plates was published a year after the first volume of the *Encyclopédie* itself.

The many faces of Voltaire: uncrowned king of the Encyclopedists.

point of view was that of the most enlightened, and it challenged sacred and hitherto impregnable institutions. Typical of its attacks was this veiled comment on the French monarchy: "A sovereign, absolute though he may be, has no right to touch the established law of a state, no more than its religion....He is, besides, always obliged to follow the laws of justice and reason."

D'Alembert, in his now famous introductory essay, the "*Discours Préliminaire*," gave full recognition to the debt the *philosophes*, or Encyclopedists, owed to their predecessors. He began with Francis Bacon, "born still in the deepest darkness" of the Middle Ages, the first who had broken the chains of scholasticism and metaphysical speculation and had placed empiricism firmly on the map. Empiricism was indeed the watchword of the Encyclopedists. It meant to explore not only the mind but all branches of knowledge and human activities: the arts, geography, zoology, botany, economics, agriculture, chemistry, architecture—even grammar and semantics. The *Encyclopédie* was truly universal, at least in its aims.

The beginnings had been very modest. Originally no more was intended than the French translation of the Quaker Ephraim Chambers' *Cyclopedia*, which had been published some decades before in London and had since been reprinted in several editions. A one-man work with modest aims and much useful information, it had shown that a public existed for this kind of dictionary. A small consortium of leading Paris publishers decided on a French edition and hired as editor Denis Diderot, who had already made himself known to the publishers as a translator of other English reference books and an author of books on mathematical problems, natural history and like subjects. Diderot at once changed the publishers' plan completely—substituting the very ambitious scheme that became the foundation of the *Encyclopédie*, and, in fact, the model for all future encyclopedias. A prospectus was printed, approved by the censor, and distributed. The response from the public was highly satisfactory, and the first virulent critics were shrugged off.

The main task for Diderot, as for any editor of an undertaking of that scope, was to find collaborators. D'Alembert, a leading mathematician who had been internationally honored with memberships in many academies, was willing to take over the section on mathematics besides contributing articles on other subjects. Other friends joined the venture: Jean Jacques Rousseau would be the author of articles on music; Baron Paul Henri Holbach would contribute articles on mining and geology; Voltaire promised his collaboration and delivered a few articles. Dr. François Quesnay, the court physician, wrote on economics, his private hobby. Quesnay proved to be one of the most valuable members of

Quesnay: influential forerunner of Adam Smith

the team; his name now figures in all textbooks on the history of economics as the influential forerunner of Adam Smith.

But the *Encyclopédie* was by no means a mere repository. It was highly original in many places, and it paved the way for further development—not only in political and religious thinking but in such seemingly modest fields as veterinary science (then in its infancy and most important for a predominantly agricultural country). Almost no subject was overlooked. Articles in the form of "letters to the editor" came in as the work progressed, and they were gratefully accepted. An anonymous lady even provided highly professional information about frills and ribbons. Diderot, son of a master cutler and deeply interested in all arts and crafts, provided an article on stockings and the method of knitting them using improved machinery.

In 1751 a first volume appeared in Paris under the title *Encyclopédie, ou Dictionnaire Raisonné des Sciences, des Arts et des Métiers*. It was in folio format, printed in double columns and comprising nearly a thousand pages. The title page mentioned Diderot as the general editor and d'Alembert as responsible for the mathematical entries. The volume carried on the title page the official line of approval by the censor: "*Avec Privilège du Roi.*" Another volume—well received by the public and fiercely criticized by powerful representatives of the Church and tradition—followed shortly. Then the first battle was lost: the censor intervened, permission was withdrawn

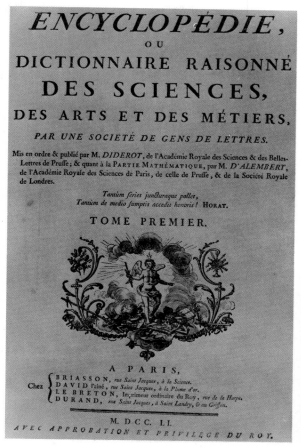

The title page of the first edition of the *Encyclopédie*, published in 1751.

Above The French dramatist Beaumarchais.

Voltaire presiding at a philosophical dinner: others present include d'Alembert, Diderot and Condorcet. The Encyclopedists were regarded by their enemies as a group of dangerous conspirators.

and the entire work was banned under order of the King.

Half a year later, however, the great work was continued, although without official permission and on sufferance, because the chief censor and director of all publications, Chrétien de Malesherbes, sympathized in secret with the undertaking. And so the next five volumes came out. The number of subscribers reached four thousand, a colossal figure for the time, especially taking into account the very high price of subscription.

In 1757 the next battle was joined—and it ended in near catastrophe for the editors. The attorney general denounced the work as dangerous and subversive from the point of view of religion as well as of politics and morals. The State Council gave the order for suppression. Worse still, some of the most important contributors deserted. D'Alembert resigned as joint editor. Jean Jacques Rousseau, who as a friend of Diderot had contributed numerous articles, attacked his former comrades-in-arms in public. The faithful band who had carried the great undertaking to such a spectacular success broke up and was scattered.

Diderot alone remained at his post and decided to continue. Many well-wishers advised him to transfer the *Encyclopédie* to some safer place, such as Berlin or

St. Petersburg, since both Frederick the Great of Prussia and Catherine the Great of Russia had taken considerable interest in the work and sympathized with its views. But Diderot stuck to Paris and his contract with the original publishers. Under his editorship, the final ten volumes of text were completed and printed in Paris. On the title page, however, Diderot's name was replaced by an anonymous "Mr.——"; an obscure firm in the possession of the King of Prussia was listed as printer.

When the final set of volumes came out, Diderot discovered that the publisher, Le Breton, had secretly employed a censor of his own who had eliminated many lines and paragraphs that seemed too dangerous. Le Breton had also taken the precaution of destroying the manuscripts and the corrected proof sheets. Diderot could do nothing but rage and curse. Nonetheless, because he wanted to see his work finished, he began editing a further set of eleven volumes containing engraved illustrations of the industrial arts. Those finely engraved plates, covering the whole field of technical development known at the time, served not only to inform the reader but also to instruct and encourage owners of factories to introduce new methods.

In 1772, after twenty-five years of almost uninterrupted effort, the *Encyclopédie* was finished. Several volumes of supplements and plates followed, and in the end the whole work comprised thirty-five large folios and filled a fairly substantial bookcase. But Diderot refused to work on the supplements or on new editions. In fact he published no more books. The great dialogues and novels of his later years were published only after his death

The fact that Diderot's *Encyclopédie* was published

The benevolent neutrality of Mme. de Pompadour

in spite of solemn public condemnation by the Church and the highest legal authorities and an official ban by the State Council was puzzling to his contemporaries, especially to the enemies of the great undertaking. One explanation for the work's successful appearance is suggested by an anecdote: One day, it was said, a discussion about powder making was going on in the salon of the Marquise de Pompadour, the King's all-powerful favorite. Since nobody knew anything of the process, some well-wisher of the *Encyclopédie* produced the appropriate volume, which had a full and highly instructive article on the topic. The text was read out and generally applauded. There was general consensus that so useful a book should not be banned but should be in the hands of anybody interested in information. The King, the indolent Louis xv, agreed, although he did not see fit to lift the official order. According to another version, the article dealt not with the making of face powder, Madame de Pompadour's sphere of interest, but with the fabrication of gunpowder, which appealed to the King, a great hunter. The story, although apocryphal, is significant: the practical usefulness of the work was certainly directly related to its success—and to the limited tolerance accorded its distribution.

The Marquise de Pompadour's actual role in protecting the publication remains rather obscure. It may be best described as "benevolent neutrality." Yet even that attitude—when held by the de facto ruler of the country—was invaluable. In one of her portraits, painted by La Tour, the Marquise saw to it that among numerous objects displayed on a table to attest to her cultural interests and gifts was a volume of the *Encyclopédie*.

Another and far more powerful influence was the fact that the battle against the *Encyclopédie* took place at the same time as the great campaign against the Jesuit order. Waged by the main Roman Catholic countries—Portugal at first, then Spain and France—it culminated in the final suppression of the Society of Jesus by the Pope. After the ban on the first two volumes of the *Encyclopédie*, there had been elements at work to seize the papers and continue the work under the supervision of the order. The chief censor, Malesherbes, prevented this intrigue by taking the papers into his personal custody and returning them after some time to Diderot. Six years later, when the *Encyclopédie*'s continuation appeared almost hopeless, the Society of Jesus suffered an equally heavy blow: all activity of the order and its members was forbidden in France. The most active adversaries of the Encyclopedists were thereby eliminated from the scene.

Enemies remained, however: churchmen, satirists, defenders of the holy rights of absolute monarchy and the traditional moral standards (although the actual morals of the time, as everybody had to admit, did not exactly conform to the time-honored precepts that were being preached). The fight continued long after the publication of the original edition and finally merged with the ferment of the French Revolution. The *Encyclopédie* has often been described as

Expérience Aérostatique faite à Versailles le 19 Septre 1783 en présence de leurs Majestés et de la famille Royale par Mr. de Montgolfier avec un Balon de 52 pieds d'hauteur sur 41 de Diamettres. Cette Superbe machine à fond d'asur avec le Chiffre du Roi pesant 900 livres. Ce balon a été enlevé avec toutes l'applaudissement de tout les Spectateurs et a tombé dans le Bois de Vaucresson

one of the dominant intellectual influences paving the way to that great event.

The Encyclopedists were widely regarded as a faithful band of brothers or suspected as a sect, or a church of their own, or a dangerous underground conspiracy. But they were by no means as united a movement as they appeared later. They had their personal squabbles, enmities and ambitions. Voltaire, as the uncrowned king of this movement, sent out exhortations and quasi-military instructions from his safe, strategically located stronghold on the border between France and Switzerland: "Form a square, gentlemen! Unity, O brethren!" However, he could not offer much more than praise for Diderot's work and diligence, although he did advise him to transfer the whole undertaking to a safer place, in Switzerland or perhaps Berlin, when the position in Paris seemed hopeless.

Yet history's view of the Encyclopedists as a movement of the greatest consequence is justified. The work came at the right time and it found the right people as collaborators. The names of the antagonists are rightly forgotten and can be found only in very detailed historical surveys of contemporary pamphlets, skits or dramatic productions of the most ephemeral kind. The Church was very poorly served; the monarchy and all traditional powers fared even worse. Half a century later, writers of caliber and standing—members of the generations that had gone through the school of the Encyclopedists—appeared in defense of traditional values. The half-century that preceded them belonged to the *Encyclopédie* and its friends.

RICHARD FRIEDENTHAL

Montgolfier's balloon: the publication of the *Encyclopédie* coincided with scientific advances in aviation and electronics.

Malesherbes, the writer and lawyer who, as Chief Censor, confiscated Diderot's papers.

While Poland is divided Frederick the

The upbringing of Frederick the Great

The French *philosophes* revered no monarch in Europe as highly as Frederick II, King of Prussia. Jean Le Rond d'Alembert, the philosopher and mathematician who contributed numerous articles to Diderot's *Encyclopédie* and edited part of it, wrote that Frederick was "a prince greater even than his fame, a hero at once *philosophe* and modest, a king worthy of friendship, in fact a true sage on the throne."

Frederick, the first son of Frederick William I, was born in

Frederick the Great under whose enlightened despotism Prussia developed into Germany's leading state.

January, 1712. The child's father was a harsh, narrow, boorish man whose eccentricities verged on insanity and whose tastes for order, regularity and the military life were reflected not only in the government of his country but in the architecture of his capital. Determined that his son should be a hardy, practical soldier, Frederick William devised a system of education for him that excluded from its curriculum all studies that he considered peripheral to that goal. And when his son displayed a keen interest in learning those very subjects that had been specifically denied him, the King looked upon the boy as an idle wastrel whose character must be molded by stronger and stronger discipline.

Frederick William's disappointment in his son soon turned to dislike—and then to positive hatred. The King did not trouble to hide his enmity, which he frequently voiced in public. He customarily referred to his offspring with contemptuous disdain—and

before the boy was twenty he had decided to run away and to seek protection at the English court. The plan was discovered, and a young friend who had been implicated in it was condemned to death. The execution took place outside Frederick's window, and Frederick William—who conceived that the experience might awaken his son's sense of responsibility—forced young Frederick to watch.

"The whole town shall be his prison," the King wrote after the execution, upon learning that his son had promised not to disobey his commands in the future. "I will give him employment from morning till night in the departments of war and agriculture and of the Government. He shall work at financial matters, receive accounts, read minutes and make extracts.... But if he kicks or rears again, he shall forfeit the succession to the crown, and even, according to circumstances, life itself."

His future thus threatened, Frederick devoted himself to his duties with so much conscientious application and such marked talent that his father's attitude toward him began to change. The young prince's interest in poetry and philosophy and his correspondence with Voltaire were not likely to arouse Frederick William I's unqualified approval, but the practical mind that Frederick brought to the business of government assured the King that he did indeed have an heir of whom he need not feel ashamed.

Frederick comes of age

For his part, Frederick recognized that his father—whom many dismissed as a violent martinet—was in fact a dutiful, economical sovereign who had done much good for his country. Indeed, Frederick William had provided Prussia with an adequate treasury, sound schools, a strictly organized system of taxation and a large and well disciplined army.

"Prussia's entire government was militarized," Frederick wrote. "The capital became the stronghold of Mars. All the industries which served the needs of armies prospered. In Berlin were established powder mills and cannon foundries, rifle factories, etc.... The military character of the Government affected both customs and fashions. Society took a military turn." After he succeeded to

Empress Maria Teresa; the Pragmatic Sanction failed to secure the succession for her.

the throne of Prussia in 1740, Frederick had good cause to thank his father for the strong army and sound finances that Frederick William had bequeathed him.

In truth, Frederick William I was not solely responsible for that legacy. Prussia had begun its climb to power in Europe in the seventeenth century under Frederick William, the Great Elector of Brandenburg and Duke of Prussia, whose efficiency in the government of his possessions was celebrated all over Europe. The Elector's son, Frederick I, obtained the Emperor's permission to adopt the title of King of Prussia, and he placed the Prussian crown on his own head in the cathedral at Königsberg in January, 1701. At that time the territories governed by the royal House of Hohenzollern were all but separate entities: Brandenburg, where Frederick's forebears had been established since 1417, lay at the center and had its capital at Berlin; to the east was Prussia, which had been won by Brandenburg in 1660; to the west, beyond

the Elbe, were the isolated duchies of Cleves, Mark and Ravensburg.

It was young King Frederick II's determination to unite and extend those hereditary possessions, and thereby to make Prussia a mighty force in European affairs. His first opportunity came within five months of his accession when, on October 20, 1740, Emperor Charles VI died without a male heir. By a document known as the Pragmatic Sanction, all the leading European powers except Bavaria had agreed to recognize the right of Charles' daughter, Maria Theresa, Queen of Hungary, to succeed him. When the time came, however, Maria Theresa's army was weak and her treasury impoverished. She was in no position to enforce the recognition of her rights if good faith were lacking and chivalry were shown to be dead.

Silesia and the Sanction

Frederick II was the first to act: in late autumn of 1740 he invaded Silesia. The Hohenzollerns' claim to Silesia was a weak one, and Frederick himself confessed that his invasion was merely "a means of acquiring reputation and of increasing the power of the state." After some initial setbacks, he was entirely successful: his armies defeated the Austrians at Mollwitz in the spring of 1741, and after further Prussian victories at Chotusitz, Hohenfriedberg, Soor, Hennersdorf and Kesseldorf, Maria Theresa was forced to concede the rich territories of Silesia—and a million German subjects—to Prussia.

Frederick, still in his early thirties, now set about the task of

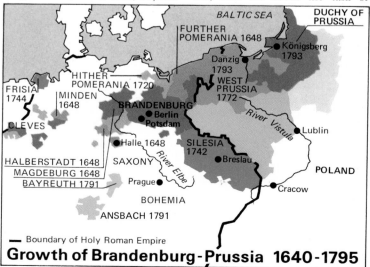

Growth of Brandenburg-Prussia 1640-1795

BALTIC SEA

DUCHY OF PRUSSIA

FURTHER POMERANIA 1648

Königsberg 1793

Danzig 1793

WEST PRUSSIA 1772

HITHER POMERANIA 1720

FRISIA 1744

MINDEN 1648

BRANDENBURG

Berlin
Potsdam

River Vistula

Lublin

CLEVES

HALBERSTADT 1648

MAGDEBURG 1648

BAYREUTH 1791

SAXONY

Halle 1648

River Elbe

SILESIA 1742

Breslau

POLAND

Prague

BOHEMIA

ANSBACH 1791

Cracow

— Boundary of Holy Roman Empire

Great's Prussia grows

building Prussia into a powerful and respected state, economically stable and militarily strong. His formidable talents in many fields earned him envy as well as admiration, while his caustic wit—which was frequently directed at the leading women of Europe, the Empress Elizabeth of Russia, Madame de Pompadour and Maria Theresa—earned him their undying detestation. "The King of Prussia," the Hanoverian King of England declared, voicing a popular opinion, "is a mischievous rascal, a bad friend, a bad ally, a bad relation, and a bad neighbor, in fact the most dangerous and ill-disposed Prince in Europe."

Because so many European rulers agreed with the English King, Maria Theresa experienced little difficulty in organizing a coalition of states to crush the Prussian upstart—a coalition that Russia, France and Saxony all willingly joined. Learning (through the treachery of a clerk in the Saxon Foreign Office) of the clandestine measures that were being taken to destroy him, Frederick attempted to forestall his enemies by advancing to the attack himself. In the summer of 1756 he marched into Saxony at the head of his army, provoking the outbreak of the Seven Years' War. In that war, Prussia found herself surrounded by enemies: France (in unnatural alliance with Austria), Russia, Saxony and Sweden. Frederick found one useful ally in England, where William Pitt—recognizing the importance of Prussia in England's challenge to France—subsidized Frederick's army and supported his one powerful ally on the Continent, the Duke of Brunswick.

Fortunes of war

The war in Europe remained Frederick's responsibility nonetheless, and the loneliness and weight of that responsibility all but overwhelmed him. There were times when it seemed that nothing could save him from crushing defeat. After victories in Saxony and Bohemia, he was driven from the field by the Austrians at Kolin, and as his enemies moved in to what seemed the certain kill, he contemplated suicide. But within weeks he and his forces had rallied, and at Rossbach, in November, 1757, he surprised and overwhelmed a French army led by the

A satire on the Treaty of Paris, 1763, which ended the Seven Years' War.

Frederick meeting the Emperor Joseph II in 1760: the two men, despite their hostility, admired each other.

Prince de Soubise. A month later Frederick's army—weak in numbers and tired out by its long campaigning—achieved an equally stunning victory over the Austrians at Leuthen.

Leaving Ferdinand of Brunswick to keep the French occupied in the west, Frederick then turned upon the Russians, whom he defeated at Zorndorf. He was less fortunate

against the Austrians at Hochkirch, and he fared so badly against the combined armies of the Russians and Austrians at Kunersdorf in August, 1759, that he became as gloomy and disheartened as he had been two years before. "All is lost," he reported to Berlin. "The consequences of this battle will be worse than the battle itself. I shall not survive the ruin of the Fatherland. Adieu for ever."

The crestfallen monarch soon recovered his spirits, however, and at Liegnitz and then at Torgau he reversed the tide of his fortunes. Nonetheless, by the end of 1761 it once more seemed that Frederick's cause was doomed. His countryside had been ravaged by Russian troops, towns had been occupied and all but destroyed, his army had suffered terrible losses, and he himself was worn out by the long and tragic war. His enemies watched eagerly for his final collapse—only to see him saved by the death of the Russian Empress Elizabeth. Elizabeth was succeeded by Peter III, who was one of Frederick's most zealous admirers, and the Russians withdrew. With the loss of Russia's support, with the Turks threatening her borders in the southeast, and with Frederick's final victory over her army at Freiberg, Maria Theresa was forced to agree to the Treaty of Hubertusburg in February, 1763. The Treaty of Paris had been signed a few days before; the war was over.

The year before that war began, a disastrous event had occurred in Europe—an event that seemed even more terrible than war itself, and one that brought an age of optimism suddenly to an end. That age, reflected so complacently in Alexander Pope's 1733 *Essay on Man* and based so contentedly on what Voltaire called the *tout est bien* philosophy, ended in November, 1755, when a shattering earthquake destroyed one of the oldest and richest cities in Europe.

Alexander Pope, poet of the age of optimism.

1755 Disaster Strikes Lisbon

November 1, 1775 was All Saints' Day in Lisbon, Portugal's bustling capital city and principal port. Thousands of Lisbon's faithful jammed the city's numerous churches to celebrate the Holy Day—and thousands of them died in their pews shortly before ten in the morning as a series of earth tremors sundered the city. Cathedral vaults collapsed, church walls cracked and buckled inward, and fires—many lit by holy candles—swept the city. As few as 10,000—or as many as 40,000—persons died in the holocaust that followed, and as Lisbon's dazed citizens began the task of rebuilding their devastated city, scientists and seers alike attempted to explain the disaster. The former could offer no answer; the latter were certain that the quake was Divine Retribution for Portugal's collective sins. Both groups recognized that the earthquake had irrevocably shattered an age of optimism.

The Marquis of Pombal who, after the earthquake had wrecked the city, took command of the situation and headed the commission that rebuilt Lisbon.

Opposite The Church of Carno which was damaged in the earthquake and remains today as it appeared in 1755.

After the event there was talk of signs and omens, of crossed swords appearing in the sky and prophesies, but on that momentous November 1, 1755—a religious holiday—the weather was perfect and an unusual stillness in the air and a certain nervousness among the animals passed almost unnoticed. No one was worried about such things on that glorious morning of All Saint's Day, a day filled with the sounds of ringing church bells, the hurrying of the faithful to the churches and the lively bustle of the town and port of Lisbon.

King Joseph and the court had gone to Belém to attend Mass at the monastery of the Jeronimos, and certain wealthy middle-class families had their own chaplain say Mass for them in their private chapels. The majority, however, preferred to go to the Carmo or the San Roque, where they sang the long Masses. All the churches were packed to overflowing.

Suddenly, just a few minutes before ten o'clock, while the Service of the Holy Ghost was being celebrated, there were three violent shocks, one after another, accompanied by a terrifying uproar. All over the city the ground was splitting apart, walls were cracking and vaults were collapsing. A blinding curtain of dust clouded the sky and tongues of fire began to curl upward from the first fires; wax candles overturned on the altars and set fire to the hangings and the gilded woodwork, and stoves vomited forth their burning embers. A strong wind arose, blowing the smoke in all directions and fanning the flames.

Those who had not been buried under the ruins or swallowed up by the crevices in the ground rushed toward the river Tagus, hoping to escape from the scene of the disaster in one of the many boats moored in the estuary. To their horror, they saw that the waters of the Tagus were rapidly receding and that the boats were breaking up, their hulls crashing into one another and becoming stuck in the oozing mud. Then, just as abruptly, the waters began to rise again and came rolling onto the banks in a rushing tidal wave that carried corpses and debris alike as far as the center of the Lower Town.

Thus, within the space of a few minutes, the four elements had joined together: the earth splitting open like an overripe fruit, the wind swirling violently through the air, fire springing up in a thousand places at the same time and the waters angrily barring the way on all sides.

It was a merciless disaster, and terror reigned supreme. No one ever established the exact number of victims, although a total of 100,000 was first suggested. The figure was later reduced to 40,000, and that too was probably an overestimation. But even if one accepts the lowest estimate, of around 10,000 victims, the Lisbon disaster was still a great tragedy.

The 1755 earthquake affected all of Europe. Its tremors had shaken the whole of the Iberian Peninsula and had reached as far as Scandinavia, affecting the springs there. More important, however, was the fact that it had destroyed a city that served as a center for European trade. It seemed that Lisbon had been especially chosen—or cursed—by God, who had used the quake to reveal His wrath toward the whole of Christianity. Such a belief was enough to provoke the less fearful into a serious examination of conscience, while the more credulous were plunged into a state of total religious hysteria. Everyone was afraid, confessed his sins and did penitence. King Louis xv of France went so far as to promise his confessor that he would break off relations with the Marquise de Pompadour; she, in turn, vowed she would give up the wearing of rouge as an atonement.

King Joseph, his family and his court—as well as the monastery and tower of Belém—had escaped the catastrophe. The pathetic King, who was concerned only for his own personal safety and the salvation of his immortal soul, abandoned the task "of burying the dead and taking care of the living" to the man who already wielded the real power behind the throne: his minister, Sebastião José de Carvalho, who was to become famous in the annals of history as the Marques de Pombal.

In 1755, Lisbon was the prosperous capital of a poverty-stricken country. Travelers who came there

4/118

A city stultified by wealth

were dazzled at the sight of so many palaces and by the treasures they contained: the rarest of goldware, silks and porcelain, paintings by Rubens and Titian and precious books. (Seventy thousand volumes and many priceless documents were destroyed when the royal palace was burned.)

The churches of the city were even more ostentatious, with their giant organs, their gilt woodwork, their panels of *azulejos* (glazed tiles) and their ciboriums and tabernacles of massive silver encrusted with precious stones.

By 1755 the huge Portuguese Empire had begun to disintegrate. Joseph's predecessor, John v, the last great king of Portugal, had squandered all the gold that he obtained from Brazil by building churches, clothing his prelates in purple and decking out religious ceremonies with pagan ostentation.

Lisbon suffocated under the weight of this inert wealth. The whole country was paralyzed by the King's narrow, pious attitude and by his total indifference to his subjects' interests. Thus paralyzed, Portugal fell without a struggle into the hands of its powerful ally, Great Britain, and was devoured alive. Indeed, the turn-of-the-century Treaty of Methuen, which laid down the terms for trading between the two countries (roughly speaking, Portuguese wines in return for British wool), was such that every Englishman who came to Portugal enjoyed a king's privileges.

A sudden shock, a violent emotion, can sometimes cure a paralyzed person. Pombal had a presentiment that the earthquake might serve as such a shock, reviving the energies of the Portuguese people and rousing the country from its state of hopeless apathy.

In attempting to restore order in Lisbon, Pombal was faced with many urgent and acute problems, all of which had to be dealt with immediately. One section of the city had been completely destroyed. The remainder was tottering on the verge of collapse, endangered by the earth tremors that followed one after another for many months, unpredictable in their timing and their volume. In spite of the rain, the discomfort and the bands of looters, the inhabitants of Lisbon who had not already fled into the country preferred to camp outside, to sleep in the open air under the stars or under any temporary form of shelter that came their way, rather than stay in the city.

With remarkable coolness and clarity of vision, Pombal immediately took the necessary steps to deal with the emergency. The dead were buried or unceremoniously thrown into the river, panic was allayed, famine averted and looters were severely and publicly punished. The complaints of the English merchants, who had lost their stocks as well as money owed to them, were coldly received. They were told that nothing prevented them from returning home to England; none of them did so, however. The situation soon improved, for Pombal had a very clear idea of both the difficulties and the resources of Portugal.

Pombal decided to rebuild the city on exactly the same site that it had occupied ever since its foundation (which, according to legend, dated back to Ulysses). Two months after the catastrophe, the plans for this new city of Lisbon had already been drafted, revealing a boldness of conception, a practical genius and a clear vision of the future.

Pombal made no attempt to reconstitute Lisbon

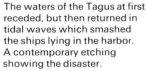

The waters of the Tagus at first receded, but then returned in tidal waves which smashed the ships lying in the harbor. A contemporary etching showing the disaster.

LISABONA

in its former medieval style, with one section of the city clustered around the port and the rest scattered between the convents and the properties of the nobles. On the contrary, he commissioned a plan for a modern city with wide, well-drained streets laid out at right angles to each other. The façades of the buildings were uniform but dignified in style. They were constructed out of prefabricated sections for the first time in the history of town planning, and they were enhanced by beautiful wrought-iron lanterns and balconies and by the harmonious lines of their mansards and roofs.

Pombal's new Lisbon was dedicated to trade—of vital importance in his plans for the future prosperity of the country—as well as to industry, the growth of which he tried to stimulate. Such a policy soon met with the strong disapproval of the nobility—who considered Pombal an upstart—and of the Church. How could Pombal concern himself with such mundane preoccupations at a time when Divine Wrath had struck down Lisbon as a warning to others? The only thing that mattered was to obtain God's mercy by repentance and resignation. Pombal's detractors wanted more public confessions, processions of penitents, mortifications of the flesh and hymns of praise to ward off even greater evils. They were all agreed that they had deserved to be punished, but at the same time they were quick to point out the guilt in others. Thus the priests were accused of simony, the nobles of corruption, the middle classes of religious apathy and avarice, and the masses of lubricity. Fanatics, acting as Jeremiahs, predicted new catastrophes and cast curses on Lisbon, which they believed should remain a city in ruins like Sodom and Gomorrah.

Pombal had the utmost difficulty in persuading people that the disaster had been caused by a natural phenomenon. His difficulties were aggravated by the fact that science—which for some years had been accepted throughout Europe as the source of all truth—found it almost impossible to provide an explanation for this phenomenon. Famous scientists suggested that the quake might have been caused by the influence of the moon, or by fire and water that had become overheated in the center of the earth or by the little known force called electricity. None of the explanations was satisfactory. People preferred to listen to the oracles and to sermons.

In defiance of Pombal's orders, the Jesuit Malagrida wrote and distributed his *Judgment on the True Causes of the Earthquake*. According to Malagrida, Lisbon—the sixteenth-century center of operations for the Jesuits—had been punished for having sought to deprive the Jesuits of the Maranhão, an area of land claimed by both Brazil and Paraguay. Malagrida was a religious visionary who had great powers of fascination. He was considered a prophet, and he might have reduced Lisbon to a state of superstitious terror had he not been banished to the port city of Setubal. He was soon surrounded by a nucleus of loyal supporters, including some of the most illustrious families of the kingdom, who hatched a plot to kill King Joseph and thereby rid themselves

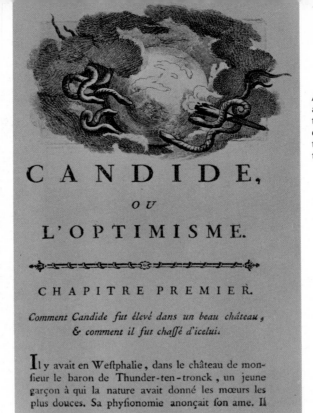

An early edition of Voltaire's allegory *Candide*. Writing twenty-three years after the earthquake, Voltaire still felt the event important enough to describe in great detail.

The city of Lisbon was almost totally destroyed. This picture shows how even the strongest buildings had crashed to the ground after the series of tremors.

of his first minister. The plot was discovered, however, and Pombal took advantage of the opportunity to bring all his enemies, aristocrats and Jesuits alike, to trial at the same time. The prisons were filled with them for the next twenty years; the Inquisition condemned Malagrida to be garroted and burned at the stake and many of the most illustrious heads in Portugal rolled beneath the executioner's blade.

Pombal's hands were red with the blood of his enemies, but at last he was free to do what he wanted: set up a government of technocrats. He founded the *Compagnie Royale* in order to wrest control over the vineyards that produced Port wine from the English. Moreover, he sent to France, Italy and Germany for specialist craftsmen to start up or revive such local industries as ceramics, silk, cutlery and smelting

The royal palace at Lisbon.

The statue of King Joseph, a timid and ineffectual ruler who fled in terror during the earthquake.

works. He was a great believer in technical progress, in individual effort and in hard work, and he overcame all obstacles impeding his plans. The Society of Jesus had become progressively weaker and lacking in authority and finally was driven out of the country altogether. An ambitious, active and dedicated middle class did its best to carry out the great aims of Pombal. Before he fell into disgrace, Pombal saw Lisbon rise once again out of the ruins and saw the statue of his master erected in one of the most beautiful squares in the world, a plaza dedicated to commerce. But Pombal was to die a slandered, ruined man, and with his death all the fragile structure of his work collapsed. For the next 150 years, Portugal sank into oblivion, disorder and decadence.

The deadly earth tremors that had destroyed Lisbon had shaken the world. It was not only buildings that had collapsed, but also beliefs; the cracks carved out abysses not only in the ground, but also in the minds of the most well-balanced men.

It was true that this misfortune, befalling a country that could count on few friends at the time, was viewed very severely by many people. The Protestants saw in the earthquake a just retribution for popish idolatry; the Jansenists were overjoyed that the "cradle of the Jesuits" was destroyed; others believed that the crimes committed by the Inquisition had been expiated in this way.

Even compassion tended to be condescending. Emergency aid was generous to begin with, but soon people grew irritated with Pombal's claim that his country was capable of recovering by its own efforts and would soon take its place again alongside the other European nations. The scientists felt resentful toward Portugal because they had been asked to find an explanation for a phenomenon that was beyond their comprehension.

The philosophers, too, were troubled. The Lisbon disaster was a deadly denial of the complacent optimism that had reigned during a century when science served merely as a diversion for the government, and when religion was a pleasant way of making sure of a place in the next world. After all, the finest minds of the time had established, mathematically, that everything was "for the best in the best of all possible worlds." God had been proven infallible as well as just and good.

Why then had God struck down so pitilessly the innocent at the same time as the guilty? Where was His justice, His goodness? If, on the other hand, He had not wanted such a catastrophe to happen—if the phenomenon had been fortuitous—how could He be the Almighty, the wisest of all? What about the perfection of His creation?

People were reluctant to accept the doctrine of collective responsibility that so carelessly sacrificed innocence in its cause. Their belief in God was shaken. They began seriously to question Divine Providence. Man became bitterly aware of his own insignificance, of the precariousness of his existence. Prayer no longer sufficed to reassure him.

Just after the event Voltaire wrote a passionate poem that is one long cry of despair, pity and revolt. Rousseau, although he did not go quite so far, declared that man, and man alone, was responsible for his own misfortunes. If he had lived as a "noble savage" in the midst of nature, instead of crowding together in the cities for sordid motives of profit, there would never have been so many lives sacrificed. Goethe, then a child, was terrified at the thought of the blind wrath of Almighty God that struck indiscriminately at both the good and the wicked. If God were not just, if there were no mercy in Heaven, if, as Voltaire had cried so passionately, "evil is in this world," then there was no longer any joy in living.

Thus, a complete way of life, of thought, of hoping had disappeared, to be replaced by a new approach to existence. Menaced by the hostility of a cruel world, man had to accept the responsibility for his own actions. Pombal had shown him how he could conquer his fear, and tackle with courage the task of rebuilding a city to make it more beautiful and prosperous than the one that had been so cruelly reduced to ashes.

A Portuguese poet advised people to "stay at home in their villages and tend their sheep"—in

Pombal's reconstruction of the capital

other words, to concentrate on making the most of their own resources without depending on others or interfering in their affairs. This philosophy still prevails in Portugal today. Man must fend for himself without expecting God's help; the existence of Heaven is doubtful.

While all these ideas were merging and blending one with another, the old established order was gradually falling apart. Like the decrepit, worm-eaten old palaces and gilded churches of Lisbon, the world was crumbling down to its very foundations. New currents of thought emerged as a result of the traumatic shock that had swept across the whole of Europe: Choiseul expelled the Jesuits from France, the Pope dissolved the Society of Jesus, and the education of young noblemen—which up to that time had been in the hands of the Jesuits—henceforth changed direction. Daring new ideas, no longer contradicted or forbidden, began to circulate.

The Lisbon disaster, by causing man to doubt the wisdom of Divine Providence, marked the end of an era, an era dominated by faith and respect for the established authorities: the head of a family, the king and God. The senseless cruelty of the disaster had not only aroused compassion, Christian solidarity and simple human love, it had also led to objective, nonmaterialistic speculation and to a disdain for individual life, which, although still precious and unique, was subordinate to larger goals. This concept was to lead directly to the conclusion that "the end justifies the means." Without a Divine Justice to separate good from evil, man was responsible for his own actions and had a perfect right to sacrifice the liberty or dignity of others in order to achieve his aims.

The reactions and shock provoked by the Lisbon earthquake in the eighteenth century can perhaps be compared to everything that man experiences in face of the horrifying reality of modern warfare: his confusion in face of the annihilation of the individual, the iciness weighing down his spirit, the despair that finds no relief in understanding. Today, as then, man's anguish is perfectly expressed in Voltaire's lines:

What am I, where am I, where am I going to and from
                                        where did I come,
A thinking atom, an atom whose eyes,
Guided by thought, have scanned the heavens?

SUZANNE CHANTAL

The Inquisition in session. For twenty years after a plot to murder Pombal was discovered the Inquisition executed the most able men in Portugal, and thus helped establish Pombal's position.

A picture painted at the time of the earthquake showing the dead and wounded inhabitants of Lisbon lying in the streets while fires rage throughout the city.

England's East India Company—a new force

For months after the Lisbon earthquake the theory that Lisbon had been destroyed by God's anger was propounded in countless tracts, sermons and moralizing poems. Such pamphleteering was particularly rife in France, where the Chevalier Joseph Cuers de Cogelin wrote that he recognized God's terrible hand in the city's destruction. According to the Chevalier, Lisbon had simply been too proud, too rich. Several French writers contended that France, like Portugal, had grown too proud and too rich, and that some terrible calamity would soon befall her. Among those prophets were some who saw the will of a jealous God reflected in the course of events in India.

In that country, the dissolution

Robert Clive, who became Governor of Bengal and Commander-in-Chief of the East India Company's Army in India.

of the Mogul Empire had provided opportunities for both France and England to extend their influence and power. The trade of the English East India Company, which had bases at Calcutta and Madras, eventually grew to be considerably greater in bulk than that of the French (whose bases at Chandernagore and Pondicherry were less advantageously placed), but in the earlier rounds of the struggle it was the French who were more successful. The talents of the French sailor Mahé de Labourdonnais and those of the brilliant governor of the French East India Company, Joseph François Dupleix, contrasted sharply with the meager talents of Nicholas Morse, the English governor of Madras who surrendered his town to the French in 1746 after a few days' half-hearted resistance. In the summer of 1748, the British attemp-

ted to recoup their losses by launching an abortive siege operation at Pondicherry, only to be obliged to withdraw.

By the Treaty of Aix-la-Chapelle, Madras was given back to the British in exchange for Cape Breton —but French prestige was greatly enhanced by her conduct of the war and French garrisons were greatly strengthened against the time of its continuance. After 1748, however, the French grip on India began to loosen. Dupleix extended French influence in southern India by manipulating numerous Indian alliances, and he set up puppet governments in the Carnatic, in the Deccan and in Hyderabad. But by 1754 he had overreached himself and all but exhausted his finances. Dupleix was recalled to France—and as he departed, another figure of remarkable talents appeared on the Indian scene. This man was Robert Clive, the eldest son of a Shropshire gentleman of modest means.

Clive had migrated to Madras at the age of eighteen to become a writer in the East India Company, and he was there—homesick and miserable—when the town was captured by Labourdonnais in 1746. He entered the army a short time later and greatly distinguished himself during the siege of Arcot (where rival claimants, supported respectively by France and Britain, were contesting for the position of Nawab). By 1756 Clive had become governor of Fort St. David and a lieutenant-colonel in the British army. He took up his post as governor on the day that the young Nawab of Bengal, Suraj-ud-Dowlah, captured Calcutta.

Like his predecessors, Suraj-ud-Dowlah had originally been on

Suraj-ud-Dowlah, Nawab of Bengal, who captured Calcutta from the East India Company.

friendly terms with the British East India Company. But when the British governor refused to remand a rich fugitive who had fled to Calcutta to escape the new Nawab's extortionate demands, Suraj-ud-Dowlah had advanced on Calcutta with an army of 40,000.

The town's defenses had been much neglected during those peaceful years, and the garrison numbered only 250 men. At the approach of the Nawab, both the governor and the military commander of Calcutta fled to the safety of the British ships anchored in the river, and the garrison was left to its fate. It surrendered on June 20 and that night—a night of stifling heat—146 prisoners were locked up in the small punishment cell of the fortress, the Black Hole of Calcutta. All but twenty-three of them died before dawn.

Clive at Calcutta

Although war with France was considered imminent, it was decided that the British forces in the area must concentrate on the immediate recapture of Calcutta. Supported by Rear-Admiral Charles Watson and five men-of-war, Clive set out from Madras with 900 European troops and 1,500 native troops. On February 4, 1757, he overwhelmed the massed ranks of the Nawab's immense army. A treaty was soon concluded, and Suraj-ud-Dowlah was forced to restore all the territory that he had taken from the British.

The long-anticipated clash finally erupted, and Clive was urged to return to Madras. He refused the summons, however, believing it was more important to capture Chandernagore, the base of the French East India Company in Bengal. He succeeded in achieving his objective only after the gallant French defenders of that city had been driven into submission by Admiral Watson's determined onslaught from the river.

Suraj-ud-Dowlah, who was known to be supporting the French, had actively sought to renew his attack on the English while they were engaged at Chandernagore, and a conspiracy was therefore arranged to replace the Nawab with Mír Jafar, a noble who was more acceptable both to the English and to his own people. While the conspirators were plotting his dethronement, Suraj-ud-Dowlah took the field with over 50,000 fighting men and more than 50 pieces of

heavy ordnance served by French artillerymen. Clive moved out of Chandernagore to meet the renegade with just over a thousand Europeans, two thousand native troops and nine field pieces. The two armies met amid the mango groves of Plassey, a few miles out-

A coin commemorating the Battle of Plassey.

side Murshidabad. Clive hesitated to move against so large an army with so small a force—but after initially voting against an immediate attack, he changed his mind. On June 23, 1757, he defeated the Nawab in one of the most fateful battles of the modern world. Suraj-ud-Dowlah fled from the field on a camel, Mír Jafar was installed as a puppet ruler in his place, and the British were masters of Bengal.

The Dutch, appalled by the sudden triumph of their rivals, responded by dispatching several armed vessels to the Ganges. When these Dutch warships seized some English merchant ships, Clive's response was immediate and determined: seven Dutch ships were

Count de Lally on the ramparts of Pondicherry.

Tortures inflicted by the Dutch on English East India Company employees.

captured and the Dutch army was defeated by one of Clive's best officers, Francis Forde. The Dutch were allowed to retain their settlement in Bengal, but the terms upon which they did so removed the threat of Dutch competition on the subcontinent.

The War in the South

The British were equally successful in southern India, where the French general Count de Lally, the son of an Irish Jacobite, vainly endeavored to prosecute an aggressive war against the British settlements with insufficient money and supplies. In December, 1758, Lally advanced against Madras, which was ably defended by Major-General Stringer Lawrence and Lord Pigot, the city's governor. Lally and his unpaid, ill-supplied and mutinous troops were forced to withdraw. A well-equipped army led by Colonel Eyre Coote defeated Lally at Wandiwash in January, 1760, and Coote went on systematically to attack the French forts in the Carnatic. By September Lally had been forced back to Pondicherry. The arrival of a British fleet ended his beleaguered force's hope of resupply, and in January, 1761, he was obliged to surrender. His surrender marked the end of French dominion in India.

Clive, who had left India the year before at the age of thirty-five, had established the base of British power. In the process, he had become an extremely rich man. He was not home long enough to enjoy the pleasures that his fortune could buy, however: in May, 1765, he returned to India as Governor of Bengal and commander-in-chief of the Army.

Corruption in the company

In Clive's absence Bengal had been notoriously governed by a succession of administrators. (Clive's own behavior had unfortunately set the precedent for such conduct.) Mír Jafar had been deposed in favor of his son-in-law Mír Kasim, from whom the Bengal Council accepted £200,000 worth of gratuities. Indeed, the whole of the English East India Company had become corrupted by the commissions and gifts its servants had grown accustomed to expect. It was to be Clive's duty to carry out extensive reforms, and he did so with a dispatch that was widely resented by those who felt that Clive himself was largely responsible for the tradition that money should be extracted from the natives through fear of Britain.

Clive raised the Company's salaries so that its employees had less reason to accept bribes; he forbade the acceptance of gifts and the participation of the Company's employees in private trade; and he reformed the army. Above all, he secured from the Emperor of Delhi —whose forces had recently been defeated by Major Hector Munro at Buxar—a document that granted the Company the provinces of Bengal, Behar and Orissa. Clive thus became the virtual ruler of 30 million people and the recipient of nearly 4 million pounds a year.

Clive left India for the last time in 1767, and on November 22, 1774, he killed himself in one of the fits of depression to which he had always been subject. Clive's work was continued by Warren Hastings, who became Governor of Bengal in 1772 and Governor-General of India in 1773. Hastings reformed the government of Bengal; supported the Nawab of Oudh against the Rohillas, who led plundering raids against his northern frontiers; and saved British India when a renewal of the French war in 1778 led to its being threatened by a coalition of Indian princes supported by France. By the time Hastings arrived back in England in 1785 (to face charges of impeachment for his supposedly ruthless conduct as Governor-General), he had succeeded in extending the East India Company's influence over even larger areas of India.

In 1784 Parliament passed William Pitt's India Act, which transferred the control of much of the Company's power to the British

Warren Hastings, Governor-General of India.

government. Responsibility for Indian affairs was given to a board of six Privy Councillors appointed by the King.

India was but part of a huge and growing English empire. Lally's 1761 surrender at Pondicherry—which marked the end of French dominion in India—was soon followed by other French territorial losses. The French and Indian War (1756–1763) had not gone well for France. In 1745 and again in 1746 the brilliant generalship of Maurice de Saxe had resulted in French victories (at Fontenoy and Lauffeld), and in the French and Indian War she had enjoyed several initial successes. But in 1759 her Mediterranean fleet had been severely damaged at Lagos and her Atlantic fleet all but destroyed in Quiberon Bay. And on the Plains of Abraham outside Quebec, her noble general, Montcalm, had been killed by a shot from a British gun. Quebec had been taken and North America lost. By the Treaty of Paris she was forced to recognize England's right to most of her former empire.

France was not the only country to be affected by England's burgeoning imperial designs. In 1768 an expedition set sail for the South Pacific that was to add a whole new continent to the Empire.

European Powers in India 1755-71

OUDH
✗ Buxar 1764
MURSHIDABAD   BENGAL
Plassey 1757
Chandernagore ●✗
Calcutta Capital of British India
MAHRATTAS
Bombay ●
NORTHERN CIRCARS
THE NIZAM
Hyderabad ●
GOA (Portuguese)
MYSORE
CARNATIC
Madras Wandiwash 1760
✗
Pondicherry Capital of French India
CEYLON
○ Dutch territory
○ British territory
● French territory
Colombo ●

"Terra Incognita"

Captain James Cook was only one of dozens of eighteenth-century Englishmen who firmly believed that an undiscovered continent lay somewhere in the South Pacific. Cook was convinced that the "Great South Land" had to exist—to balance the known land masses in the northern hemisphere and thereby preserve the earth's orbital stability. Dutch and Portuguese navigators had purportedly touched the shores of Terra Australis Incognita *in the preceding century, but the continent remained virtually unexplored when Cook sailed south from Tahiti in 1769. On April 19, 1770, a crewman aboard Cook's ship, the* Endeavour, *sighted a low promontory on Australia's southeast coast—and before returning to England, Cook investigated and mapped most of the new continent's eastern and northern coastlines. The captain's journals aroused considerable interest at home and led, less than half a century later, to England's annexation of the entire continent.*

It was originally a matter of stargazing that led James Cook to the shores of Australia. A rare occurrence called the "transit of Venus" was to take place in 1769. (During a transit, Venus passes directly between the earth and the sun and appears projected on the sun's disk as a small black dot. Important deductions—such as the scale of the solar system and the distance of the earth from the sun—can be made from its passage.) Astronomers' charts recorded only two previous transits, the first of which had occurred in 1639. The next had taken place in 1761, but observation of the 1761 phenomenon had been unsuccessful and it was therefore of particular importance that the 1769 event be properly charted.

The Royal Society, which was devoted to the cause of natural enlightenment, took a lively interest in the coming transit and petitioned King George III not to neglect the chance of furthering the fame of British astronomy, "a science," the members pointed out, "on which navigation so much depends." Several European nations, among them Russia, wanted to establish points of observation, and England, the Society argued, should certainly do the same. The Royal Society was considered the world's most distinguished scientific body, and its petition carried weight with the King, who was particularly interested in science and exploration.

Because it was essential that the observers follow the transit from a point south of the equinoctial line, the recently discovered island of Tahiti was suggested as a suitable place. The idea of sending an expedition to the Pacific appealed to the King. He promptly gave the project his approval, and the Royal Society approached the Admiralty for a ship and a competent man to sail it. James Cook, a forty-year-old British naval officer who had already surveyed the coasts of Newfoundland and Labrador, was chosen to command the H.M.S. *Endeavour*.

In 1768 the expedition set out. Sailing with Cook were Joseph Banks, a young naturalist of twenty-five with an independent fortune who was later knighted

by the King; Charles Green, an astronomer; Doctor Daniel Charles Solander, a Swede who had been Linnaeus' favorite pupil; and two artists, twenty-five-year-old Sydney Parkinson and Herman Dierich Spöring, another Swede who joined the ship at Capetown and seems to have acted as Banks' secretary. In his journal Cook always referred to Banks and members of his party simply as "the gentlemen."

The transit of Venus was successfully observed from Tahiti, but it proved to be a task of secondary importance to the expedition, for Cook had been given secret instructions by the Admiralty. After exploring Tahiti and the neighboring islands, he was to search for the Great South Land that was supposed to exist in the South Pacific. Known as the *Terra Australis Incognita*, it was a shadowy area sketched in around the South Pole on many old charts.

Geographers had been struck by the fact that, unlike the northern hemisphere, the southern Pacific had no large land masses. Having accepted the spherical nature of the earth, they came to the conclusion that in order for the earth to keep its stability, the amount of solid land in the two hemispheres must balance. Hence there must be a great unknown continent in the southern part of the Pacific. Dutch mariner Abel Tasman was supposed to have touched it when he sailed along the western shores of New Zealand, and many believed that Portuguese navigator Pedro Fernandes de Queiros had seen yet another part of it when he landed on Espiritu Santo in the New Hebrides in 1606—but no one was quite certain. Beyond these tentative probes, nothing definite was known about the mysterious continent.

Cook and Banks between them had an extensive geographical library on board, and among the books was Charles de Brosses' useful *Histoire des Navigations aux Terres Australes*, published in Paris in 1756. In his work de Brosses explained, "I call Austral lands all that is beyond the three southern points of our known world in Africa, Asia and America." Accompanying

An engraving of a kangaroo from Banks' *New System of Geography*. Kangaroos were first sighted on Cook's first expedition on the coast of Australia.

Opposite A Wedgewood cameo portrait of Captain Cook made in 1784.

Attacked by natives

The *Endeavour*, after narrowly escaping shipwreck, is laid up on the banks of the Endeavour River in New South Wales.

the text were maps by the celebrated French cartographer Robert de Vaugondy.

In one of his maps, Vaugondy marked out Tasman's discoveries: the southern part of Van Diemen's Land (now Tasmania) and the western coast of New Zealand's North Island. The imaginary eastern coast of New Holland (the early name for Australia) was shown by vague hatchings and was joined to the discoveries of de Queiros, which were displaced westward. Van Diemen's Land was also shown connected to the mainland.

These, then, were the geographical uncertainties that faced the crew of the *Endeavour* as the ship left Tahiti. Cook sailed from the Society Islands in August, and by the end of March of the following year, 1770, he had already charted New Zealand and had circumnavigated its two islands, thus disproving any continental connection. By April 1 he had turned northwest toward Tasmania, but strong southerly gales drove the *Endeavour* north, so that the English arrived at the southeast corner of Australia

itself. Had the weather been fair, Cook would almost certainly have discovered Bass Strait, which separates Australia from Tasmania.

On Wednesday, April 18, certain birds were spotted—a sure sign, Cook noted, of the nearness of land. The following day Lieutenant Hicks sighted a low hill and Cook named the point after him. (Few modern maps bear Hicks' name; the British ship's landfall is known today as Cape Everard.) Sailing northward, the *Endeavour* hugged the shore, looking for a safe anchorage. The calm, noble landscape that they saw had a certain haggard beauty of its own— green and wooded, but with a shore of white sand. Dark figures could be distinguished against the glare. Smoke curled up through the dusty green hanging foliage of the eucalyptus, only to be lost against a pale sky. At night fires pricked the flat shoreland.

Cook, Banks, Solander and Tupaia, a Tahitian chief whom Banks had persuaded to join the expedition, tried to land in a yawl but were prevented from doing so by the heavy surf. Banks noted the parklike aspect of the land, the trees separate from each other "without the least underwood." Passing within a quarter of a mile of the shore, he was surprised at the total lack of interest that their presence had aroused in the natives; they did not seem to notice the passing of the yawl, although an old woman who was gathering sticks and was followed by three children "often looked at the ship but expressed neither surprise nor concern." On Sunday, April 29, the *Endeavour* stood into Botany Bay and anchored off the south shore. Midshipman Isaac Smith, Mrs. Cook's cousin (and later an Admiral of the British Fleet), was the first to land. Young Isaac, eighteen at the time, later recalled how Cook, on the point of stepping ashore, said, "Isaac, you shall land first." Cook was forced to fire a musket loaded with small shot between two natives when a party of them threatened the explorers with spears.

Cook originally called their anchorage Sting Ray Harbor, "occasioned by the great quantity of these sort of fish found in this place." Banks' and Solander's prodigious haul of new plants later provoked him to change the name to Botany Bay. The plants were kept fresh in tin chests, wrapped in wet cloths, while Parkinson and Spöring drew them. (Parkinson worked with such alacrity that he averaged seven meticulous drawings a day.) Banks, who preserved his specimens by spreading them out on sails to dry in the sun, wrote that the aborigines "seemed never to be able to muster above fourteen or fifteen fighting men." He seemed undecided about their actual color—"they were so completely covered with dirt, that seemed to have stuck to their bodies from the day of their birth"—and on one occasion he spat on his fingers and tried to rub it off. His actions altered the color very little, and he judged their skin to be chocolate-colored.

The *Endeavour* remained at Botany Bay just over a week. On May 7 Cook resumed his voyage. A few miles north he passed present-day Sydney Harbor, which he named Port Jackson in honor of one of the

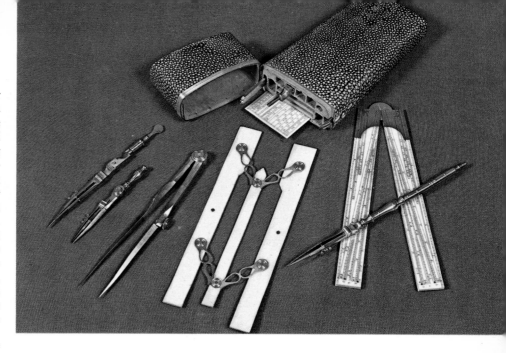

Above Navigational instruments used by Cook on his voyages.

A model of the *Endeavour*, the ship in which Cook made his first expedition in 1768–70.

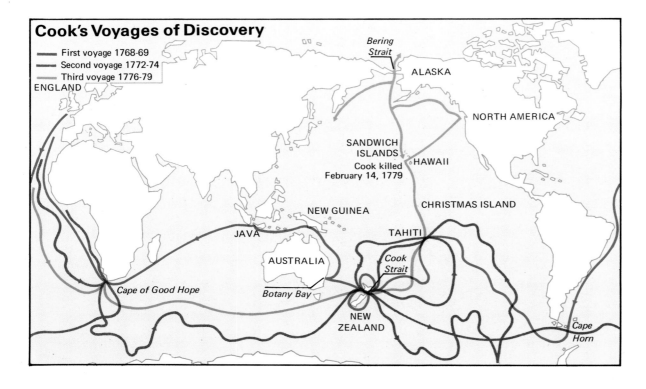

Cook's Voyages of Discovery

First voyage 1768-69
Second voyage 1772-74
Third voyage 1776-79

ENGLAND
Bering Strait
ALASKA
NORTH AMERICA
SANDWICH ISLANDS
Cook killed February 14, 1779
HAWAII
CHRISTMAS ISLAND
NEW GUINEA
JAVA
TAHITI
AUSTRALIA
Cook Strait
Cape of Good Hope
Botany Bay
NEW ZEALAND
Cape Horn

Colonizing Botany Bay

secretaries of the Admiralty. Cook slowly worked his way north, charting the coast. He frequently landed, and he never sailed very far without sending boats ahead to cast shoreward and seaward and take bearings.

As they neared the northern end of the island continent, the voyage nearly came to an abrupt end when the ship grounded on a coral reef twenty miles from land. Cook's seamanship was, however, equal to the occasion: the *Endeavour* was freed and, much damaged and leaking severely, was guided up the estuary of a small nearby river, where she was banked and careened. There the men saw their first kangaroo, which Cook described as "an animal something less than a greyhound, of a mouse color, very slender made and swift of foot." During Cook's stay, natives came to the camp, but they always left their women on the opposite bank of the river. Banks, busy with his glasses, commented on their nudity, noting that they "did not copy our Mother Eve even in the fig-leaf."

Although repairs on the ship finally were finished, a strong wind further delayed Cook's departure. Eventually he managed to creep out and slowly threaded his way through the tortuous mazes of the Great Barrier Reef. Inch by inch the group advanced to the northern point of Australia, which Cook named Cape York in honor of the King's late brother. Sailing west, they rediscovered Torres Strait, and before departing for Batavia and England they landed on a small island off the coast of Cape York. Cook made no claim regarding the strait, but he did claim the land. Accompanied by Banks and Solander, he made for the island and climbed the highest hill—from which he saw nothing but islands to the northwest.

Cook admitted that to the west he could make no new discoveries "the honor of which belongs to the Dutch navigators; but the east coast I am confident was never seen or visited by any Europeans before us." He had already claimed several places along the coast; now he "once more hoisted the English colors and in the name of His Majesty King George III took possession of the whole eastern coast," christening it New South Wales. Three volleys of small arms were fired, and they were answered by a like number from the ship. Why, one asks, did Cook pick on so improbable a name? It has been suggested that since there already was a New England and a Nova Scotia, and since Cook wanted to associate the recent discoveries with his own country, he decided on New South Wales.

The most immediately striking aspect of early maps of Australia is the marked Dutch flavor of their nomenclature. The earliest explorers—before Cook's time—had been Dutch captains serving the East India Company, and rather naturally they perpetuated their sightings by their own names or those of their employers or ships. Some fifteen different landings took place during the first half of the seventeenth century. The first was made in 1606 by the *Duyfken* under the command of Willem Janz, who sighted the present Cape York Peninsula and advanced down the west shore as far as Cabo Keer-Weer, or Cape Turn-Again. Ten years later Dirck Hartog, sailing from Amsterdam in the *Eendracht*, entered present-day Shark Bay, which he named after his ship. Hartog left a pewter plate nailed to a post to commemorate the event; the plate, crudely carved with the men's names and the date, still exists.

Other landfalls followed in quick succession. In 1619 Jacob Dedel came in sight of the mainland in

The island of Huahine, one of the Society Islands, from Banks' *System of Geography*.

the vicinity of Perth, and in 1622 the *Leeuwin* discovered Australia's westernmost point. Later came Tasman's two voyages. His second, in 1644, proved the most rewarding: he sailed along the whole north coast from Cape York to the North West Cape, some three thousand miles—a greater distance even than Cook's northward passage up the eastern side.

By the middle of the seventeenth century three-quarters of Australia's actual coast had been mapped, and one wonders why it took another century and a quarter before Cook completed its outline. The answer is simple: the Dutch regarded this enormous island, about the size of the United States, as completely valueless. No place had been found where they could revictual their ships, and more often than not the crews, in their searchings for water, had been obliged to dig in the sand, unearthing only an evil brackish fluid. From the reports of the time one pictures a low, desolate shoreline dotted with burning fires but otherwise apparently uninhabited. On the rare occasions that the aborigines did make their appearance, they were judged to be "a race of savages more miserable than any creatures in the world." Further discoveries would cost money, and the expeditions had brought in no returns. It was obvious that to establish colonies in a land of this size would be a prodigious undertaking, more than the East India Company or even the Republic of Holland could manage. It was thought best to drop the whole matter.

William Dampier, the first Englishman to visit Australia, agreed with the Dutch about the inhospitable nature of New Holland's shores. A merchant-sailor as well as a privateer, Dampier had visited Australia twice—once in the *Cygnet* in 1688, and again in the *Roebuck* ten years later. Both times he had touched the country's arid northwest shore, and his two celebrated books, *A New Voyage Around the World* (1697) and *A Voyage to New Holland* (1703), did nothing to excite the British government's curiosity. No one in London thought much about Australia until Captain Cook's expedition discovered the well-watered, attractive eastern coastline seventy years later. His report was far more favorable and it led to the British taking possession of the continent.

The first suggestion for establishing a Pacific colony in Australia was made by Joseph Banks before a committee of the House of Commons in 1779. In 1776 the United States had declared its independence, and the loss of her American colonies meant that England could no longer send her convicts across the Atlantic. Nevertheless, English judges continued sentencing convicted persons to transportation, and jails were overcrowded; a new outlet for offenders had to be found.

It was at this point that Banks enthusiastically recommended Botany Bay for that purpose. "The proportion of rich soil was small in comparison to the barren," he noted, "but sufficient to support a very large number of people ... The country was well supplied with water. There were no beasts of prey," and the natives were peaceful when compared with those in New Zealand. Banks did make the proviso

Sir Joseph Banks, a naturalist, accompanied Cook on his first voyage in 1768.

A drawing of a breadfruit or Uru by Sydney Parkinson, a naturalist-artist who worked for Banks on his voyage with Cook.

A picture of many of the natives discovered by Cook during his expeditions.

War-boats on the island of Ulietea, one of the Society Islands.

"The finest natural harbor in the world"

that any body of settlers going to the country must take a full year's allowance of such things as victuals, raiment, tools, seeds and stock. Cook, in his journals, had stated similar views. "We are to consider that we see this country in the pure state of nature, the industry of man has had nothing to do with any part of it and yet we find such things as nature hath bestow'd upon it in a flourishing state. In this extensive country it can never be doubted but what most sorts of grain, fruit, roots etc. of every kind would flourish were they once brought hither."

By 1786 Lord Sydney, the Secretary of State, had appointed forty-nine-year-old Captain Arthur Phillip, a man with a fine naval record, to lead a fleet to Botany Bay. His fleet consisted of six transports, three storeships and two ships of war, carrying a total of 1,138 people, of whom 820 were convicts.

When Captain Phillip sailed into the bay, he realized that it had an exposed situation with an indifferent supply of water, and that settling there could lead only to disaster. Instead, exploring a few miles to the north, he entered Port Jackson, the future Sydney, an infinitely more satisfactory location—"the finest natural harbor in the world," according to Phillip, "in which a thousand sail of the line may ride in the most perfect security."

At this point Great Britain, still under the belief that New South Wales might be separated from what the Dutch called New Holland, did not lay claim to the whole of Australia, but just to the eastern coast and all the islands adjacent in the Pacific. But by 1815 Australia's entire perimeter had been examined—and by 1820 Britain had formally annexed the entire country.

Thus the ultimate result of Cook's exploration of the Australian coast was to give Great Britain a whole new continent. But this was not his only achievement in the southern hemisphere. The 1768 expedition had proved that New Zealand was an island group and had closed off Australia's missing coastline—but it also disproved the existence of one enormous southern continent to counter-balance Europe and Asia.

Cook's second voyage, begun in 1772, settled that question once and for all: in the three years Cook was absent, he sailed between 60,000 and 70,000 miles and made vast sweeps in hitherto unexplored parts of the Pacific. He traveled in a giant, irregular zig-zag, penetrating as far south as 70° 10′ latitude, a record not bettered until 1823. During that voyage he made numerous major geographical discoveries, one of them being New Caledonia, the largest island in the South Pacific after New Zealand. Ironically, it was what Cook did *not* discover that was to count as his most important contribution on that voyage: his conclusive proof that there was no great southern continent put our knowledge of the South Pacific on a sound basis. Indeed, maps of that part of the world remain essentially as Cook left them.

RODERICK CAMERON

The death of Captain Cook. Cook was killed by natives on the island of Hawaii on February 14, 1779.

Catherine the Great, Empress of Russia, ambitious and dominating, who succeeded her poisoned husband.

While England continued to expand her empire overseas, Russia was extending her frontiers in Europe. Aided by Austria, Russian troops invaded Prussia during the French and Indian War (1756–1763), inflicting an overwhelming defeat on Frederick the Great at Kunersdorf. The Russians captured Colmar, advanced as far as Frankfurt-on-Oder and Berlin, and occupied Prussian Pomerania. Frederick's tenacity (despite the fact that by the end of 1761 his army was reduced to a meager 30,000 men)—combined with Russia's inability to coordinate plans with the Austrians—spelled doom for the Russian campaign. With the death of the Empress Elizabeth and the accession of her half-German nephew as Peter III in 1761, Russian troops withdrew from Prussia.

Catherine the Great

The new Tsar, a weak and incompetent ruler, was poisoned within a few months of his accession by supporters of his dynamic German wife, Catherine, who succeeded him to the throne. A worthy successor to Peter the Great, she is also known to history as "the Great." Catherine's determination to modernize and Westernize Russia was clearly influenced by the ideas of the French *philosophes*. Indeed, the Empress claimed that Voltaire was her master and Diderot's *Encyclopédie* her bible. But the vast size of her empire, the political power of the nobles and her own determination to extend Russia's frontiers blocked any full attempt to implement the ideas of the Enlightenment. When Diderot (whose library she bought) pressed Catherine to institute more reforms, she retorted: "You only work on paper, while I, poor Empress, work on human skin which is much more ticklish."

Catherine did succeed in abolishing most of the state monopolies and in reforming the provincial administration of Russia. She increased the number and efficiency of the *gubernii*—local authorities administered by a governor and elected councils—and she subordinated the Orthodox Church to the State by secularizing Church lands and granting religious freedom to non-Church members. When Pope Clement XIV's bull, *Dominus ac Redemptor*, dissolved the Society of Jesus in 1773, she refused to expel the Jesuits from Russia.

Compared with her over ambitious and liberal *Instructions to the Commissioners for Composing a New Code of Laws*—most of which she plagiarized from Montesquieu's *Spirit of Laws* and Beccaria's *Crimes and Punishments*—the legal reforms that Catherine actually instituted were minor: the establishment of a new system of courts and the separation of civil from criminal cases. The Empress had more success in reforming the educational system. She established free

Pugachev, an illiterate peasant who claimed to be Tsar Peter III.

public primary schools in the towns, extended the scope of Peter the Great's Academy, and set up a College of Medicine.

Peasant discontent

Despite the benefits certain sections of Russian society gained from her rule, Catherine did little to improve the lot of the serfs. In fact, she increased their number—not only by giving estates to discarded lovers but also by introducing serfdom into new territories conquered by her armies. The extent of peasant discontent was dramatically revealed in 1773. An illiterate Cossack named Pugachev, pretending to be the murdered Peter III, announced that he was marching to St. Petersburg to punish his wife and place his son Paul on the throne. Pugachev gained so much support from the salt miners, Cossacks and peasants of the lower Volga that he was able to capture and pillage several towns, and to hang hundreds of priests, officers and government officials before his eventual defeat. Captured in 1775, he was taken in an iron cage to Moscow, where he was executed for his crime of lese majesty.

The discontent that generated Pugachev's revolt was to last throughout Catherine's reign and was, in fact, to be exacerbated by her aggressive and extremely expensive foreign policy. Determined to expand Russia both west and south, she used the Duke of Courland's refusal to allow Russian troops returning from the French and Indian War to pass through his territories as a pretext to invade his duchy. She replaced the Duke, a son of King Augustus III of Poland, with her own nominee. The death of Augustus himself in 1763 gave Catherine the opportunity to interfere directly in Polish politics. She chose her former lover, Stanislas Poniatowski, to succeed Augustus—and by spending a fortune in bribes and by threatening military action, Catherine obtained his unanimous election in September, 1764.

The French government, which was disturbed by Russia's territorial ambitions and alarmed by the friendship between Catherine and Frederick of Prussia, persuaded Turkey to attack Russia. The Turkish Army was overwhelmed on the Dnieper in 1768 and the Russians occupied Bucharest; the

Stanislas Poniatowski, a former lover of Catherine of Russia, who was elected King of Poland.

Turkish Navy was defeated off Chios and the Russians moved into the Crimea, occupying Moldavia and Wallachia. By the terms of the 1774 Treaty of Kuchuk Kainardji, Turkey ceded Azov and Kertsch to Russia, thereby extending its frontiers to the Black Sea and the lower Danube. Victory in a second Turkish war confirmed Russia's earlier annexation of the Crimea and secured her hold on the Black Sea.

Catherine's success in Turkey was made possible by her role in the War of the Bavarian Succession. Upon the death of the Elector Maximilian Joseph in 1775, the Emperor Joseph II claimed Lower Bavaria for Austria, offering to compensate the Elector Palatine Karl Theodore, the legal heir to the throne, with money and titles for his illegitimate children. But Frederick the Great, having persuaded Karl Theodore's nephew

makes Russia a force in Europe

Gustavus III, King of Sweden, who built up Sweden's strength to avoid Poland's fate.

and legitimate heir, the Duke of Zweibrücken, to reject the Emperor's arrangement, invaded Bohemia. The Treaty of Teschen, which ended the war, guaranteed the rights of the Elector Palatine and the Duke of Zweibrücken in Bavaria, and gave Austria only a small slice of Bavarian territory. Russia, having acted as mediator in the dispute, was in a position to influence Austrian affairs. She obtained the support of Joseph II in her designs on Turkey. Thwarted in his attempt to add Bavaria to his Empire, Joseph decided that an alliance with Russia might win him parts of Turkey's possessions. As we have seen, Russia's gains in the war were considerable, but Joseph's ill-led and disease-ridden army was defeated.

Partition of Poland

Meanwhile, Catherine's protégé in Poland, Stanislas Poniatowski, was

Emanuel Swedenborg.

hampered in his attempts to rule as an enlightened monarch by a constitution that inhibited his initiative. This constitution was guaranteed by both Catherine and Frederick the Great, neither of whom wanted the resurgence of a healthy Polish state.

Early in 1772, Catherine and Frederick agreed that the time had come to partition Poland, and in August of that year they signed the First Treaty of Partition. Russia took the area known as White Russia, east of the Düna and Dnieper rivers; Prussia took West Prussia; and Austria, which had already seized Zips—the Polish enclave to the north of Hungary—took Galicia. Although the King of Poland declared that his country was not "a nation near its fall," a Second Partition Treaty was forced upon him less than a year later. Russia acquired another vast area of eastern Poland, from Polozk to the Dniester, and Prussia absorbed Danzig and a large area in western Poland.

Reduced to about a third of her

Partitions of Poland

--- Frontiers of Poland before partitions
Territorial gains of Prussia
Territorial gains of Russia
Territorial gains of Austria

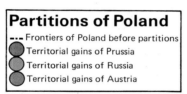

Poland partitioned by Catherine of Russia and Frederick of Prussia.

former size, Poland bravely rose in revolt against her oppressors. Under the leadership of General Kościuszko, the Poles won several battles against the Russians and recaptured large tracts of territory. Warsaw and Vilna were liberated and Kościuszko was proclaimed dictator. Prussia then joined the Russians to suppress the patriots. And after Kościuszko's defeat at Maciejowice and the fall of Cracow and Warsaw, the last Polish field unit capitulated in November, 1794. The final partition of Poland came in 1795. Russia moved still farther west, occupying what remained of Lithuania; Austria moved farther north, beyond Cracow and up to the river Bug; and Prussia swallowed the rest, including Warsaw. Thus, Poland ceased to exist as a nation, but for generations it remained an area of dispute among Austria, Prussia and Russia.

Sweden

Frederick the Great and Catherine planned to partition Sweden as well. When Gustavus III succeeded to the throne in 1771, Sweden was close to anarchy. The previous fifty years had been a period of remarkable artistic and scientific achievement. Societies of science, painting and sculpture flourished; the great botanist, Carl von Linné, known as Linnaeus, published his *Species Plantarum* in 1753; Anders Celsius, professor of astronomy at the University of Upsala for fifteen years, invented the centigrade thermometer; Emanuel Swedenborg,

the Swedish philosopher, inventor, scientist and mystic, also studied at Upsala and began his work there. But this intellectual ferment coincided with ruinous political party rivalry. In a forceful yet bloodless coup d'état, Gustavus III arrested the Council, dissolved the Diet, and promulgated a new constitution. He pushed forward reforms in agriculture, commerce, administration and law, encouraged the study of science, and built up a powerful and well-equipped army and navy. Gustavus thus demonstrated to Prussia and Russia that Sweden would not submit passively to Poland's fate.

By 1787, Gustavus' forces were strong enough for a full-scale war. Suspecting that Catherine was subsidizing his enemies, he attacked her while the Russian army was heavily engaged in the second Turkish war. Gustavus' navy did well, and his army was preparing to march on St. Petersburg when an attack by Denmark—from which Gustavus wished to wrest Norway—forced him to withdraw his forces to defend Göteborg. Peace was finally achieved through the mediation of Prussia and England—both of which feared Russia's growing power in the Baltic.

To Gustavus—and to his enemy, Catherine the Great—England's own power, which had appeared irresistible in 1763, seemed irretrievably weakened. The empire England had so recently carved out for herself was crumbling: Wolfe's capture of Quebec in 1759 preceded by only sixteen years the convening of the second Continental Congress at Philadelphia.

The Declaration of Independence

The angular and garrulous delegate from Virginia seemed an unlikely candidate for the vital task of drafting the Second Continental Congress' proclamation of independence. At thirty-three, Thomas Jefferson was one of the youngest of the representatives who had gathered in Philadelphia —and he was a notoriously ineffective public speaker. Yet Jefferson single-handedly drafted a declaration that not only evoked patriotic fervor in American readers but voiced the rebellious colonies' grievances with consummate diplomatic skill. So artfully worded was Jefferson's document that even the supremely autocratic King of France was able to support it. Ignoring the lanky Virginian's declaration that "governments derive their just powers from the consent of the governed," Louis XVI openly assisted the colonists—and in so doing, ensured the spread of the revolutionary spirit that toppled his own government twelve years later.

The Declaration of Independence, unlike the United States Constitution and most other such famous documents of history, is the work of one man. John Adams of Massachusetts and Benjamin Franklin of Pennsylvania suggested a few changes in the wording, but the responsibility for phrasing the sentiments expressed in that momentous manifesto fell to Thomas Jefferson, a gentleman from Virginia who possessed, to a greater degree than any of his colleagues, what John Adams termed "a happy talent of composition."

Jefferson had arrived in Philadelphia in June, 1775, as one of Virginia's delegates to the Second Continental Congress. The Second Congress was far more radical than the First, which had met in Philadelphia from September 5 to October 6, 1774, to protest Britain's colonial policy. The First Congress had sent several petitions of grievances to King George III, and it had formed the "Continental Association" to boycott British imports into the colonies and bar colonial exports to the Empire. But although the First Congress called for a thorough revamping of the Empire, few of its members contemplated a complete break with England when the Congress was adjourned.

By the time the Second Congress convened in May, 1775, however, England had rejected the petitions of the First Congress and had decided to end the rebellion with force. Armed skirmishes between colonial militia and British troops already had broken out at Lexington and Concord, and as the radicals in the Congress gained support, the delegates adopted measures that moved them inexorably toward the final break with the mother country. A Continental Army was formed; diplomatic feelers were sent to France; American ports were opened to foreign shipping; and finally, in June, 1776, a committee was appointed to draft a formal declaration

of independence from Great Britain. The committee was composed of Adams, Franklin, Roger Sherman of Connecticut, Robert Livingston of New York and Jefferson.

Tall, sandy-haired, loose-jointed, Jefferson had not made a good first impression upon his arrival in Philadelphia. He seemed awkward. His clothes were ill-fitting and his talk was as loose and rambling as his gait. At a time when the ability to sway an audience counted heavily, he revealed himself as an ineffective public speaker. Fortunately for the cause of independence, he was blessed with other qualities. If he did not shine in public debate, he did show himself to be well informed, outspoken and incisive in committee work. Obviously the reputation he had made for himself in the House of Burgesses at Williamsburg was well earned.

Intellectually and physically the thirty-three-year-old delegate, one of the youngest men in the Congress, was a curious blend of the Old World and the New. Although he had grown up on the fringe of western settlement—which accounted for his fierce opposition to a government that fostered rank and privilege—he inherited from his mother, Jane Randolph, a member of one of the most distinguished families in the province, a taste for the good things of life. A lover of good books, good music and good wine, and at the same time an accomplished linguist, architect, farmer, naturalist and administrator, the extraordinarily versatile Jefferson could have made a name for himself in any one of half a dozen different professions.

There may have been a grain of truth in the wry comment of one critic that Thomas Jefferson was "a martyr to the disease of omniscience." But if like so many men of varied talents he flitted too easily over too many fields of knowledge, for at least once in his life—in the month of June, 1776—he was utterly and

A five shilling stamp of 1765. The Stamp Act of 1765, requiring almost every paper document to have an official stamp, created anger among all sections of the community.

Opposite Thomas Jefferson, author of the Declaration of Independence and third President of the United States.

An address to the civilized world

George III. He unnecessarily alienated his colonial subjects.

Lord North, British Prime Minister from 1770 to 1782. He tried to limit the freedom of the colonists and thus provoked them to oppose British authority by force.

exclusively engrossed in the task that had been assigned to him. Robert Livingston and Roger Sherman agreed with Adams and Franklin that the wording of the Declaration had better be left to the young delegate from Virginia. Jefferson retired to his lodging on Market Street and was not seen again until June 28, when he emerged with his first draft.

As he sharpened his quill, he may well have reminded himself that the primary purpose of the document over which he was laboring was not so much to declare independence as to proclaim to the world the reasons for declaring it. Jefferson's colleague, Richard Henry Lee, already had submitted a resolution to the Continental Congress on behalf of the Virginia delegation, declaring that "these United Colonies are, and of a right ought to be, free and independent States, that they are absolved from all allegiance to the British Crown, and that all political connection between them and the State of Great Britain is, and ought to be, totally dissolved." But before Congress would pass Lee's resolution, it had appointed the drafting committee to prepare a justification for independence.

Conscious that he was addressing not just the people of England and America but the whole civilized world, Jefferson began his justification with a lofty statement of purpose:

When, in the course of human events, it becomes necessary for one people to dissolve the political bands which have connected them with one another, and to assume among the powers of the earth the separate and equal station to which the laws of nature and of nature's God entitle them, a decent respect to the opinions of mankind requires that they should declare the causes which impel them to the separation.

There is nothing of the passionate rebel in this statement; indeed Jefferson would have denied that the colonists were rebels at all. On the contrary, they were a free people maintaining long-established rights against a usurping king.

Jefferson was writing with one eye on France, from whom it was essential that the colonists should get supplies if they were to make good their assertion of independence. For if the colonists seemed to be rebelling against rightful authority, no state in Europe would deal with them. Jefferson therefore had to persuade readers of the Declaration that the act of separation was legitimate—and more than that, he had to excite sympathy for a downtrodden people who had submitted for many years to the oppression of an unnatural tyrant. Sympathy for the downtrodden and indignation against the oppressor would, he hoped, culminate in active French support of the American cause. While it was too much to expect a king of France to smile upon the strange theory that "governments derive their just powers from the consent of the governed," it was possible that Louis XVI and his ministers might ignore what they did not like in the Declaration in view of the pleasing prospect of taking a hand in the disruption of the British Empire.

In the second paragraph of the Declaration, Jefferson set out to formulate a general political philosophy upon which to rest his case.

We hold these truths to be self-evident: that all men are created equal; that they are endowed by their Creator with certain inalienable rights; that among these are life, liberty, and the pursuit of happiness; that to secure these rights, governments are instituted among men, deriving their just powers from the consent of the governed; that whenever any form of government becomes destructive of those ends, it is the right of the people to alter or to abolish it, and to institute new government, laying its foundations on such principles, and organizing its powers in such form, as to them shall seem most likely to effect their safety and happiness.

The reader of the Declaration of Independence must even now be on guard against the haunting cadences with which Jefferson beguiled his readers. The truths that he called self-evident were not self-evident at all, either to his contemporaries or to later generations. As for the notion that all men are created equal, posterity is still wondering just what Jefferson meant by those words. Certainly men are equal in the eyes of God and in the eyes of English common law, but in every other way they are obviously and distressingly unequal. Even assuming that Jefferson did not include Negroes as men, he would have done better to have adopted the phrase used by his friend George Mason in the Virginia Bill of Rights—"all men are born equally free."

Yet, while it is easy to cavil over certain statements in the Declaration, we must remember that Jefferson was inspired by an ideal that he believed could be attained, for the first time in history, by the people for whom he was speaking. He was trying to harmonize the conduct of human affairs with what he believed to be the laws of the moral universe. However, like all great statesmen he was at the same time a shrewd, practical politician. The Declaration must also be regarded in another light, therefore, as a propaganda document whose purpose was to invigorate the rebellion. Its utterances must be viewed not only as a noble affirmation of the rights of man, but also as a political platform. Taken together they represented an ideal to which the writer and his party aspired.

Having affirmed the right of revolution under certain conditions, and having set forth the theory upon which the colonies would base their republican government, Jefferson moved from the abstract to a specific justification for exercising the rights enumerated in the first part of the document. Namely, he set forth a long list of grievances—not against Parliament, as might have been expected, since the dispute between the colonies and the mother country had

Above The Boston Massacre. This incident was exaggerated to arouse the colonists' discontent.

Below The attack on Bunker Hill and the burning of Charlestown in 1775.

The Declaration of Independence, signed by delegates from the thirteen states.

A satire on the Boston Port Act of 1773, by which the port Boston was closed as a result of the Boston Tea Party: in the picture Lord North pours tea into the mouth of America.

always centered on the question of parliamentary authority—but against the King. The reason for transposing the odium from Parliament to the King was that Congress had decided that Parliament was the legislative body only of Great Britain.

Jefferson cited the King's interference with representative government in the colonies, the harshness with which he administered colonial affairs, his restrictions on civil rights, his stationing of troops in the colonies and his restrictive tax and trade policies. The list also included some grievances that were not very serious, and others that were untrue—in particular the charge that George III had encouraged the slave trade against the wishes of the colonies.

Congress was only too happy to blame King George for every sin in the calendar, but considering that the slave trade was carried on by New England shipowners and supported by Southern purchasers, it would have seemed better not to mention it in the Declaration. John Adams, who acted as Jefferson's spokesman on the floor of Congress, fought hard for

A slave-holding devotee of freedom

the retention of the passage on slavery, but Congress decided against him and the offending passage was struck out. The word "slavery" therefore does not occur in the final text. There was perhaps an indirect reference to it in the charge that the King had deliberately fomented domestic insurrection in America—a charge that might have been taken as referring either to Indians or to Negroes. To have been more specific would have been embarrassing. Slavery was not a topic to be discussed in a document whose keynote was human freedom.

It was especially curious that Jefferson had inserted the section on slavery in light of his own attitude toward the institution. He never denied that slavery was a great evil, as harmful to the white man as to the Negro, but there was a vein of complacent optimism in Jefferson that allowed him to think that slavery would die a natural death. It was already dying out in the North, and in God's good time it would disappear in the Southern states as well. That he owned from one hundred to two hundred slaves, while at the same time maintaining as a self-evident truth that all men are created equal, does not seem to have disturbed him. He was a kind master, and his slaves were devoted to him, which may explain why he was so unconcerned by the equivocal role he continued to play, from July 4, 1776, to the day of his death exactly fifty years later, as a slaveholding devotee of freedom.

The debate in Congress over the provisions of the Declaration was an agonizing ordeal for the author. His committee had been very complimentary; they made only a few changes, which Jefferson promptly incorporated into a new draft. But the other members of Congress were not so easily satisfied. They cut out a quarter of what he had written, altered about two dozen words, and made two insertions in the peroration—references to a "Supreme Judge" and a "Divine Providence." Jefferson had already mentioned the Deity twice, but Congress wanted God in the peroration as well.

Monday Morning, December 27, 1773. THE TEA-SHIP being arrived, every Inhabitant, who wishes to preserve the Liberty of America, is desired to meet at the STATE-HOUSE, This Morning, precisely at TEN o'Clock, to advise what is best to be done on this alarming Crisis.

Lee's resolution of independence was approved on July 2, but the debate over the wording of the Declaration lasted another two days. Jefferson himself said nothing—he was busy making notes on the weather and on his current expenses. On July 3, the temperature was 76 degrees Fahrenheit—not a hot afternoon for Philadelphia in July. On that same day Jefferson spent 103 shillings, most of which went toward a thermometer. He also bought seven pairs of women's gloves and gave one shilling and sixpence "in charity." On the evening of July 4, the debate was closed, and all the members present with the exception of John Dickinson of Pennsylvania signed the Declaration. The thirteen colonies now became thirteen independent states.

Jefferson had succeeded in imparting a quality of timelessness and universality to what might otherwise have been merely a national document. His colleagues in Congress sensed they were doing far more than repudiating a king: they were founding a new order of society that had as its cornerstone the rights of free individuals. Jefferson had based his ideal of government on the philosophy of natural rights. According to that philosophy, man originally lived in a state of nature without benefit of civil authority. Possessing the right of life, liberty, property, and the pursuit of happiness, each man enforced those rights as best he could. Since the strong often took advantage of the weak, the time came when men were glad to surrender the state of nature for the civil state. In other words they acknowledged their inability to enforce their natural rights themselves, but in so doing they did not surrender them to anybody else. Those precious rights, frequently identified with God's will, no ruler could take from them. Implicit in this contract theory of the origins of civil authority were the doctrines of the consent of the governed and the right of revolution.

American colonists maintained that their philosophy was part of their inheritance, that it had come down to them in the writings of John Milton and John Locke. So obvious was that line of reasoning to the Founding Fathers that John Adams, who as he grew older was sometimes irritated by the eulogies that Fourth of July orators lavished on Jefferson, complained that there was not an idea in the Declaration "but what had been hackneyed in Congress for two years before." Jefferson did not deny it. He was not aiming at originality of principle or sentiment. The essential thing, he said, was "to place before mankind the common sense of the subject in terms so plain and firm as to command their assent, and to justify ourselves in the independent stand we are compelled to take."

Above A notice calling a meeting which resulted in the famous Boston Tea Party, when all the tea aboard the East India Company tea ships was dumped into Boston harbor.

Below Thomas Paine, author of *The Rights of Man*. In 1774 he went to America and took up the cause of the colonists.

Left Messengers ride through the thirteen states in July, 1776, reading the Declaration of Independence to the colonists.

The cause of all mankind

John Adams, delegate from Massachusetts, appointed a member of the committee to draft the Declaration of Independence.

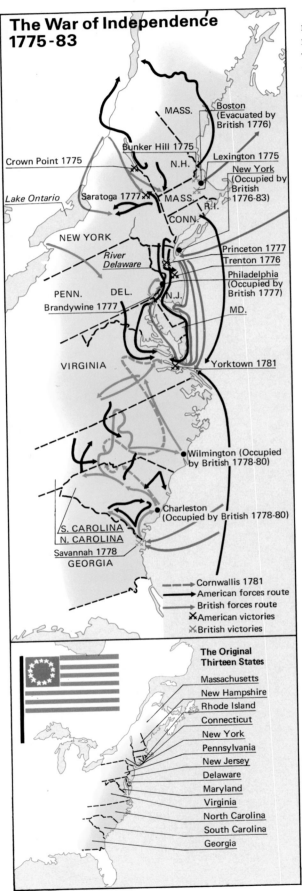

The War of Independence 1775-83

Boston (Evacuated by British 1776)
Bunker Hill 1775
Crown Point 1775
MASS.
N.H.
Lexington 1775
New York (Occupied by British 1776-83)
Lake Ontario
Saratoga 1777
MASS.
R.I.
CONN.
NEW YORK
River Delaware
Princeton 1777
Trenton 1776
Philadelphia (Occupied by British 1777)
PENN.
DEL.
N.J.
MD.
Brandywine 1777
VIRGINIA
Yorktown 1781
Wilmington (Occupied by British 1778-80)
Charleston (Occupied by British 1778-80)
S. CAROLINA
N. CAROLINA
Savannah 1778
GEORGIA

- - - Cornwallis 1781
→ American forces route
→ British forces route
✕ American victories
✕ British victories

The Original Thirteen States

Massachusetts
New Hampshire
Rhode Island
Connecticut
New York
Pennsylvania
New Jersey
Delaware
Maryland
Virginia
North Carolina
South Carolina
Georgia

While Jefferson was right in insisting that the chief merit of the Declaration lay in its expression of commonly shared beliefs, both he and John Adams were wrong in assuming that the Declaration did nothing more than state what everyone was thinking, in the tone and spirit called for by the occasion. Even those who agreed with Jefferson—and there were many who did not—must have been aware that the truths he proclaimed as self-evident were far from being as axiomatic as he supposed. In substituting "life, liberty, and the pursuit of happiness" for the familiar formula, "life, liberty, and property," he made a significant departure from John Locke and all the other philosophers from whom he is said to have borrowed. No other state paper had ever suggested that one of the essential functions of government is to make men happy, or that one of man's natural rights is the pursuit of happiness. That was indeed a revolutionary doctrine.

It may be argued that the "pursuit of happiness," whatever it may be meant to include, is already implicit in "liberty." If a man is secure in life and liberty he can pursue anything he pleases. To many of Jefferson's contemporaries, the pursuit of happiness may well have seemed too cheap a thing to mention in a proclamation of human rights. As Aldous Huxley once put it, "happiness is like coke—something you get as a by-product in the process of making something else." Evidently Jefferson did not think of happiness as a by-product, but whether we agree with him or not, there is no question but that in specifying the pursuit of happiness as one of man's inalienable rights he launched America on uncharted seas. Today young people, not only in America but all over the world, are taking Jefferson's dictum more seriously than he may have intended.

In at least one other respect the Declaration was startlingly original, not in what it said but in what it omitted. It made no mention of the rights of British subjects. This was a significant omission, since throughout the entire controversy between the colonies and the mother country, beginning with the imposition of the Stamp Tax in 1764, those rights had been the mainstay of the American case. "No taxation without representation": Parliament had no right to tax British subjects without their consent. While his colleagues were still fighting it out along that line, Jefferson had shifted his ground. In his diatribe against George III he pointed out that the King had committed a worse crime than violating the rights of his subjects. He had violated the rights of man. Jefferson was now appealing to a higher court. Mankind in general might not be vitally interested in a controversy between Great Britain and her colonies involving intricate questions of constitutional law. There must be a more inflammable issue than that, and it was part of Jefferson's genius to identify it and present it as he did.

Possibly he was influenced by Thomas Paine, an Englishman recently arrived in America who had taken up the cause of the colonists with all the ardor of a convert. In his pamphlet *Common Sense*, Paine had pointed out that "the cause of America is in a

great measure the cause of all mankind." Many were won over by his eloquence, but Paine was essentially a rabble-rouser; Jefferson, of course, was not.

The argument that Jefferson made before the bar of world opinion has been attacked again and again, either in anger or contempt, by friends as well as enemies of the American Revolution. The critics have in general agreed with Rufus Choate, one of the great lawyer-statesmen of the nineteenth century, that the famous Declaration was after all nothing but a series of "glittering generalities." Jefferson's champions have been no less insistent and no less vocal than his critics. Perhaps the most famous is Abraham Lincoln. In 1861, on his way to Washington to take up the Presidency, Lincoln said:

I have never had a feeling politically that did not spring from the sentiments embodied in the Declaration of Independence. .. Something in that Declaration giving liberty, not only to the people of this country, but hope for the world for all future time....And that all should have an equal chance.

In those words, spoken in Independence Hall,

Philadelphia, where the Declaration was signed, Lincoln suggests why it is that all leaders of nationalistic movements and all champions of liberal reform inevitably hark back to the Declaration of Independence. To them it stands for hope:

"till hope creates
From its own wreck the thing it contemplates."

Jefferson may have been overoptimistic when, in his old age, he wrote to John Adams that "the flames kindled on the fourth of July, 1776, have spread over too much of the globe to be extinguished by the feeble engines of despotism; on the contrary, they will consume those engines and all who work them. . . ." Unfortunately, the "engines of despotism" and those who work them have not yet been consumed, but wherever they still exist, and wherever they may appear in the future, they will always have to withstand the challenge of Jefferson's devastating rhetoric.   ARNOLD WHITRIDGE

The Battle of Yorktown, 1781. Britain's defeat at this battle made it finally clear that she must accept America's independence.

European Possessions in North America

1713

HUDSON'S BAY COMPANY
NEWFOUNDLAND
NEW FRANCE
NOVA SCOTIA
NEW ENGLAND
VIRGINIA
CAROLINA
FLORIDA
NEW SPAIN
LOUISIANA
NEW GRANADA

○ English territory
○ French territory
○ Spanish territory
○ Independent territory

1783

HUDSON'S BAY COMPANY
NEWFOUNDLAND
NOVA SCOTIA
QUEBEC
UNITED STATES
LOUISIANA
TEXAS
FLORIDA
NEW SPAIN
CALIFORNIA
NEW GRANADA

The Peace of Versailles, signed in January, 1783, recognized the independence of the American republic and renounced colonization on the American mainland. The Earl of Shelburne, whose position as England's Prime Minister had made him responsible for the conduct of the negotiations, had been anxious to keep America within the British sphere of influence. Shelburne hoped to see Britain and America become partners in Atlantic commerce, with America assuming the expensive responsibilities of governing North America and Britain becoming the accepted link between the United States and the Continent. He had consequently striven to obtain the Americans' goodwill and to provide them with an extensive market for British goods by granting them all the territory they wanted. Such largesse angered the Prime Minister's critics, who failed to understand its economic implications. Shelburne countered their attacks by pointing to the relatively small concessions that he had made to England's other enemies in the recent war—and considering the country's fortunes in that war and

the exhausted state in which it had left her, those concessions did indeed seem slight.

The war between England and her American colonies had been welcomed in France. Louis XVI's foreign minister, Charles Gravier Vergennes, hoped that the struggle would reverse the advantages that England had gained from the French and Indian War and provide a fitting retort to the Treaty of Paris. By the time that General John Burgoyne was forced to surrender to General Horatio Gates at Saratoga on October 17, 1777, the French were already supplying the Americans with muskets and gunpowder; the following year, war was formally declared

The widening war

France was but one of England's enemies. The League of Armed Neutrality—which was established in 1780 to prevent British ships from searching neutral vessels for contraband of war—eventually included Russia, Sweden, Austria, Prussia, Denmark, Spain and Holland in addition to France. And of those powers, Spain and Holland

actively joined in the hostilities against their traditional rival. Spain declared war on England in June of 1779 (after obtaining guarantees of French assistance in recovering Gibraltar and Florida) and immediately laid siege to Gibraltar. England declared war on Holland in November, 1780, in a vain attempt to prevent her from joining the League.

The British Navy—faced with the problem of relieving Gibraltar, supplying the army in America, fighting the French in the West Indies and guarding the Channel—was strained to the limit of its resources. The Caribbean island of St. Vincent fell to the French on June 20, 1779 (two days after Spain declared war on England), and Grenada capitulated a fortnight later. In January, 1780, Admiral George Rodney defeated a Spanish squadron off Cape St. Vincent, temporarily relieving Gibraltar and offering the British some respite. But later on that year the British fought three indecisive naval engagements with the French in the West Indies, and in April, 1781, the French, under the Marquis de Grasse-Tilly, captured Tobago. A French fleet led by

Pierre-André de Suffren Saint-Tropez prevented England from seizing the Dutch post on the Cape of Good Hope, and later captured a Ceylonese port that the Dutch had recently surrendered to the British. In July, 1781, the Spaniards captured Pensacola, Florida, and on October 19 Lord Cornwallis' forces at Yorktown surrendered to George Washington.

By February, 1782, the British seemed to be on the verge of collapse. The Spaniards followed up their victory in Florida by capturing Minorca on February 5, and a week later the French captured the West Indies island of St. Christopher. On February 22 a parliamentary motion that was harshly critical of the continuing war in America was defeated by only one vote—and a month later the Prime Minister, Lord North, handed in his resignation.

Tom Paine, the prophet of revolution.

Back from disaster

Late in 1782, however, the tide began to turn. Admiral Rodney defeated the French in the April 12 battle of The Saints, captured de Grasse and saved the West Indies. Seven months later, Admiral Lord Howe relieved Gibraltar. Within a year, Benjamin Franklin, the American minister in Paris, John Jay, who was to become Secretary for Foreign Affairs in 1784, and John Adams, the future President of the United States, were all in

Nelson at the Battle of St. Vincent, 1797.

excitement mounts

Paris to negotiate a peace settlement.

By the Peace of Versailles, England recovered her West Indian possessions and retained Gibraltar; France, while saving her trading posts, agreed to abandon her other ambitions in India. She retrieved St. Lucia and gained Tobago in the West Indies, added Senegal and Gore in Africa and secured fishing rights off Newfoundland. Spain regained Florida and Minorca. Holland, in accordance with the terms of a separate treaty, retrieved all her former possessions, including the Ceylonese port of Trincomalee, but granted the British the right of navigation among the Dutch spice islands.

Age of achievement

In the year that the Peace of Versailles was signed, Ludwig van Beethoven published his first composition, Wolfgang Amadeus Mozart published his Mass in C Minor, William Blake his *Poetical Sketches*, Immanuel Kant his *Prolegomena zu einer jeden Künftigen Metaphysik*, William Herschel his *Motion of the Solar System in Space*, and Moses Mendelssohn his *Jerusalem*. The quarter-century that elapsed between the Treaty of Paris and the outbreak of the French Revolution—a quarter-century that was divided into two almost equal halves by the War of American Independence—was extraordinarily rich in artistic achievement, philosophical debate and scientific discovery.

Those years saw the ascendancy not only of Voltaire, Rousseau and Diderot, but of Sterne, Smollett, Goldsmith, Burns, Cowper, Johnson and Boswell. In Germany, Goethe and Schiller were rising to prominence. Johannes Ewald was writing for the Danish theater, Beaumarchais for the French, Alfieri for the Italian and Richard Brinsley Sheridan for the theaters of London. Guardi, Greuze and Fuseli were painting in Italy, Chardin, Fragonard and Boucher in France, and Reynolds, Romney and Gainsborough in England. Thomas Rowlandson and James Gillray had begun to lift the caricature into the realm of high art. Bach, Haydn, Beethoven, Gluck and Mozart were composing music for the churches, concert halls and operas of the world. Robert Adams and William Chambers were transforming the architecture of

Gluck, whose music broke away from the Italian tradition.

London, and Jacques Ange Gabriel was altering the face of Paris. In London, George Hepplewhite, Thomas Sheraton and Thomas Chippendale were providing exquisite furniture for the houses of the well-to-do.

The Royal Academy was founded in London in 1768, the Royal Academy of Sciences was established in Lisbon in 1779, and a national theater was set up in Stockholm in 1773. In 1780 Sebastien Erard made the first pianoforte in France; the first gymnasium was opened at Breslau in 1765; and the first carriage-traffic crossed the Brenner Pass in the Alps in 1772. In 1770 a Scottish explorer named James Bruce reached the headstream of the Blue Nile; in 1773 James Cook set out upon his third voyage into the Pacific; in 1783 the Montgolfier brothers ascended in a fire balloon at Annonay and the Marquis Jouffroy d'Abbans sailed down the Saône in a paddle-wheel steamboat; in 1785 Jean Blanchard and John Jefferies crossed the English Channel in a balloon; and in 1787 Horace de Saussure reached the summit of Mont Blanc.

Developments in science during the period were equally remarkable. Between 1764 and 1775 James Hargreaves invented the spinning jenny, Joseph Priestley published his *History of Electricity*, Richard Arkwright set up his spinning machine at Preston, Daniel Rutherford discovered nitrogen, Joseph Priestley discovered oxygen, and James Watt perfected the steam engine.

Revolution!

In the midst of all this intellectual ferment, the threat of international revolution arose: there were several uprisings outside France before 1789, and in 1775 there was a serious peasant uprising in Bohemia. In 1780 London experienced the worst riots in English history when Lord George Gordon, the unbalanced and vehemently Protestant son of the Duke of Gordon, led an angry mob of some 50,000 men to the House of Commons to protest a recently passed act that granted some minor relief to Roman Catholics. In several days of wild rioting at least seven hundred people lost their lives, and the damage done to property was incalculable. Many of the targets of the mob's fury were Irish immigrants, but the outbreak was essentially a revolt of the poor against authority, and it is possible to detect in the riots the first symptoms of the quasi-revolutionary movement that was to end the political system of George III.

There was unrest in the United States and the Low Countries as well during this period. In 1786 a Continental Army veteran named Daniel Shays led a rebellion against the United States government. Shays' Rebellion found widespread support among the people of Massachusetts, who were dismayed by the evident incapacity of both the state and federal governments to solve the economic ills of the territory and to lessen the crippling taxation. In September Shays and roughly a thousand followers converged on Springfield to prevent the Supreme Court from convening, and the insurrection was not quelled until the Governor had raised an army of 4,400 men.

In Holland, the objects of resentment were the weak and unpopular Prince of Orange and his wife, the intensely disliked Frederika Wilhelmina of Prussia. Holland's commerce had been severely weakened by the recent war against England, and the peace that followed greatly strengthened the influence of the anti-Orange or Patriot Party. The insulting attitude of the Patriots toward the Prince and Princess, whose position by 1787 had become impossible, induced the Princess' uncle, the King of Prussia, to invade Holland, to place William V firmly back on the throne by force and to dissolve the Patriot Party.

There was trouble too in the Austrian Netherlands where there was passionate opposition to the Austrian Emperor's high-handed attempts to reform the Church and the administration without reference to the susceptibilities of the Flemings and the Walloons, and to his contempt for the "antediluvian rubbish" of the people's treasured rights and privileges. In 1787 their feelings burst out into violent riots which forced the Emperor to give way.

Two years later there was trouble in Sweden where Gustavus III, increasingly autocratic, established a new constitution by the Act of Unity and Security (February 17, 1789), thus granting to himself almost absolute powers.

But it was in France in the summer of 1789 that the revolution for which Europe had been waiting began.

Riots in London: three hundred prisoners were released from Newgate in 1780.

"Liberté, Egalité, Fraternité"

In the decades following its conversion into a prison, the crenelated confines of the Bastille served the political whims of four French kings. In the process, the fourteenth-century fortress became the detested symbol of France's arrogant and arbitrary autocracy. Its unfortunate inmates were arrested on lettres de cachet *issued by the King, spirited through the streets of Paris in closed carriages and incarcerated without trial. Not illogically, the ancient fortress became the focal point of anti-royalist ire during the popular risings of July, 1789—and when the fort's entire garrison surrendered to a mob of armed Parisians on July 14, the profound weakness of Louis XVI's government was at last revealed. The King had lost the support of his army—which would not fire upon the citizens—and from that moment, both he and his dynasty were doomed.*

Louis XVI and his son while they were in prison.

Opposite The attack on the Bastille. The prison was thought of as the main bastion of injustice.

Sunday, July 12, 1789. The best of summer was still to come. The day was fine but showery with a hint of coolness in the air. In Paris huge crowds were making their way to the bridges of the Seine. People were saying that Necker—who had been the commoners' favorite minister from the time he persuaded Louis XVI to double the number of deputies representing the Third Estate in the States-General—had been dismissed. What was going to happen next? Already there was a shortage of corn and the price of bread was higher than it had ever been within living memory. Did the enemies of the people—the aristocrats—want to starve French citizens in order to force them to give in? Or was the state on the verge of bankruptcy? Would the States-General, which had been convened on May 5, be dissolved before it even had a chance to debate the situation?

Instinctively, the crowd hurried to the Palais-Royal, a favorite meeting place for eighteenth-century Parisians. Inside, in the gardens, there were so many people crushed together that it was almost impossible to move. Self-appointed orators were standing on the tables, haranguing the crowds with inflammatory speeches. In order to hear the speakers, some of the onlookers had perched themselves precariously on the branches of chestnut trees.

In spite of his stammer, one particular orator seemed to be holding the attention of the crowd, and he had attracted a large group of interested listeners:

Do you realize that, although the Nation demanded that Necker should be kept on as a minister, they threw him out all the same! How much more insolently can they defy our wishes? They will stop at nothing after such behavior! Who knows whether they may not even be planning, arranging, at this very moment, a new Saint Bartholomew's Eve for all patriotic citizens! To arms! Let us all wear the green cockade, the symbol of hope. No doubt, the wretched police are present among us here! Well, let them watch me, listen to me, observe me carefully,

for it is I who proudly urge my brothers to seek their liberty!

At this point, the orator—an unemployed lawyer named Camille Desmoulins whose name was being whispered by everyone in the crowd—drew a pistol from his pocket and shouted: "At least, they will never take me alive! I shall die a glorious death! My one fear is to see France become enslaved!"

Chanting "To arms, to arms!" the crowd swarmed out of the Palais-Royal. A huge procession surged through the streets of Paris to the theaters, and demonstrators went inside and stopped the performances. Joined by the theater audiences, the crowd pressed on to the Musée Curtius, where waxwork figures of the most famous personalities of the age were exhibited. Some of the demonstrators went inside, only to emerge shortly afterward carrying the busts of Necker and the Duke of Orleans.

They continued on to the Tuileries gardens, where an enormous, frenzied crowd was shouting "Long live Necker!" and "To arms!" Suddenly there was pandemonium. People ran off in all directions, shouting that the "Royal Allemand" cavalry regiment had entered the gardens and was charging the crowd. At that moment it became obvious that if the people were to defend themselves, they had to be armed. It was rumored that a militia was to be formed, and that the district committees in Paris would be distributing arms and ammunition on the following day. The militia would be able to force the King and his evil counselors to recall Necker.

Very early the next morning, Jean-Baptiste Humbert—a watchmaker who eventually recorded his experiences during the turbulent days of July, 1789—went to his district committee headquarters in the parish of Saint-André-des-Arts, only to find that the group had already distributed the small quantity of firearms at its disposal. Nevertheless, Jean-Baptiste volunteered to join the citizens' militia

The opening of the States-General in 1789. Popular feeling was expressed at the assembly that led to outbreaks of revolt.

Below The Fall of the Bastille on July 14, 1789. The event was seen by many as a symbol of liberty.

A record of the Revolution

Revolutionary Paris

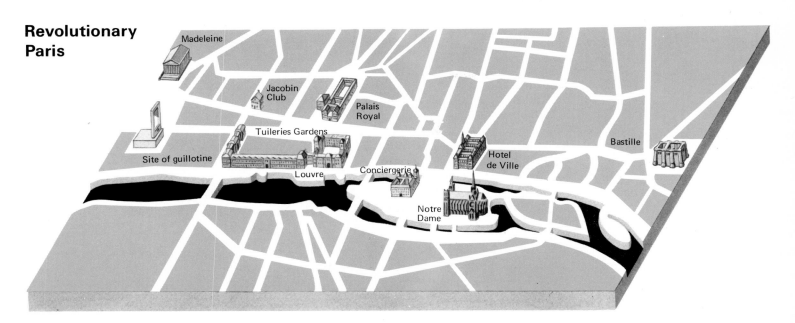

Releasing a prisoner from the Bastille.

Below The Bastille in September 1789. During the summer demolition work on the prison began.

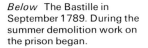

that was being formed. The "electors"—men chosen by each district assembly to elect the deputies representing Paris in the States-General—had decided that every district of the city should raise two hundred men. According to their plan, a total force of 12,000 men could be recruited from the sixty districts of Paris. Those men were badly needed, for news had just come that during the previous night the majority of the customs posts at the gateways to the city had been pillaged and burned down.

It was vital to prevent any repetition of such scenes, and the unarmed watchmaker spent the whole day patrolling the streets of his district. In the evening, the local committee received orders to recruit an additional six hundred men. The anxious electors had decided that the citizens' militia must be increased to 48,000 men. But how were they going to arm all these volunteers? Where could they find the firearms and ammunition?

When daybreak came at last, Humbert and the other exhausted members of his patrol returned to the Assembly. After a short rest, Humbert rose and went out into the street, where he learned that firearms were being distributed at the Invalides. He immediately rushed off to find Monsieur Poirier, the commander of the local militia, and asked him to lead the members of his group to the Invalides. Poirier, pestered with thousands of questions, seemed in no hurry to leave. Impatiently, Humbert seized him by the arm and, followed by five or six other citizens, escorted the reluctant commander to the Invalides.

An enormous crowd had collected on the parade ground in front of the building, and it proved impossible to remain together. Humbert soon found himself separated from his companions, and he entered the huge building by himself. Following the surging crowd through the corridors, he eventually reached the cellars where the weapons and ammunition were stored. As he gained the bottom of the staircase, Humbert caught sight of a man holding

The Bastille surrenders

The Petit Trianon at Versailles, where Queen Marie-Antoinette played at being a milkmaid.

Below The march to Versailles in October 1789. Officers of the Royal Guard who tried to prevent the march were decapitated and their heads carried on pikes by the marchers.

two muskets. He seized one of them and turned to the stairs—only to find that it was impossible to move. The crowd had become so dense that anyone trying to climb up the stairs was pushed down again. It became almost impossible to breathe and terrible shrieks and cries could be heard above the tumult. In desperation, some of those who had obtained muskets advanced with fixed bayonets on the others, forcing those who still had no arms to clear a passage.

Humbert lost sight of his companions in the chaos. He left the Invalides on his own and returned to the Hôtel de Ville, where powder was purportedly being dispensed to the citizens. The watchmaker succeeded in obtaining a quarter of a pound of powder but no musket balls. The clock struck three. Suddenly, the sound of shooting was heard coming from an easterly direction. "They must be fighting at the Bastille," someone said. Humbert rushed into a nearby grocer's shop and bought some little nails, which he planned to use as projectiles in his musket. As he emerged from the shop, a citizen announced that the Hôtel de Ville had finally received a supply of ammunition. Humbert therefore turned back, and was given six pellets of buckshot. Equipped with ammunition, he hurried off to the Bastille.

It was half-past three by the time that Humbert arrived. The outer drawbridge had already been pulled down by the attackers, who were now trying to drag two cannon into the outer courtyard. Humbert gave them a hand and soon found himself in the front of the crowd. Cannon were placed in position at the main gate of the fortress, the drawbridge was raised and the firing began. Humbert fired six rounds of ammunition. As he did so, a hand appeared through a small oval opening on one side of the gate, waving a piece of paper. One of the citizens fetched a wooden beam from a nearby carpenter and placed it across the moat. A man began to walk across the plank but lost his balance and fell. Another man followed him, grasped the paper and read it out loud: "We have about twenty thousand pounds of gunpowder, and we intend to blow up the garrison and the whole district if you do not capitulate. The Bastille, 5 p.m., July 14, 1789."

The note, which was signed by de Launay, the commander of the fortress, did not produce the desired effect. On the contrary, it provoked unanimous shouts of "Lower the drawbridges! We shall never give in!" The citizens began to reload the cannon, and they were on the point of firing when the drawbridge was suddenly lowered. (Later on it was learned that the Invalides soldiers, who formed part of the garrison in the Bastille, had forced the commander to open the gates.) The crowd poured into the fortress; Humbert was in the vanguard. Nine hundred and fifty-four craftsmen, shopkeepers and common citizens, all of whom lived in Paris but many of whom had come from the provinces, earned themselves the title of "conquerors of the Bastille."

The building of the Bastille had been started in 1370, during the reign of Charles V. By the seventeenth century, the fortress had lost most of its importance as a citadel of defense, and Cardinal

L'arrestation du Roi a eu lieu à Varennes, à cinq lieues de France, vers une heure après nuit, au moment où l'on venait d'en être prévenu par M. Drouet, maître de poste de ...nie-Menehoult, qui a rendu un service essentiel à la France, qu'elle surprise pour les ...itifs de se voir arrêtés au milieu de la nuit, par deux braves gardes nationaux

LA RECOMPENCE ACORDÉE A Mr DROUET EST DE 30 MILLE LIVRE ET A Mr SAUCE 20 MILLE LIVRE

qui ont bravé les menaces d'un détachement de-hussards, qui avoit été commandé par ... traître Bouillé! M Sauce, Procureur de la Commune, a invité le Roi d'entrer che... lui et de s'y reposer lui et sa famille Le généreux citoyen de Varennes n'a poin... accepté les offres du Roi, disant qu'il devoit tout à sa patrie.

Richelieu, the chief minister of Louis XIII, had converted it into a prison. The Bastille was no ordinary prison, however—it was a state prison. The old fort's unfortunate inmates were not being held for crimes or offenses committed under the common law. They had—without exception—been summarily arrested on *lettres de cachet*—in other words, at the direct and arbitrary order of the King.

In Richelieu's time the Bastille housed as many as fifty-three prisoners, but the number of arrests made by *lettres de cachet* had decreased, and under the reign of Louis XVI the prison held an average of only sixteen prisoners a year. Indeed, on July 14, 1789, the day the Bastille was captured, the victorious citizens found only seven prisoners inside. Moreover, these prisoners had a fairly easy time of it. A prisoner with private means was allowed to send for his own furniture, servants and meals. Poorer prisoners received enough money to provide themselves with the necessities of life. In the eighteenth century the cells were furnished by the state, although prisoners were allowed to add their own personal articles. The food, supplied by the prison, was good, and on occasions prisoners were invited to dine with the warden. It is true that there were some damp, unhealthy dungeons underground—as well as prison cells exposed to bitter cold in winter and the heat of summer, located at the top of the towers of the fortress—but none of them had been used since 1776.

Nevertheless, the Bastille remained an object of great hatred. It symbolized the absolutist authority of the King in its most despotic form. Moreover, its operation was shrouded in secrecy. Prisoners were arrested clandestinely and driven to the Bastille in closed carriages. The soldiers on guard duty were obliged to stand with their faces to the wall, and the prison warders were forbidden to have any conversation whatsoever with the prisoners. Moreover, the latter were not interrogated when they were arrested and never knew how long they were going to be imprisoned in the Bastille. They might be released several weeks, several months or even several years after they were arrested, upon receipt of another *lettre de cachet* from the King.

By the end of the eighteenth century, most of the prisoners in the Bastille were writers who had publicly denounced various corrupt practices of the regime. Voltaire spent a year in the Bastille in 1717-18, and was incarcerated for another twelve days in 1726. The Abbé Morellet, one of the leaders of the *Parti Philosophique*, was imprisoned for six weeks in 1760. The journalist Linguet remained there from

The arrest of the Royal family at Varenne in 1791. The failure of Louis' attempt to escape led to his execution.

A "religious procession" under the Directorate. Despite anti-clerical feeling in France, religious rights and ceremonies remained popular.

The army supports the populace

Louis XVII as the Dauphin.

The trial of Marie-Antoinette. Although her life had estranged her from the people, many were impressed by her courage during the trial.

1780 to 1782, and during that time he wrote *Mémoires sur la Bastille*, which he published upon his release from prison. For those who believed in free speech, free thinking and free writing, therefore, the Bastille represented everything that was shameful in the *ancien régime*.

Those reasons do not fully explain why the storming of the Bastille should have brought about the capitulation of the monarchy and the victory of the French Revolution. For an explanation of why the government toppled, one must examine a remarkable result of the capture of the old fort. The fall of the Bastille served to illustrate—better than any other event during that stormy period—a fact that was both obvious and almost incredible: the army

did not want to fight against the revolutionaries. On June 24, two companies of "Gardes Françaises" had refused to go on duty. They were followed on June 28 by other companies of soldiers, who laid down their firearms and ammunition and joined the people assembled in the Palais-Royal, assuring the crowds of citizens that they would never fight against the Parisians. Fourteen grenadiers, believed to be the ringleaders, were put in prison, only to be released by the demonstrators. Seventy-five members of the Swiss regiment of Salis-Samade deserted to the citizens' side during the first fortnight in July.

The army's reluctance to fight was graphically demonstrated on the morning of July 14, when the crowd attacked the Invalides and seized the 40,000 muskets that were stored there. Five thousand well-armed soldiers were encamped some four hundred yards from the Invalides at the time. Their commander, the Swiss general Besenval, intended to defend the Invalides. In fact, as soon as he received word that the rioters had arrived, he sent for his corps commanders—who informed the general that they could not rely on the cooperation of their men. According to one witness, the Count of Salmour, "from that moment onwards, the generals were agreed that it was impossible to subdue Paris and that the only prudent course of action was to withdraw." Thus, when de Launay surrendered the Bastille, he did so for two reasons: first, because the Swiss soldiers who garrisoned the Bastille refused to fight, and second, because he knew that he could expect no help from the army outside the fortress. In truth, the fall of the Bastille was due far more to the defection of the troops stationed in Paris than to the enthusiasm and bravery of the attackers. If the 30,000 troops that Louis XVI had concentrated in and around the capital had made the slightest attempt to stop the citizens from attacking, the Bastille would never have been taken. But the defection of the soldiers and their fraternization with the revolutionaries was a clear indication that they too were infected with revolutionary zeal. From that day on, the French monarchy, deserted by its defenders, had no choice but to capitulate.

The fall of the Bastille served as the perfect symbol of royal surrender. The Duke of Dorset, British ambassador to Paris, wrote to the British foreign secretary on July 16: "So, My Lord, the greatest revolution ever known in the history of mankind has just taken place and, relatively speaking, taking into consideration the results as a whole, it has cost very little in the way of bloodshed. At this moment we can consider France as a free country, the King as a monarch whose powers are restricted and the nobles as being reduced to the level of the rest of the nation." In explaining the situation to President Washington, Gouverneur Morris, the new United States ambassador to Paris, noted: "You may now consider the revolution to be over since the authority of the King and the nobles has been utterly destroyed."

The consequences of the fall of the Bastille soon made themselves felt. On July 17, Louis XVI visited Paris in person and was forced to recognize the

Permanent Committee, or new revolutionary municipal council, as well as the citizens' militia known as the National Guard. Before July 14, revolutionary municipal councils and citizens' militias had been formed in some of the provincial towns of France. After the fall of the Bastille, this revolutionary movement spread like wildfire. In the country, the peasants attacked the chateaux and destroyed the ancient charters that recorded the peasants' feudal obligations to their masters. In the towns, the bourgeois seized power from the King's representatives and formed National Guard companies to defend themselves. In order to keep the people calm and under control, the States-General, which had become the constituent national assembly, proclaimed the abolition of the "feudal regime." On August 26 they published a "Declaration of the Rights of Man and of the Citizen" that laid the foundations for the new regime: liberty, equality and the sanctity of property.

The movement grew in violence, and soon reached the point of no return. On October 5 the citizens of Paris, fearing fresh counterrevolutionary action on the part of the King, marched on Versailles and took Louis XVI and his family prisoner. The constituent assembly gave France a new constitution and new institutions, based on the rational ideas and beliefs that the French *philosophes* had been developing since the beginning of the century.

The revolutionary fervor soon spread to other countries, including the United States, Great Britain, the Netherlands, Germany, Switzerland, Italy, Hungary and Poland. At the same time, the forces of reaction and conservatism began to organize a counterrevolutionary movement. The clash between revolution and counterrevolution proved disastrous for Europe. From April 20, 1792 onward, that clash took the form of an international war—one that was to last for twenty-three years almost without a break. The counterrevolution's apparent triumph at Waterloo in 1815 proved to be an illusion. In reality, revolutionary ideas, principles and institutions had taken firm root not only in France but in all Europe, and in North, Central and South America.

JACQUES GODECHOT

A Play for All Seasons — William Shakespeare's reworking of a familiar folk legend gives the stage its most famous tragedy

1601

1609

Revolt of the Netherlands — After eighty years of determined resistance, the Dutch win their independence from Europe's mightiest monarch, Philip II of Spain

Jan van Oldenbarneveldt 1547-1619
Dutch statesman

William Laud 1573-1645
Archbishop of Canterbury

William Bradford 1590-1657
Governor of Plymouth Colony

Louis XIII 1601-43
King of France

Charles IX 1550-1611
King of Sweden

Inigo Jones 1573-1652
English architect

Duke of Buckingham 1592-1628
Favorite of James I

Jules Mazarin 1602-61
Italian cardinal and French minister

Boris Godunov 1552-1605
Muscovite boyar, later Tsar

Peter Paul Rubens, Sir 1577-1640
Flemish painter

John Eliot 1592-1632
English statesman

Abel Tasman c. 1603-59
Dutch explorer

Richard Hakluyt 1552-1616
English geographer

Christian IV 1577-1648
King of Denmark and Norway

Shah Jahan 1592-1666
Mogul Emperor

John IV 1603-56
King of Portugal

Francisco, Duke of Lerma 1552-1625
Spanish minister

Philip III 1578-1621
King of Spain

Thomas Wentworth, Earl of Strafford
1593-1641 *English statesman*

Philip IV 1605-65
King of Spain

Matthias 1557-1619
Holy Roman Emperor

Ferdinand II (of Styria) 1578-1637
King of Bohemia, Holy Roman Emperor

Gottfried von Pappenheim 1594-1632
Imperial general

Rembrandt van Rijn 1606-69
Dutch painter

Johann, Count of Tilly 1559-1632
Imperial general

William Harvey 1578-1657
English physician

Gustavus II Adolphus 1594-1632
King of Sweden

Pierre Corneille 1606-84
French dramatist

Jacobus Arminius 1560-1609
Dutch theologian

Frans Hals 1581-1666
Dutch painter

John Hampden 1594-1643
English statesman

Anne of Austria 1607-66
Queen, Regent of France

Duc de Sully 1560-1641
French statesman

Albrecht Wallenstein 1583-1634
Imperial general

Frederick V "the Winter King" 1596-1632
Elector Palatine, King of Bohemia

Michel de Ruyter 1607-76
Dutch admiral

Francis Bacon, Earl of Verulam, 1561-1626
English philosopher and statesman

John Pym c. 1583-1643
English Puritan leader

Michael Romanov 1596-1645
Tsar of Russia

George Monk 1608-70
English general

William Shakespeare 1564-1616
English dramatic poet

Hugo de Groot (Grotius)
1583-1645 *Dutch jurist*

René Descartes 1596-1650
French philosopher

John Milton 1608-74
English poet

Galileo Galilei 1564-1642
Italian astronomer

Axel Oxenstierna 1583-1654
Swedish Chancellor

Marten Harpertzoon Tromp
1597-1653 *Dutch admiral*

John Casimir 1609-72
King of Poland

James I 1566-1625
King of England (James VI of Scotland)

Frederick Henry 1584-1647
Prince of Orange, Stadholder of Netherlands

Giovanni Bernini 1598-1680
Italian sculptor

Henri Turenne 1611-75
Marshal of France

Count of Gondomar 1567-1626
Spanish diplomat

Cornelis Jansen 1585-1638
Dutch Catholic theologian

Anthony Van Dyck 1599-1641
Flemish painter

Henry Vane 1613-63
English Puritan administrator

Claudio Monteverdi 1567-1643
Italian composer

Duc de Richelieu 1585-1642
French cardinal, statesman

Oliver Cromwell 1599-1658
Lord Protector of England

André Lenôtre 1613-1700
French landscape gardener

Ambrose, Marquis de Spinola
1569-1630 *Italian general*

Mohammed Kuprili 1586-1661
Turkish Grand Vizier

Robert Blake 1599-1657
English admiral

Cardinal de Retz 1614-79
French politician

John Donne 1572-1631
English poet and clergyman

Gasper de Guzmán, Count Olivares
1587-1645 *Spanish minister*

Diego Velasquez 1599-1660
Spanish painter

Ben Jonson 1572-1637
English dramatic poet

Thomas Hobbes 1588-1679
English philosopher

Charles I 1600-49
King of England, Scotland and Ireland

Marie de Medici 1573-1642
Queen of France

Ahmed I 1589-1617
Ottoman Sultan

Pedro Calderón 1600-81
Spanish dramatist

● **1600**
Tokugawa period in Japan:
capital Tokyo

● **1609**
Invention of microscope
(or ? 1590)

1602-18 ●
Persian-Turkish War (Persian
territorial gains in war with
Turkey)

● **1610**
Assassination of Henry IV
of France

● **1611**
Brandenburg acquires
Prussia

1605 ●
Gunpowder Plot: failure leads to
Catholic persecution in England

● **1612**
Accession of Romanov
dynasty in Muscovy

● **1598**
Edict of Nantes

● **1609**
All Moriscos expelled
from Spain

The Pilgrims at Plymouth — An intrepid band of expatriate Englishmen establishes a new atmosphere of religious diversity in the New World

1620

1631

The Rape of Magdeburg — The Protestant citizens of Magdeburg defy their Catholic Emperor and spark a religious war that engulfs the Continent

1649

"A Cruel Necessity" — Decades of bitter dissension between Parliament's Puritan radicals and England's fumbling monarch culminate in the execution of Charles I

1661

1666

Cambridge's Young Genius — One of Trinity College's least promising graduates, Isaac Newton, lays the foundation for modern physics

"L'état c'est moi" — Declaring that he *is* the state, Cardinal Mazarin's astonishing pupil, Louis XIV, guides the French nation through its golden age

Aurangzeb 1618-1707
Mogul Emperor

Christiaan Huyghens 1629-95
Dutch mathematician and physicist

Sheng Tsu - K'ang Hsi Emperor 1654-1722
Manchu Emperor of China

Frederick Augustus the Strong 1670-1733
Elector of Saxony, King of Poland

George William 1619-40
Elector of Brandenburg

Charles II 1630-85
King of England

Jean Racine 1639-99
French tragic poet and dramatist

Charles XI 1655-97
King of Sweden

John Law 1671-1729
Scottish financier in France

Prince Rupert of the Rhine 1619-82
General and admiral

John Dryden 1631-1700
English poet

Leopold I 1640-1705
Austrian Emperor

Edmond Halley 1656-1742
English astronomer

Peter I the Great 1672-1725
Tsar of Russia

Jean Baptiste Colbert 1619-83
French statesman

Jan Vermeer 1632-75
Dutch painter

Sophia Alexeyevna 1657-1704
Regent for Peter I of Russia

Philip Duke of Orleans 1674-1723
French Regent

Frederick William "the Great Elector"
1620-88 *Elector of Brandenburg*

John Locke 1632-1704
English philospher

Mehemmed IV 1641-91
Ottoman Sultan

Frederick I 1657-1713
First King of Prussia

Jean de La Fontaine 1621-95
French poet

Christopher Wren, Sir 1632-1723
English architect and mathematician

Michel de Louvois 1641-91
French statesman

George I 1660-1727
King of Great Britain

Masaniello (Tommaso Aniello)
1622-47 *Neapolitan rebel leader*

Isaac Newton, Sir 1641-1727
English physicist

Charles II 1661-1700
King of Spain

Charles X 1622-60
King of Sweden

Antony van Leeuwenhock 1632-1723
Dutch natural historian

Robert Harley, Earl of Oxford
1661-1724 *English statesman*

Jean Baptiste Molière 1622-73
French Comic dramatist

Charles V of Lorraine 1643-90
General in Imperial service

Mary II 1662-94
Queen of England

Blaise Pascal 1623-62
French scientist and philospher

Baruch Spinoza 1632-77
Portuguese Dutch philospher

William Penn 1644-1718
English Quaker

George Byng 1663-1733
English admiral

John III Sobieski 1624-96
King of Poland

James II 1633-1701
King of England

Prince Eugène of Savoy 1663-1736
Imperial general

George Fox 1625-91
Founder of Society of Friends

Jules Hardouin Mansart 1645-1708
French architect

John Vanbrugh 1664-1726
English dramatist and architect

Christina 1626-89
Queen of Sweden

Marshal Vauban 1633-1707
French military engineer

Giulio Alberoni 1664-1752
Italian minister to Philip V of Spain

Marie de Sévigné 1626-96
French noblewoman, writer

Ahmed Kuprili 1635-76
Turkish Grand Vizier

Gottfried Leibnitz 1646-1716
German mathematician and philosopher

Anne 1665-1714
Queen of Great Britain

Sivaji Bhonsle 1627-80
Maratha leader

John Churchill, Duke of Marlborough
1650-1722 *English general and statesman*

Ivan V 1666-96
Joint Tsar of Russia

Jacques-Bénigne Bossuet 1627-1704
French preacher and historian

Marquise de Maintenon 1635-1719
Second wife of Louis XIV

Jonathan Swift 1667-1745
English satirist

Nicolas Fouquet 1615-80
French statesman

John Bunyan 1628-88
English writer

Johan Gyllenstjerna 1635-80
Swedish minister

William III (of Orange) 1650-1702
King of England

William Congreve 1670-1729
English dramatist

Bartolomé Murillo c. 1617-82
Spanish painter

Duke of Luxembourg
1628-95 *French general*

Maria Teresa 1639-83
Queen of France

François de la Mothe Fénelon 1651-1715
French writer, theologian

Francesco Morosini 1618-94
Venetian commander and Doge

Alexis 1629-76
Tsar of Russia

Louis XIV 1638-1715
King of France

André Hercule de Fleury 1653-1743
French statesman

1618 ● Defenestration of Prague: beginning of Thirty Years' War

● African slaves first brought **1619** to North America

1622 ● English take Hormuz and gain influence in declining Persian Empire

1621 ● Gustavus Adolphus conquers Livonia

1624 Foundation of New Amsterdam (New York)

1621 ● Resumption of Dutch War of Independence

1624 ● Virginia becomes royal colony

1621 Conflict between English and Dutch East India Companies

● **1631** Franco-Swedish Treaty of Bärwalde

● Galileo condemned **1633** by the Inquisition

1640 ● Portugal gains independence from Spain (Braganza Dynasty)

1630 Treaty of Madrid ends Anglo-Spanish War

1630 Massachusetts colonization begun

● **1629-40** Charles I of England rules without Parliament

1644 ● Mandarin dynasty established in China

1645-64 ● Turkish-Venetian War

1648-53 Fronde revolt in France

1648 Peace of Westphalia: end of Thirty Years' War

Treaty of Münster divides Netherlands **1648**

● **1641** Dutch capture Malacca and establish supremacy in East Indies for 150 years

Swedish ambitions curbed by **1660** treaties of Oliva and Copenhagen

Peace of the Pyrenees **1659** ● between France and Spain

1658 ● Battle of the Dunes: French and English **1660** defeat Spanish

1652 ● Capetown founded by Dutch settlers

1657 ● English cripple Spanish fleet off Teneriffe

1655-7 ● Swedish-Polish War

1651 First Navigation Act gives English shipping monopoly and opens Dutch-English War (-1659)

Stuart Restoration

1664 Treaty of Vasvar: twenty year Austrian-Turkish truce

● **1670** Secret Treaty of Dover between Charles II and Louis XIV against Holland: formation of Whig party in England.

● Acute Anglo-French rivalry **1664** in India begins

● **1673** Test Act: Catholics excluded from public office in England (till 1828)

● **1667** Peace of Breda ends second Dutch-English War

● **1669** Aurangzeb prohibits Hinduism in India: Maratha rising under Sivaji till 1707

1683

Vienna Under Siege — Kara Mustafa leads the "invincible" armies of the Ottoman Sultan in a final — and nearly successful — assault on Vienna

A Window on the West — Traveling incognito through Europe, Peter the Great learns technological skills that enable him to Westernize his empire
1698

1713

Twilight of the Sun King — The treaties of Utrecht and Rastatt curb the Sun King's territorial ambitions and restore peace to Europe

The South Sea Bubble — The spectacular collapse of the South Sea Company ruins thousands of stock speculators and topples the English government
1720

Alexander Pope 1688-1744
English poet

Elizabeth 1709-62
Empress of Russia

Ahmed Shah 1724-73
Afghan ruler

George Washington
American general,

Nadir Shah 1688-1747
Turcoman Shah of Persia

Louis XV 1710-74
King of France

Immanuel Kant 1724-1804
German philosopher

Jacques
French

John V "the Magnanimous" 1689-1750
King of Portugal

David Hume 1711-76
Scottish philospher

Robert Clive 1725-74 *British soldier serving East India Company*

Joseph Priestley
English chemist

Charles de Montesquieu 1689-1755
French political philosopher

Louis-Joseph de Montcalm 1712-58
French general

James Wolfe 1727-59
British soldier in Canada

Elizabeth Farnese 1692-1766
Queen of Spain

Jean Jacques Rousseau 1712-78
French philosopher

Anne Robert Jacques Turgot 1727-81
French economist and statesman

François Marie Voltaire 1694-1778
French philospher

Frederick II the Great 1712-86
King of Prussia

Thomas Gainsborough 1727-88
English painter

Robert Walpole 1676-1745
English Whig statesman

Maurice de Saxe 1696-1750
French general

Denis Diderot 1713-84
French philospher

John Wilkes 1727-97
English politician

Stanislas Leszcznski 1677-1766
King of Poland

Joseph François Dupleix 1697-1763
Governor of French East India Company

Peter III 1728-62
Tsar of Russia

Joseph I 1678-1711
Austrian Emperor

William Hogarth 1697-1764
English artist

Christoph von Gluck 1714-87
German composer

James Cook 1728-79
English navigator and explorer

Charles XII 1682-1718
King of Sweden

Antonio Canaletto 1697-1768
Italian painter

Charles III 1716-88
King of The Two Scilies, then of Spain

Gotthold Lessing 1729-81
German writer

Philip V 1683-1746
King of Spain

Mahé de Labourdonnais 1699-1753
French naval officer

Robert Adam 1729-92
English architect

George II 1683-1760
King of Great Britain

Sebastian Pombal 1699-1782
Portuguese statesman

Maria Theresa 1717-80
Queen of Bohemia and Hungary

Catherine II the Great 1729-96
Empress of Russia

Charles VI 1685-1740
Austrian Emperor

Anders Celsius 1701-44
Swedish astronomer

Jean d'Alembert 1717-83
French mathematician and philosopher

Johann Sebastian Bach 1685-1750
German composer

John Wesley 1703-91
English preacher

Charles Vergennes 1717-87
French statesman

Edmund Burke 1729-97
British historian and statesman

George Berkeley 1685-1753
British philosopher and bishop

Benjamin Franklin 1706-90
American statesman and scientist

Etienne de Choiseul 1719-85
French statesman

Stanislas Augustus
1732-98   *King of*

George Frederic Handel 1685-1759
German-English composer

Linnaeus 1707-78
Swedish botanist

Antoinette de Pompadour 1721-64
Mistress of Louis XV of France

Warren
Governor

Anthony Heinsius d. 1720
Grand Pensionary of Holland

Georges Buffon 1707-88
French naturalist

Adam Smith 1723-90
Scottish economist

Franz Joseph Haydn
Austrian composer

Emanuel Swedenborg 1688-1722
Swedish theological writer

Francis I 1708-65 *Austrian Emperor, Duke of Lorraine and Tuscany*

John Burgoyne 1723-92
British general in North America

Richard Arkwright
English inventor

Frederick William I 1688-1740
King of Prussia

William Pitt the Elder 1708-88
English statesman

Joshua Reynolds 1723-92
English painter

Frederick, Lord North
English statesman

● **1678-79**
Peace of Nijmegen ends Franco-Dutch War, confirms Swedish territorial gains

● **1685**
Revocation of the Edict of Nantes: persecution of French Huguenots

League of Augsburg ●
against France   **1686**

Glorious Revolution ●
in England   **1688**

● **1679**
Habeas Corpus Act: protection against arbitrary arrest in England

●
1689 Bill of Rights gives political supremacy to Parliament in Britain

● **1690**
Battle of the Boyne: conquest of Ireland by William III

● **1694**
Gold discovered in Minas Gerais, Southern Brazil

● **1694**
Bank of England founded

● **1697**
Treaty of Ryswick: Louis XIV recognizes defeat by League of Augsburg

● **1700-21**
Great Northern War

● **1701**
Elector of Brandenburg becomes King of Prussia

● **1699**
Treaty of Karlowitz: Austria obtains Hungary, Poland regains Podolia from Turks

1701-14
War of Spanish Succession

● **1703**
Methuen Treaty between England and Portugal, giving England commercial advantage

● **1707**
Act of Union (with Scotland) creates Great Britain

● **1713**
Asiento Treaty gives Britain monopoly in supplying African slaves to Spanish colonies

● **1713**
Pragmatic Sanction reserving Hapsburg succession to Maria Theresa

● Sicily becomes Austrian possession: Duke of Savoy
1718 obtains Sardinia in exchange

● Afghan-Persian War: Persia
1722-30 dismembered by Turks and Russians

● Treaty of Nystadt, Russia gains
1721 control of Baltic littoral and unofficial protectorate over Poland

● **1717-20** Rise and fall of John Law's financial system in France

1721-42
Rise of Walpole and establishment of cabinet government in Britain

● **1724**
China closed to Westerners: missionaries expelled

An Encyclopedia for the Enlightenment — Hounded by government censors and condemned by the Church, Denis Diderot edits his thirty-five volume encyclopedia

1751

1755

Disaster Strikes Lisbon — When a series of earth tremors shatter Lisbon, mystics insist that the disaster is Divine Retribution for Portugal's sins

1771

1776

The Declaration of Independence — Thomas Jefferson drafts the American colonies' proclamation of independence to justify rebellion and win French support

"Terra Incognita" — Certain that an undiscovered continent lies somewhere in the South Pacific, James Cook sets out in search of the "Great South Land"

1789

"Liberté Egalité Fraternité" — The French monarchy is doomed when troops garrisoning the Bastille refuse to open fire upon a mob of armed citizens

1732-99
President

Thadeus Kościuszko 1746-1817
Polish general

Necker 1732-1804
banker and statesman

Johann Wolfgang von Goethe 1749-1832
German writer, statesman and scientist

1733-1804

James Madison 1751-1836
U.S. President

John Adams 1735-1826
U.S. President

Camille Desmoulins 1760-1827
French revolutionary

James Watt 1736-1819
Scottish inventor

Kao Tsung — Ch'ien Lung Emperor 1736-96
Manchu Emperor of China

Luigi Galvani 1737-93
Italian scientist

Louis XVI 1754-93
King of France

Edward Gibbon 1737-94
English historian

Ludwig van Beethoven 1770-1827
German composer

Thomas Paine 1737-1809
Political writer and theorist

William, Earl of Shelburne 1737-1805
British statesman

Charles Cornwallis 1738-1805
British general

Wolfgang Amadeus Mozart 1756-91
Austrian composer

George III 1738-1820
King of Great Britain

Joseph II 1741-90
Austrian Emperor

Alexander Hamilton 1757-1804
American statesman

Joseph Banks, Sir 1743-1820
British naturalist, promoter of African exploration

William Blake 1757-1827
English poet and artist

(Poniatowski)
Poland

Thomas Jefferson 1743-1826
U.S. President

Friedrich Schiller 1759-1805
German writer

Hastings 1732-1818
General of India

William Pitt the Younger 1759-94
English statesman

1732-1809

Antoine Lavoisier 1743-94
French chemist

1732-92

John Jay 1745-1829
American statesman

1732-92

Gustavus III 1746-92
King of Sweden

● **1740-48**
War of the Austrian Succession

● **1745**
Prussia gains Silesia by Treaty of Dresden

● **1739-41**
Anglo-Spanish War of Jenkins' Ear

● **1746**
French capture Madras

1750-77 ●
Pombal institutes administrative reform in Brazil and promotes trade

● **1747**
Afghanistan under Ahmed gains independence from Persia

● **1739**
Nadir Shah of Persia defeats Afghans and sacks Delhi

French naval defeats — loss of Canada to Britain

Battle of Plassey: British gain control of Bengal **1757**

British defeat Emperor of Delhi, obtain control of Bengal, Bihar and Orissa **1764**

Imposition of Stamp Tax in American Colonies **1764**

Invention of spinning jenny by James Hargreaves **1764**

Clive's reforms in India **1765-66**

Stanislas Poniatowski placed on Polish throne by Catherine the Great ● **1764**

Seven Years' War **1756-63** ●
(French and American War)

1759
British Museum opened

● **1759** Gustavus III's coup d'état and reforms in Sweden **1772**

First Polish partition by Russia, Prussia and Austria **1772**

1773 ●
Jesuit Order dissolved by Pope Clement XIV

1774
Treaty of Kuchuk Kainardji: Russia obtains Azov Kertsch and navigation rights in Turkish waters

1773 ● **1774**
Boston Tea Party

Pugatchoff rebellion in Russia **1773-75**

● **1768-73**
James Bruce's exploration along Nile promotes British interest in Ethiopia

● **1774**
Placatory Quebec Act ensures Canadian loyalty to Britain

● **1775-83**
American Revolutionary War

● **1774**

● **1778-79**
War of Bavarian Succession

1783
Peace of Versailles: recognition of American Republic: France renounces India

Continental Congress: American grievances presented in petition to George III

● **1775** Watt's steam engine

● **1787-92**
Second Russian-Turkish War: Russia's possession of Crimea confirmed

1784 ●
Pitt's India Act: East India Company's power transferred to British Government; interference in native affairs forbidden

● **1787** United States Constitution

● **1788**
Sydney founded as first Australian penal settlement

● **1788-90**
Gustavus III of Sweden attacks Russia

Acknowledgments

The authors and publishers wish to thank the authorities of the following museums and collections by whose kind permission the illustrations are reproduced:

AMSTERDAM: Rijksmuseum, 24/1, 91/2, 94/2
ANGLESEY: Marquess of, 93
BERLIN: Germanisches National Museum, 41/2
BOWDOIN COLLEGE: Museum of Art, Brunswick, Maine, 137/1
EDINBURGH: National Museum of Antiquities of Scotland, 48
　　Scottish National Gallery, on loan from Lord Roseberry, 55/1
LENINGRAD: Hermitage, 84/1, 88/2
LONDON: Admiralty, 132/2
　　British Museum, 32/1, 50/1, 52/1, 53/1, 55/2, 86/1, 87/1, 96, 97, 109/1, 146/1, 150/2, 153/1
　　Dulwich College, 16/3
　　Guild Hall Museum, 102/1
　　Hudson's Bay Company, 98/1
　　National Gallery, 25
　　National Maritime Museum, 129, 133
　　National Portrait Gallery, 14/2, 15, 17/2, 17/3, 46/1, 47/4, 50/2, 51/2, 73/2, 95/2, 99/3, 103/1, 104/1, 106/2, 138
　　Natural History Museum, 131/2
　　Parker Gallery, 139/2
　　Royal Society, 68, 69
　　Science Museum, 71/2
　　Talbot Collection, 89/1
　　Victoria and Albert, 54/1, 107/2
　　Wallace Collection, 64/3
NEW YORK: Metropolitan Museum of Art, 139/1
　　Public Library, 34/1
PARIS: Bibliothèque Nationale, 121/1
　　Louvre, 111/1, 114/2
　　War Office, 82/1

PHILADELPHIA: Collection of the Library Company of Philadelphia, 35/1
PLYMOUTH, MASS: Pilgrim Hall, 29
　　Plimouth Plantation, 28
PORTLAND: Duke of, 15/2
PRIVATE COLLECTIONS: 126/1, 131/1, 132/1
RADNOR: Earl of, 49
ROME: Pecci Blunt Collection, 75/1
STOCKHOLM: National Museum, 19/2
VERSAILLES: Musée de, 58/1, 143/1, 147
VIENNA: National Bibliothek, 79/2
WASHINGTON D.C.: National Gallery of Art, 142

Photographs were kindly supplied by the following:

Aldus Books, 109/2, 145/1
Anderson, 19/2
Blainel, 41/1, 44/3
Photo Bulloz, 57/2, 60/3, 153/2
Centre Cultural Portugaise, 118/1
Collection Viollet, 27/1, 44/1
Evans, Mary, Picture Library, 13, 14/1, 16/2, 18/3, 19/1, 21, 23/1, 23/2, 26/3, 27/2, 37/2, 37/3, 30/1, 42/2, 47/1, 57/1, 58/1, 61/3, 66/1, 67/2, 71/3, 73/1, 75/3, 78/3, 79/1, 83/1, 87/2, 88/1, 90/2, 103/2, 104/2, 105/1, 108/1, 114/1, 116/3, 127/2, 128, 130, 148/1, 149/1
R. B. Fleming, 40/2, 115/1, 147, 150/2, 153/1
Foliot, Françoise, 91/3
Freeman, John R., 24/2, 46/2, 47/3, 50/1, 52/3, 53/1, 64/3, 69, 78/4, 87/5, 88/3, 89/1, 90/1, 91/1, 96, 97, 106/1, 133, 134/2
Giraudon, 59/2, 61/2, 63/1, 64/1, 67/4, 95/3, 99/2, 110/1, 111/1, 114/2
Halliday, Sonia, 76, 77, 80, 81/2

Holford, Michael, 25, 34/4, 63/2, 107/2, 109/1, 126/1, 131, 132/1, 150/1
Lisbon Tourist Board, 119/1, 121/2, 122, 123
Mansell Collection, 12, 17/1, 18/1, 18/2, 22/1, 22/2, 26/1, 26/2, 27/3, 30/3, 31, 33/2, 33/3, 36, 37/1, 40/1, 42/3, 43/1, 46/3, 51/1, 52/2, 56, 57/3, 61/1, 64/2, 66/3, 67/2, 67/3, 70, 71/1, 81/1, 82/2, 83/2, 83/4, 87/3, 91/2, 92/1, 94/1, 95/1, 99/1, 100/2, 100/3, 101/1, 101/3, 105/2, 107/1, 108/2, 112, 113/1, 113/3, 115/2, 116/1, 117/1, 120, 124, 125, 134/3, 135/3, 140/1, 141/1, 141/3, 144/2, 145/2, 146, 148/2, 149/2, 151, 152
Musées Nationaux, Photo de, 62/1
Novosti, 85/1, 86/2, 88/2
Powell, Josephine, 75/1
Radio Times Hulton Picture Library, 16/3, 21/1, 30/2, 34/2, 34/3, 35/3, 47/2, 67/1, 74, 75/1, 82/1, 83/3, 100/1, 101/2, 108/3, 113/2, 117/2, 117/3, 135/1, 135/2, 137/1, 140/2, 141/2, 144/1
Ronan, Colin, Picture Library, 72/2, 73/3
Swedish Institute for Cultural Relations, 39

Picture research by Enid Moore, Patricia Quick and Michèle Rimbeaud

Index